*f*P

ALSO BY NADINE COHODAS

Strom Thurmond and the Politics of Southern Change

The Band Played Dixie

Race and the Liberal Conscience at Ole Miss

NADINE COHODAS

THE FREE PRESS

New York   London   Toronto   Singapore   Sydney

THE FREE PRESS
A Division of Simon & Schuster Inc.
1230 Avenue of the Americas
New York, NY 10020

Designed by Carla Bolte

Manufactured in the United States of America

10   9   8   7   6   5   4   3   2   1

Library of Congress Cataloging-in-Publication Data

Cohodas, Nadine.
    The band played Dixie / Nadine Cohodas.
        p.   cm.
    Includes bibliographical references and index.
    ISBN 0–684–82721–2
    1. University of Mississippi—History. 2. College
integration—Mississippi—Oxford—History.   I. Title
LD3413.C65   1997
378.762'83—dc21   97-3685
                                                      CIP

Contents

1

The Mystic Chords of Memory

October 29, 1994, was a picture-perfect day in Oxford, Mississippi: blue skies, sunshine, a fresh breeze. Oak and maple leaves in their full autumn glory fluttered throughout the Grove, the central gathering place at the state university.

Since daybreak students and alumni had been streaming onto the campus. Traffic was backed up for blocks, and parking lots were filled to capacity. Picnic tables in the Grove were laid out with buckets of fried chicken and bowls of potato salad for lunch before the homecoming football game. By noon the place was packed with fans, the vast majority of them white, most of them too young to remember that thirty-two years earlier this same Grove held federal troops battling the rock-throwing rioters who protested the admission of James Meredith, a Negro.

As I surveyed the homecoming scene I was reminded of photographs from Oxford's days of rage, when young white men, their faces plastered with hate, hoisted Confederate flags to signal their anger at Meredith's arrival. I looked around now, and the same flags were flying, but the faces were smiling. Today the battle was not over a way of life but a football score, and the Rebels the flag celebrated was the football team. The benign spirit on this beautiful day stood in contrast to the darker purpose that came to mind when Byron de la Beckwith had worn the same Confederate flag in his lapel months earlier during his third trial for murdering Medgar Evers.

The University of Mississippi had once been a training ground for white supremacy. Now it was proud of its black athletic stars, nearly half of the ninety-seven-member football squad. By 1995 the dean of the law school was black; so were the basketball coach and an associate vice chancellor. Ten percent of the student body was black, and between 1990 and 1994 two editors of the *Mississippian,* the campus newspaper, were young black men.

On this homecoming day, members of the Black Student Union, the organization of black undergraduates, were among the revelers. Their presence in the Grove was evidence of how the campus had changed since 1962, their party in a separate tent a hint of how this modern student body operated.

Matched against the obvious signs of racial progress at the school were incidents from the recent past that served as reminders of the intense bigotry of years gone by. In the fall of 1989 one white student had been expelled and four were suspended after participating in a blatantly racist fraternity prank: dumping two nude pledges, racial epithets scrawled on their chests, at the campus of a nearby historically black college. And the year before that the house intended for the first black fraternity to reside on Fraternity Row, the social and political hub of the campus, was burned to the ground by arsonists on the day the group was to take possession.

What could all of this tell us about race?

I had come to Oxford to find out, an outsider from the homogeneous Upper Midwest. I had been fascinated by the South from afar, struck by the brutality that was broadcast in March 1965 as civil rights protesters tried to make their way across the Edmund Pettus Bridge in Selma, Alabama. I was transfixed a week later as I watched a determined Lyndon Johnson promise, "We shall overcome." But I had not experienced firsthand the contradictions of life in a racially mixed world, and I could only imagine what native son Willie Morris meant when he said of his beloved homeland that in the same moment one could find "severity and tenderness, meanness and nobility."

He must have been referring to events like the summer of 1949, when a university art professor happened on a talented young black artist from nearby Ecru. There was no way that M. B. Mayfield could study formally at the school, so the teacher arranged for him to get a job as a janitor and handyman in the art department. When he finished his chores, he set up an easel and his equipment—all donated—in the janitor's closet next to the classroom. By leaving the door slightly ajar, he could participate in the class: the severity of segregation tempered by the tenderness of a teacher and students coping with the unforgiving system that was their way of life.

I knew this was only one of many telling stories from the university, and I was sure that its rich history and its struggle to reconcile this controversial past offered a splendid testing ground for reexamining assumptions about race.

Twenty-five years earlier as a student at the University of Michigan, when black students went on strike for increased admissions and curriculum changes, I thought that once the civil rights laws were in place, the ideal of integration would be a reality—blacks and whites working and living together on shared and common ground.

After writing about civil rights for more than ten years and living for seventeen in Washington, D.C., a city with more than its share of racial tensions, I came to question whether the goal had been realistic.

The legal apparatus of segregation has been dismantled and replaced by laws with noble goals and the mechanisms to enforce them, and although minorities had integrated all facets of life, most visibly the political world, the reality of the 1990s, with rising resegregation in schools and neighborhoods and continued racial hostility, was not the one so many of us envisioned two decades ago.

What had gotten in the way?

I thought the story of the University of Mississippi could help provide some of the answers.

Before the homecoming festivities were over on that October day in 1994, I began to understand that the celebration was not just about sports but culture, history, and tradition. To an outsider, the display of Old South symbols was overwhelming even amid the obvious presence of black students and alumni.

It wasn't just the Confederate flags, waved and worn—long skirts and short—but the ubiquitous sound of "Dixie," the school's unofficial fight song. As if on cue from some unseen conductor, the miniature flags went into the air as soon as the revelers heard the pep band play the distinctive "Da-Da-Dum" of Dixie's opening bars.

The song had been written by an Ohio man in 1859 for a minstrel company. Three years later it became the battle hymn for the Confederate states, and in 1948 it was the anthem of the States' Rights Democrats—popularly known as Dixiecrats—who walked out of the Democratic party over civil rights. So "Old times there are not forgotten," the well-known lyric from the second line, conjured up very different memories for the white and black football fans gathered in the Grove.

Like the waving of the rebel flag, the singing of "Dixie" on this lovely fall day was not the same "Dixie" the States' Righters roared in defiance in 1948. It was simply another manifestation of school spirit sung by people who seemed to be either oblivious to or unconcerned about the controversy it sometimes generated.

I held this thought as I wandered over to one postgame party, where a group of students and alumni were enjoying a snack in a corner of the Grove cordoned off with a dozen Confederate flags. A white man playing a guitar with a synthesized backup brought his small audience to their feet when he struck up "Mustang Sally." I wondered whether he knew the song was made famous by soul singer Wilson Pickett at a time when blacks had their "place" at the university as hired help to cook for the students and clean up after them.

I was reminded at that moment of some other white musicians who had played "Mustang Sally"—the Irish working-class band the Commitments, celebrated in a movie of the same name. They considered soul music to be "the language of the streets" and believed they had a special connection to it. In one of the movie's pointed moments, the band manager, acutely aware of his low status in Dublin society, explains "The Irish are the blacks of Europe and Dubliners are the blacks of Ireland and the northside Dubliners are the blacks of Dublin." So when the Commitments played "Mustang Sally" it was not only with affection for the song but appreciation for the man who made it.

4

The homecoming version illustrated the transcendent power of music, but something was out of sync. It was discomfiting to hear "Mustang Sally" performed by a white man for an all-white audience in the midst of so much Confederate memorabilia, with no appreciation for the irony of the scene, no nod to the history of the music and the place where it was being played. Perhaps I was being too harsh. This was, after all, entertainment at a football celebration, not a political event or sociology class. But I later realized that the moment, so rich in divergent symbols, held clues to the fractious issues of race I wanted to explore.

Synthesized music and traffic jams were beyond even the most vivid imaginations of the eighty young men who converged on Oxford on November 6, 1848, to begin their education at the University of Mississippi. The founders had picked this rural town for the state school because they thought it an appropriate "sylvan exile" to foster serious study. One early settler had described the area as a "fairyland [of] parklike forests and waving native grasses."

The new students, all but one from Mississippi, were considered by their elders to be a vital link between the past and the future, and it was for these young men the university had been created—not to challenge the status quo but to preserve it.

"Send your sons to other states and you estrange them from their native land [and] our institutions are endangered," one Mississippi educator had warned, an oblique reference to the rift in the young country over slavery and the growing fervor of abolitionists anxious to impose their will on the slaveholding states. And another had warned that "those opposed to us in principle cannot be entrusted to educate our sons and daughters."

Implicit in such comments was the understanding that education was more than learning and refinement. It was survival: "the process by which a culture transmits itself across the generations."

By the 1940s, a century after the first classes began on the Oxford campus, the university would have more than met this goal, infusing generations of young white Mississippians with an immutable pride in their heritage and a belief in a social order accepted as divinely ordained. It would take a crisis of monumental proportions, a revolution really, to expose the flaws and limits of the old order and require the rebuilding of the university into the racially diverse campus on display at the 1994 homecoming, a campus its creators could never have imagined. But the "mystic chords of memory," in the apt phrase of Abraham Lincoln, would always be heard on the campus, making harmony among the modern student body sometimes illusory, occasionally impossible.

From the day the university opened, the center of the campus had been the Lyceum, an imposing three-story structure with a front portico supported by six large columns. It was named after the garden at Athens where Aristotle taught, a good fit for a building that matched its Greek forerunner in architectural style and function.

During the Civil War, the Lyceum, like the small dormitories and faculty residences beside it, would be used as a hospital for wounded Confederate soldiers. A century later, when a civil war of a different sort broke out, the Lyceum symbolized a long-lost way of life, calling up ghosts of a past battle to witness the fury of a new.

Race was a fixture at the University of Mississippi from the beginning. The campus, like the town of Oxford and the rest of the state, reflected the twin ingredients of southern cultural cohesion: white supremacy and black slavery. Some slaves even accompanied their masters to school, to perform the same chores there as they had at home. Any breach, real or perceived, of the self-styled "peculiar institution," the benign euphemism for slavery, was unimaginable and would not be tolerated, as the university's third president—the only "damn Yankee" ever to head the school— found out.

Frederick A. P. Barnard was a Massachusetts native, a graduate of Yale, a scientist and an Episcopal minister. He had come to Oxford to teach science after making a name for himself at the University of Alabama, where he had been recognized for a sharp mind and energetic spirit. He had gained prominence for adjudicating the boundary line between Alabama and Florida, serving as the scientific expert for both sides. He was widely considered to be "a scholar of the first rank."

When the previous president resigned, Barnard was named to succeed him. He was committed to making the University of Mississippi one of the best schools in the country. A man "challenged not threatened by change," in the words of one admirer, he worked tirelessly to get more money to expand the curriculum and the campus. But he often found himself at loggerheads with a less ambitious board of trustees.

In 1858, Barnard wrote a long open letter to the trustees outlining in detail plans to reorganize the university so it could better meet a changing world. The hundred-page report was widely disseminated by Barnard's supporters but tepidly received overall. The only suggestion the board ultimately accepted was to change the title of president to chancellor.

When Barnard had been one of several professors, his northern credentials had not mattered so much. Loyal Mississippians even ignored a speech he had made while teaching in Alabama supporting the Union against southerners who were threatening to secede. But now that he was president of the university, the fact that he was a northerner, along with his apparent pro-Union sympathies, made him suspect. Heightening the tension was the fact that Barnard had become president as conflict between the South and North was rising. An incident concerning a student and a female slave at the president's house only confirmed the doubters' negative views, offering a clear reminder that where one stood on matters of race was the ultimate barometer of acceptability.

One May evening in 1859, while Barnard and his wife were away, two students entered their residence on campus, and one of them assaulted Barnard's female slave. She was unable to work for several days after the attack, and the bruises she sustained lingered for two months. The young woman was referred to in campus records only by her first name, Jane, accorded neither a last name nor a courtesy title.

The student was eventually identified (a professor had seen him leaving the house, and the young woman herself had told Barnard's wife of the incident). The faculty declined to punish the student even though they believed he was guilty. They were concerned, they noted in an official resolution, that the evidence against the student was not legally sufficient. Under Mississippi law slave testimony was inadmissible against a white person. But Barnard expelled the offender and would not allow him to be readmitted. The chancellor's critics had accused him of using the young woman's testimony as the basis for expelling the student, a charge Barnard denied.

But the anti-Barnard forces agitated long enough to force an investigation by the legislature and the board of trustees. It was obvious to Barnard what lay at the heart of his detractors' criticism: not whether he had exercised his authority properly but whether he abided by the "peculiar institution." He demanded a chance to show that he did and to clear his name. "I was born at the North," he told the trustees. "That I cannot help. I was not consulted in the matter. I am a slaveholder, and if I know myself, I am sound on the slavery question."

The board ultimately exonerated Barnard and gave him a vote of confidence as "trustees and Southern men." But the president was nonetheless disheartened by his treatment, considering it, perhaps with some hyperbole, "an outrage without parallels in the annals of civilization." He knew his days in Oxford were numbered. In little more than a year, he would be gone.

The Barnard episode put in microcosm the tensions between the South and the North that were escalating month by month. They were driven by the pronounced economic differences between the two regions and compounded by the slavery issue. The North had a manufacturing sector that was growing in size and clout, while the Southern economy was still based on large plantations that used slave labor. Southerners opposed any effort to limit slavery in the country's new territories; more and more northerners wanted to outlaw it completely.

When Abraham Lincoln won the presidential nomination of the anti-slavery Republican party and then prevailed in the 1860 election over a split Democratic party, southern leaders, who had threatened to secede from the Union, made good on their threat. South Carolina was the first state to leave. Mississippi was second, adopting its articles of secession on January 9, 1861. They were drafted by L. Q. C. Lamar, a prominent Mississippian and mathematics professor at the university. It was the first of many bonds that would be forged between the Oxford campus and the Confederate cause.

News of secession was greeted with enthusiasm at the school. The flag of the United States had been replaced by the flag of the newly independent state of Mississippi, waving triumphantly from dormitory windows. A campus literary society showed its sentiments by approving a motion that "two abolition books in our library be burnt" and then voting to buy a copy of the secession ordinance. One professor was dismissed for writing a letter that appeared to express "Northern sentiments."

In anticipation of the coming hostilities, a military company of students had organized a few weeks before secession became official. They called themselves the "University Greys," and they begged to be pressed into service even though their elders opposed the move. So did Confederate president Jefferson Davis, who called it "grinding the seed corn of the republic" to send these young men to fight.

Hostilities between the North and South began April 12, 1861, when Confederate artillery fired on Fort Sumter in Charleston, South Carolina. Two weeks later the University Greys became part of the Confederate army, the excitement of war overriding all concerns about their youth and inexperience. Many were killed at Pickett's charge at Gettysburg. But they had made an indelible mark on the school with their youthful but fatal enthusiasm, serving as an inspiration to later generations of white university men who battled on the athletic fields.

A month after the war began, all but five students had left the campus. "We are indeed inhabitants of solitude," Barnard wrote a friend in Washington, D.C. "Our University has ceased to have a viable existence. Its halls are completely deserted, and its officers are without occupation."

The board of trustees hoped they could keep the school open, but by the fall it was clear that the campus would have to shut down. The faculty had already recommended suspending operations, and by mid-October, only four students had applied for admission. It was unlikely very many more would be coming.

The board had been reluctant to close the school, fearing that an empty campus would be looted and damaged. But by November the trustees realized it was a risk they would have to take. Two professors would remain on campus to watch over the buildings. On November 21, 1861, Barnard made his last report to the trustees. While criticized in some quarters, in Oxford he had earned appreciation for his efforts on behalf of the university. In their final act before closing the school, the members bestowed on the chancellor an honorary doctor of divinity degree, a decent gesture befitting a man who would go on to great acclaim as head of Columbia University.

Within six months of closing, the university's buildings were turned into hospitals. The care of the wounded and dying only deepened the pain of the entire war for survivors, turning the campus into one of the many shrines to the lost battles.

The first Confederate wounded were sent to Oxford in March 1862. Their number grew considerably a month later after the battle of Shiloh, fought over two days in southwestern Tennessee near the Mississippi border. Casualties on both sides were heavy; the Confederacy lost more than 1,750 men, with more than 8,000 wounded. The Union casualties were nearly identical.

Every building on the campus was used to care for the sick, and every available space was crammed with pallets holding the wounded. There was barely a passageway for attendants to move between the ailing soldiers. Oxford residents willingly offered their help, sending over mattresses, cots, and bedding to supplement the provisions the Confederate army was sending in from New Orleans and Vicksburg until the Union army cut off supply routes.

The doctors made available to the makeshift hospital had to rely on the women of Oxford to act as nurses, each of them taking turns carrying food from their homes to the wards. Survivors remembered it as a period of "self-sacrifice and deprivation" willingly accepted "for the cause was a common cause."

In November the hospital had to be hastily disbanded when word came that the U.S. Army under General Ulysses S. Grant was advancing on Oxford. The wounded were rushed to outposts south of the campus.

Before Grant arrived, however, a band of Kansas soldiers invaded the town, destroying many stores before they rode at full gallop onto the campus. They burst into the building used as headquarters and destroyed much of the medical equipment before their commanding officers arrived and ordered them back to camp.

Grant came into Oxford early in December 1862 intent upon burning the buildings because they had been used for "war purposes." But he abandoned that plan when one of the two professors still on campus persuaded the general that using a building as a hospital was not really a "war purpose." Besides, the Union army might have similar use for the buildings. There was also widespread speculation that "damn Yankee" Barnard, the recently departed chancellor, tried to help, appealing to Grant to spare the school.

The general subsequently honored another request to put a guard around the university buildings, ensuring their protection. (Oxford itself was not so lucky. Eighteen months later federal forces burned the town, including the courthouse and all the local public records in it.)

Grant stayed at the university only three weeks. He was forced to return to Memphis after Confederate troops outflanked him to the west and cut off communications with other Union forces.

Shortly after Grant left, the campus became a hospital again, but the building housing the wounded was in terrible shape, its walls defaced, its floors crumbling from neglect, and its furnishings barely usable—the "poorest of cots and covers; one dilapidated chair for each occupant, and a few tables and washstands scattered about, all make my heart ache, as I remember them yet," recalled one Oxford woman who had volunteered as a nurse.

By the time General Robert E. Lee surrendered to Grant on April 9, 1865, roughly 1,850 patients had been cared for at the university. More than 700 of them had died. They were buried in a cemetery on campus, but their grave markers were later destroyed when workmen carelessly failed to protect them during a cleanup of the area. The mounds covering the bodies were leveled, and grass was planted over the entire spot, obscuring the fact that it was the final resting place for the dead soldiers.

Several years after the war, a monument to their memory was put up by the United Daughters of the Confederacy. Later events made clear the UDC need not have worried that the Confederate dead would be forgotten. The debate would be over how they were remembered and for what.

The university officially reopened the first Monday in October 1865, three years and eleven months after the war had closed its doors. Only 24 of the 135 University Greys who had signed up survived. None returned to Oxford to study. The memorial to them on the campus—a large stained glass window in a classroom building—reflected the reverence for tradition and fealty to place that would inform and inflame later crises on campus: "In honor of those who with ardent valor and patriotic devotion to the Civil War sacrificed their lives in defence of principles inherited from their fathers and strengthened by the teachings of the Alma Mater."

Reminders of war were everywhere as the university resumed classes. Most of the students and teachers had been in the Confederate army, and several bore the scars of the experience. Many dressed each day for class in parts of their army uniforms.

The war had also changed the university's student body. Before the fighting, students were almost exclusively the sons of wealthy white parents; antebellum per capita wealth in Mississippi was higher than in any other state. After the war, students, according to the university's official catalog, were "the sons of parents who had been wealthy but whose wealth had been entirely swept away" during the fighting.

Although there were no graduates at the end of the first postwar term, the university held a commencement ceremony anyway, an opportunity to honor the vanquished and defy the conquerors. The presiding clergyman had been carefully chosen to symbolize the moment: the Right Reverend R. H. Wilmer, an Episcopal bishop from Alabama who had forbidden his clergy to pray for northern occupying forces. In retaliation, union military authorities suspended Wilmer and the other clergymen from their duties and closed their churches for six months. Northern bishops treated Wilmer as an outlaw. Flouting this opprobrium, the university awarded Wilmer an honorary doctor of divinity degree.

The mildly defiant act was just one of many such actions across the South in the immediate aftermath of the war, each indicative of southerners' effort to make some sense, rational and emotional, of their devastating defeat. Eleven states had seceded from the Union to form a political nation built on the heritage bequeathed to its citizens by their forefathers. Lee's surrender to Grant ended that dream, but in its place in these postwar years was the creation of a cultural nation whose binding force was the elevation of the losing battle to sacred status. This worship of the "Lost Cause" was played out in annual memorial ceremonies, through literature and music—hymns to the Confederate general Stonewall Jackson were especially popular—and by a proliferation of monuments to honor those who had died in its service on the battlefield. By 1914 more than nine thousand of them had been put up in the South, along with a proliferation of stained glass church windows whose designs commemorated the Confederate sacrifices.

The Confederate Museum in Richmond was a special sanctuary with a room for each seceding state, each filled with medals, flags, uniforms, and weapons from the Confederacy. One section of the museum, named the Solid South Room, displayed the great seal of the Confederate States.

At the University of Mississippi, one of many postwar shrines, the religion of the Lost Cause was evident at commencement exercises in 1867, barely two years after the fighting stopped. The Reverend T. D. Witherspoon, a university graduate, was the main speaker, his florid prose typical of so much of the Lost Cause literature and reflecting a deep suspicion of outsiders. He called on the young men to preserve and revere the past in a speech he titled "The Appeal of the South to Its Educated Men." It was an appeal, he explained, "which comes up from her wasted fields, her desecrated altars, and her smoking ruins—from her darkened homes, her smitten hearts and the graves of her unknown dead. . . . If I can but call up the spirit of this desolated and suffering land, and bid it speak to your hearts, I know that I shall not fail to have attentive hearers, and that my words will not be spoken in vain." The first thing the young graduates must do, he counseled, was "to embalm in literature, and thus preserve in fragrant memory at least that peculiar type of civilization which has been the ornament of the south, but which is now to pass away."

Of particular importance was to set the record straight about slavery. Enemies of the South, Witherspoon said, had tried "to represent the influence of slavery as having been degrading both to master and to slave; to picture Southern society as corrupt and debased through the presence and contact of this vile enormity; to represent Southern people as embruted in their instincts, rendered cruel, mercenary and vindictive by their traffic in human flesh. . . . It must be ours," Witherspoon continued, "to give the world a true portraiture of those brighter days . . . when our very slave states were happier than those who came to liberate them—far happier than they will ever be in that freedom, falsely so-called, into which they have been introduced."

Second, these graduates must "transmit to posterity in permanent form a fair and impartial record of the struggle which has just closed." Although historians would later cast doubt on this assertion, Witherspoon contended that there was "unanimity of sentiment" in waging the war and that "right or wrong, the hearts of the Southern people were as the heart of one man." To portray the four-year battle as simply over slavery was to foster "an entire misconception," he added, and it was the "educated men of the south" who had to put a stop to the "determined effort being made to write a history of this revolution as a fractious and causeless conspiracy against a peaceful government."

Finally they must be willing to replace old school books with new ones, to aid in the "preparation of an educational literature for the youth of the South. . . . All the text books in prominent use among us have been compiled by Northern scholars and issued by Northern publishers," he said, and in these books was a "spirit of fanaticism" that threatened "to poison the minds of the people with false views of the struggle that has closed. . . . We must have an educational literature of our own, or we have no security for the future against a thraldom far worse than that of the bayonet."

Witherspoon had no way of knowing that his alma mater would provide future generations with the "security" he was looking for. Nor could he have foreseen the later political fights on the campus about what would be taught and by whom. But his emotional address was evidence that the university, barely twenty years old, was already fulfilling the mission its earliest supporters had hoped for, transmitting culture—customs, values, history, and habits—"across the generations."

The war, as Witherspoon noted, had changed more than the student body. It had remade the social order, at least on the surface. Slavery was gone; blacks were now free and in theory entitled to the same educational opportunities, among other things, that whites were. The entitlement would prove illusory.

White leaders feared that too much education for newly freed slaves might be dangerous. The more overtly racist among them disparaged blacks as not having the ability to learn. But the more privately expressed concern was that blacks would learn too much in school, not too little— and what they learned might make them dissatisfied and more likely to challenge the status quo. "White people want to keep the negro in his place," noted Thomas Pearce Bailey, one of the university's own highly regarded professors, and the problem with education, he observed, is that "educated people have a way of making their own places and their own terms."

No one better understood this than James K. Vardaman, one of the state's most virulently racist politicians. "Literary education—the knowledge of books—does not seem to produce any good substantial results with the negro," he said, "but serves rather to sharpen his cunning, breeds hopes that cannot be gratified, creates an inclination to avoid honest labor." It was a view that would be carried well into the twentieth century. (In 1940, state legislators nearly adopted legislation that would have stripped textbooks for black students of all reference to democratic political procedures, a move driven by white opposition to "teaching Negroes about voting and other matters pertaining to running the government.")

In post–Civil War Mississippi, a black person had to struggle to get any education at all; the prospect of getting a college education was even more daunting. Two private colleges, Shaw University and Tougaloo, had been established in 1866 and 1869, respectively, and each received small state subsidies to support their teacher training programs. They were hardly full-fledged colleges, however. Shaw was largely a secondary school until well after World War I, and Tougaloo did not issue its first baccalaureate degree until 1901. For the next thirty years it averaged only two a year.

Immediately after the war questions loomed about whether greater state support for black education would be required under the Reconstruction government, and if so what that might mean for the Oxford campus. University loyalists were concerned because this new government included blacks, hated "carpetbaggers" from the North, and "scalawags," the unsympathetic southern whites. To the university's new chancellor, John Waddel, they were nothing but "alien controllers."

L. Q. C. Lamar, the professor who had drafted Mississippi's secession ordinance, resigned from the faculty when he saw who was appointed to the university's board of trustees. (Lamar eventually would be pardoned for his role in the Confederacy and appointed to the U.S. Supreme Court, one of the more striking examples of postwar reconciliation.) Although others did not follow Lamar's lead, there was vigorous debate around the state about whether "sound Democrats" should step down from their positions of power and influence and whether Mississippians should decline to send their sons to Oxford, "where they would be in danger of being corrupted politically."

Edward Mayes, a tutor at the university, recalled some years later that even in 1870 there was "a strong undercurrent of nervous apprehension lest at any time some aggressive negro should ignore the provision made for his race elsewhere, and demand admission to the university, in which case an explosion was regarded as inevitable." It was a prescient observation.

For the moment, however, the focus was on keeping the university a white man's province. One resident was so concerned about the prospect of integration that he wrote Chancellor Waddel to ask, "Will the University, as now composed, receive or reject an applicant for admission as a student on account of color or race?"

With faculty approval, Waddel wrote back a firm reply: Should a black apply for admission, "we shall without hesitation reject him." The chancellor stated in unequivocal terms that the university "was founded originally and has been conducted exclusively, in all its past history, *for the education of the white race*." (Italics his) No one, Waddel said—not Congress, the state legislature, the board of trustees, or the faculty— "for a moment, conceived it possible or proper that a negro should be admitted to its classes, graduated with its honors or presented with its diplomas."

Waddel's letter was subsequently sent to newspapers around the state, and the chancellor recalled later that when he went to Jackson for a meeting, he was told by one supporter that "the University was saved" by his strong position. One contrary voice was Robert W. Flournoy, a former slaveowner and Confederate colonel who was editor of a newspaper called *Equal Rights*. A scalawag by Mississippi standards, he wanted the legality of the university's admission policy to be settled by the federal courts under the newly ratified Fourteenth Amendment, which guaranteed all citizens, former slaves included, equal protection under the laws. Flournoy used *Equal Rights* to encourage black students "competent to enter the university" to seek admission and "test the question whether the professor [Chancellor Waddel] or the Constitution is supreme."

No black student sought admission during Reconstruction or in the succeeding ninety years, and when the question would finally come before the federal judiciary in the summer and fall of 1962, the Constitution, not university policy, would be ruled supreme. Then the "explosion" that Edward Mayes had prophesied in 1870 would tear through the campus.

Leery as they were of the concept, white Mississippians did not completely ignore higher education for black residents. But it was as much a strategic decision to preserve white institutions as it was a beneficent gesture. The thinking was that if state-supported schools for blacks existed, then there would be no reason for them to seek admission to white colleges. It was clear to the white community, however, that higher education for blacks would be different from that for whites—geared, in the view of white educators, "to meet the 'peculiar' aptitudes and needs of a race of manual laborers."

Within months of Waddel's reassuring letter, the state established Alcorn University for young black men, named in honor of Governor James L. Alcorn. (Women were admitted unofficially in 1884 and officially in 1903; over five hundred applied for admission for far fewer slots and only one dormitory.)

Alcorn opened with commendable state support: annual allocations from the legislature, scholarships, and $100-a-year stipends for students who qualified. It also had a broad mandate. In addition to industrial arts and agriculture courses, which were taught at the school's ninety-acre demonstration farm, Alcorn offered the basic courses to train teachers.

This auspicious beginning was short-lived. Within three years of its founding, Alcorn was rife with discord centering around racial politics. Its president, Hiram Revels, who had been Mississippi's first black senator, was unpopular in the black community because he was thought to be too deferential to whites. Not only that, his narrow vision of what was possible for young black men conflicted with their rising aspirations, and they finally rebelled against his leadership.

There was enough unrest on campus to trigger a legislative investigation in 1874. The Alcorn board of trustees, the faculty, and Revels were removed, and the entire school was reorganized. Two years later the Republican-dominated Reconstruction government was out and Democrats reasserted power. Revels was reinstated as president, but a short time later Alcorn was again reorganized. Renamed Alcorn Agricultural and Mechanical College, its educational mission was diminished. Along with these administrative changes came drastic cuts in funding that would persist for decades, turning Alcorn, as one observer noted, into "not so much a stepchild of Mississippi higher education as an orphan."

When the school's funding was cut while Vardaman was governor, he provided his chilling approval: "I am not anxious even to see the Negro turned into a skilled mechanic. God Almighty intended him to till the soil under the direction of the white man, and that is what we are going to teach him down there at Alcorn College."

The state's neglect of Alcorn, until 1940 the state's only black four-year public college, was made even more apparent in 1925 when the school was unable to take advantage of a $100,000 offer from a northern foundation. The money was available if the state would provide an additional $200,000, but the state legislature refused to provide its matching share. Three years later, the offer was renewed, and this time the state legislature provided the funds. But when another foundation offered a $2,500 grant to buy books, the legislature once again refused to come up with the money.

Black Mississippians knew they were relegated to second-class educational status. One well-known Alcorn alumnus, Charles Evers, bluntly asserted that a degree from Alcorn was "the equivalent of a good eighth grade education—maybe."

While blacks may have been prevented from attending the University of Mississippi, admission of white women was a different matter. But the decision to do so was made with due deference to the idealized role of southern women, an implicit acknowledgment that it was not only blacks who had their "place" in Mississippi society. After an on-and-off debate over twenty-five years, the school opened its doors to women in 1882. No housing arrangements were available, however, and only eleven young women attended in this first year of eligibility. The number would not exceed thirty until the end of the century.

The prime mover behind state-supported education for women was Sallie Eola Reneau, who first raised the subject before the Mississippi legislature in 1856. Her comments seemed intended to reassure politicians that she understood and appreciated tradition. "We are not teaching women to demand the 'rights' of men nor to invade the place of men," Reneau promised. What was sought was the "higher training of the mind, of the sensibilities of her aesthetic faculties, of the moral and religious parts of her being, which fits her for the ways of modest usefulness . . . and which invests her with that true womanly character and those beautiful Christian graces that constitute her the charm of social life and the queen of the home."

The first female students seemed to follow Reneau's prescription, choosing such courses traditionally associated with women as home economics, needlework, and spinning.

After enrollment picked up at the school, there seemed to be so many appealing coeds that campus leaders one year sent movie mogul Cecil B. DeMille a stack of pictures of female students and asked him to pick the top ten. DeMille obliged, writing back that it was "a very special pleasure to pass judgment on these special representatives" of the school. A few years later the honor of selecting the campus beauties was given to Bing Crosby, who wrote in his letter to the yearbook that because of his movie experience he could vouch for the fact that Mississippi's reputation for beautiful women was deserved.

A photographic layout of campus beauties became a regular feature of the annuals. Three university women eventually were named Miss America, an honor the university always listed along with those more traditionally associated with academic institutions such as the number of Rhodes scholars.

The first yearbook had been published in the 1896–1897 academic year by fraternity men. The men's social clubs had been in existence for nearly thirty years, and publication of the annual was one more sign of the clubs' influence on campus. The early yearbooks also provided evidence that memories of the Civil War were constantly being rekindled and were not dependent for survival on the aging campus monuments. Though they had chancellors and distinguished alumni to choose from, the editors of the first volume dedicated it to the University Greys. Like the stained glass window installed in their honor, the inscription bespeaks a reverence for the past: It honors the young men who "resigned their college labors to battle for the cause of their fathers."

A few years later another yearbook was dedicated to Jefferson Davis. Although he had no direct connection to the school, he was honored posthumously as "an epitome of the patrician South, her natural leader in the struggle for constitutional freedom."

Though no blacks were students, they were fixtures of campus life, invisible but "in their place." They did the same work as free Americans they had done as slaves. Caricatures of blacks frequently showed up in the annuals in the form of cartoons or literary offerings, generally written in ungrammatical black dialect. One entry, "Negro Philosophy," featured a sketch of a black speaker telling his audience: "Brer'en' some pussons say dat dere war no niggers in de Bible. But I kan prube dat dey is wrong . . . dey larn about dot nigger Demus." "Nicodemus" was added in parentheses for those who needed a translation.

Another annual featured a picture of the blacks on the dining room staff, lined up and wearing starched white jackets. They were called the "skid professors, the really important ones on campus." Still another annual included a page of head shots of black employees with short descriptions of each, apparently intended to demonstrate the affection they had earned on campus. There was, however, a distinctly patronizing tone to the entries. One, for Charlie Webb, noted his forty-three years on the campus with the comment, "Never missed a trunk, never missed a train."

The name of the yearbook was as telling as the content. The title had been selected after a campus contest. The winning entry came from Emma Meek, a student from Oxford, who submitted "Ole Miss." It was not a diminutive form of "Mississippi" but rather a takeoff on the title given to the mistress of a plantation. It derived from the southern custom of courtesy titles that referred not only to marital status but also applied to names. The wife of the plantation owner, for example, might be Mrs. Jones but she would also be Miss Mary—called that by her husband and certainly by her slaves. If her daughter had the same name, she would be "Little Missy" and the mother would be "Old Missy."

The name for the annual not only remained, but from that point on, though nothing was ever done officially, "Ole Miss" became a synonym for the university. It was a fitting moniker given the goals of the school's founders, for with its obvious reference to the plantation aristocracy, when whites were masters and blacks were slaves, it was another "mystic chord of memory" that would echo throughout the university's troubled future.

2

A Tattered Shrine in Oxford

The 1927 gubernatorial campaign in Mississippi included much discussion about higher education, most of it prompted by a recently published study critical of the state's colleges. It was known as the O'Shea report, named for its principal author, Professor Michael V. O'Shea of the University of Wisconsin. The report took particular aim at Ole Miss for the low quality of its faculty and a curriculum in need of drastic change. One education specialist bluntly noted that the school "was not a great university . . . nor was it even a good university."

Theodore Bilbo won election to a second term as governor in the November vote and had made clear in his campaign that he would focus on education issues. By this time Alfred Hume, the chancellor of the university, had been a fixture on the Oxford campus for thirty-seven years. The clashes over the next three years between these men and the interests they represented highlighted the role Ole Miss had come to play as the conservator of a cherished heritage for so many white Mississippians. They would not countenance anything that in their eyes might diminish it.

Hume and Bilbo had much in common. Both were gifted speakers, though Hume was the more erudite; both had a deep feeling for Mississippi; and both defended with vigor the state's racial order. Each man had his own following, though Bilbo, who had been a state legislator and lieutenant governor, was by far the more controversial of the two given that he already had been charged twice with violating Mississippi laws. He had been acquitted of one charge but served a ten-day jail sentence for the other.

There were also important differences between the men. Bilbo was a politician, and a profane one at that, tweaking his audiences by sprinkling "hells" and "damns" throughout his stump speeches and telling stories often geared more for the good ole boys than mixed company. He was a diminutive man who favored well-cut suits and always wore a diamond tie tack. Hume had a more commanding and sedate presence. He was an educator steeped in a strong Presbyterian tradition that left little room for the kind of excesses that made Bilbo beloved by some, cursed by others. One enemy called him "a pert little monster."

Most important, the two men had very different views of what the university should be and do, and their divergent ideas precipitated a clash that would throw the school into turmoil. Hume believed in history and tradition—in other words, not rocking the boat. He viewed the university as a citadel for the state's white elite, a place to build their moral character, the better to preserve their heritage.

Bilbo considered himself a populist insofar as white Mississippi was concerned. He wanted to improve the lot of the common folk and believed that shaking up the state's public institutions, particularly Ole Miss, was the way to do it. Candidate Bilbo had promised in his stump speeches to act on the many recommendations made in the O'Shea report, stirring concern that bordered on enmity among those already secure in the academic community. One Ole Miss law professor wrote letters to friends and alumni urging them to help defeat Bilbo. He warned that "a vote for Bilbo is a vote against Chancellor Hume"—a warning based on rumors that if elected, Bilbo intended to fire Hume.

An angry Bilbo pressed Hume to rein in faculty members openly critical of him during the campaign; Hume refused, asserting that the teachers' private comments were not his concern. The entire conflict was one more manifestation of how much politics had infected higher education in Mississippi. Thirty years earlier, the university and four other public colleges had been governed by separate boards of trustees, with the governor appointing all the members. Back then, many board members were politicians, and in 1896, for example, the board that governed Ole Miss included the governor, the state superintendent of education, the state treasurer, two former governors, a congressman, and one former senator. This meant that college presidents were drawn into political contests and could be dismissed if they had supported the losing candidate.

By 1910 legislators, at the prompting of educators, had consolidated the boards into a single governing body and barred elected officials from serving on the new board of trustees. But politics still played a role in higher education given the governor's ability to choose the trustees. Indeed Hume had become chancellor in 1924 because the man then serving in the position, Joseph Neely Powers, was a long-time adversary of Henry Whitfield, who had been elected governor in 1923. Hume must have seemed especially appealing to Whitfield. In addition to his academic credentials—three degrees from Vanderbilt, math professor at Ole Miss, a dean, and the vice chancellor—he was the father-in-law of Whitfield's campaign manager.

Hume felt amply prepared to be chancellor. He had come to the post with clear ideas, long envisioning a tightly run school for Mississippi's upper classes. When he finally got the job in 1924, he announced that his singular goal for the university was "the exalting of character, by putting the emphasis on things moral, by stressing religious and spiritual values." In this time and from this man it was a way to signal preservation of the social and political status quo.

By his own admission—this in a report to trustees—Hume had not been interested in putting up new buildings (though he admitted more were badly needed), increasing enrollment, or beefing up the faculty, "however necessary and desirable both may be," or even in pursuing academic or athletic excellence, "however much I want these, too." They simply were not his focus. He was, however, attuned to the deep attachment many Mississippians had for the university, and he would play on that attachment with considerable skill in the coming clash with Bilbo.

Known fondly to his biggest fans as "Little Allie," Hume had applied his strong Presbyterian beliefs about "religious and spiritual values" to campus activities, prohibiting students from smoking, drinking, dancing, wearing shorts on campus, or playing tennis on Sunday. Daily chapel was required. Some joked that Ole Miss was really "Hume's Presbyterian University."

Anyone who ran afoul of his proscriptions could be in trouble, as two yearbook editors found out. One year Hume declared that some of the poetry and puns in the annual amounted to "libelous slurs at girlhood and womanhood. . . . I do not know what to think of people who dedicate a book to their mothers, beautify it with scenes of the old home—their alma mater—together with pages of pictures of lovely young women . . . and then print and publish right alongside of these, scurrilous statements about women which should bring the blush of shame to every right minded person," he said. Hume impounded the book, expelled the editors, and set up a board to censor future student publications. Roundly criticized for handling the matter so arbitrarily, Hume subsequently reinstated one of the students, contending that he was not responding to pressure but meting out "mercy not justice" for a student who had approached him as a "penitent child or sinner."

Hume also had specific ideas about academic freedom at the school, generally subscribing to the concept but within limits. In his mind "fundamentally and historically the University of Mississippi is essentially a Christian institution. . . . It goes without saying that anything tending toward atheistic teaching will never be tolerated by me."

At one board of trustees meeting, he offered an example of an appropriate dismissal of a faculty member. Although it did not suggest atheism in the traditional sense, Hume's hypothetical case did illustrate how "religion" at Ole Miss embraced the political. The chancellor's example was a teacher who suggested that secession was treason and that Robert E. Lee was a traitor. If an Ole Miss professor propounded such views, Hume said, his place in the history department would be "instantly vacant." And if the professor raised the issue of academic freedom, "the emphatic answer, coming quick and hot," would be: "'Sir, you are entitled to your opinions and you may teach them in a college of your own, but not in ours. . . . You are free, but so are we, and you may not trample under foot what we regard as sacred as long as you hold a position in our institution.'"

Hume was firmly anchored in a present defined by the past. Bilbo was, in his own mind, "looking fifty years ahead for Mississippi," and he was ready to take on all opponents, Hume included. He understood that he would have only a short time to seek change at the university and that there was no guarantee that whatever he put in place would survive the next administration.

Like other white Mississippians of note, certainly the politicians, Bilbo believed in white supremacy. Indeed as pressure to break down racial barriers began to seep into Mississippi, Bilbo would emerge as one of the most virulent and vocal racists in the entire South. But when it came to the hopes and aspirations of common white folk, Bilbo considered himself an energetic populist, and toward that end he wanted to reorganize the university into a more progressive institution committed to building programs that could help solve the state's economic and social problems—albeit within the framework of segregation. Hume's attitude and opposition to Bilbo from Ole Miss teachers had deepened his conviction that the school catered to the state's old aristocracy.

Even before Bilbo was elected, rumors surfaced that the university might be moved to Jackson, the state capital, to make it more accessible to potential students and facilitate its expansion. In an effort to derail this idea, Hume struck the "mystic chords of memory" with an exquisite touch that illustrated his understanding of how important a sense of place was to so many in Mississippi. His appeal on behalf of Ole Miss could have come straight out of the literature of the Lost Cause a half-century earlier.

"The University of Mississippi is rich in memories and memorials, in a noble history, and in worthy traditions," he said in a statement printed in newspapers around the state. "Were it robbed of these or separated from them, it would be a heavy loser and would become poor even if endowed with millions. A school without sacred memories and holy traditions," he continued, "can never be more than a school in the making. . . . If its children do not come to its defense," he added, the memorials on campus—the stained glass plaque honoring the University Greys, the monument to the Confederate dead, and the Confederate cemetery—"would cry out." He called them "as sacred as any ancient shrine, altar or temple. Instead of moving the University away that it might be a little easier to reach, ought not the people of Mississippi to look upon a visit here as a holy pilgrimage?"

Bilbo had little patience with this sentimental approach. He didn't want a shrine in Oxford. He wanted a vibrant learning center in Jackson. He believed rebuilding Ole Miss into a modern institution was "the one thing that would do more to develop Mississippi and bring her to glory than anything else."

The day after his inauguration, legislation was introduced to relocate the school. Hume and his allies in Oxford were not about to let such a thing happen without being heard. Within three weeks, town leaders raised several thousand dollars to invite the entire legislature—via special train—to visit the university. After a day of touring the campus to view its sacred memorials and soak up its "noble history," the lawmakers were feted at a banquet featuring a peroration by Chancellor Hume that once again infused the political with the religious. "Gentlemen, you may move the University of Mississippi. You may move it to Jackson or anywhere else," he told them. "You may uproot it from the hallowed ground on which it has stood for eighty years. You may take it from these surroundings that have become dear to the thousands who have gone from its doors. But gentlemen, don't call it Ole Miss."

Hume apparently moved the legislature. When the proposal came up for consideration in Jackson, lawmakers voted overwhelmingly to leave the university in Oxford. Two weeks later, Bilbo conceded that the school would not be moved. But if the governor could not move it, he could try to improve and change it, and one of the major changes was to fire Hume. It would prove to be no easy task.

Hume had been popular in some quarters in spite of the O'Shea report—certainly among the faculty he hired and protected and those who appreciated his style and shared his educational views. But the O'Shea report had shown demonstrable problems under his stewardship. Not only was the physical plant in need of repair, its academic programs were floundering as well. The law school was a case in point. Started in 1854, the school had grown steadily despite a three-year hiatus during Reconstruction. By 1921 the curriculum required three years of study, and the next year the school became a full member of the Association of American Law Schools. But four and half years later, in January 1927, the accreditation was removed because of inadequate physical facilities and poor administration. A report by the law school association cited an inadequate library, insufficient classrooms, and insufficient offices for instructors. It noted further that the school was even short on such basics as bookshelves, chairs, and desks.

The association's inspector said record keeping was particularly poor, pointing to four lists of students enrolled, with no two the same. Five students had enrolled without the knowledge of the dean. The faculty was criticized for not being informed about modern methods of legal instruction and not being "alert or aware of what was being done in legal education elsewhere."

The medical school had also been placed on probation by its accrediting organization, further tarnishing the university's luster.

All of this was ammunition for Bilbo. Making good on his promise to improve Ole Miss, he immediately had secured a hefty appropriation for the school, and Hume promised that "a transformation is being wrought." His few detractors on campus were dubious.

One of them was W. A. Lomax, the editor of the *Mississippian,* the weekly campus newspaper. When the chancellor announced that some of the state appropriation would be used for new steel library shelves, Lomax took on the chancellor in an editorial. "Let's first get a library," Lomax wrote. He ridiculed its holdings, noting that most of them had either been donated or bought at an auction; in any event, the inventory was inadequate. "Outstanding among the deficiencies," he went on, "is the spirit of conformity, which rules and prevails. . . . If a book even hints at disturbing the established political, social or religious questions of the day, it is not on the University Library shelves." Such a situation, Lomax said, "should not be the case in a great University, the alleged home of free thought."

One department chairman learned firsthand of Hume's limited view of transformation. Aware of the new infusion of cash to the school, he asked the chancellor to approve a $125 expenditure to buy back issues of an important professional journal. Hume turned him down, telling the teacher he had found it hard enough to make students read textbooks, much less outside reading, so there was "no reason why $125 should be spent on old periodicals."

By the summer of 1928 Bilbo announced that he wanted to replace Hume. But the board of trustees, a majority of whom were appointees of the former governor and Hume loyalists, refused to fire him. His contract was extended for a year. In the meantime the Southern Association of Colleges and Schools determined that the university's general academic program did not meet required standards. The faculty came in for special criticism because a "large proportion" had gotten their degrees at Ole Miss. The organization, which was run by southern school administrators, many of them good friends of Hume, nonetheless took a gentlemanly approach to the problems: It did not rescind the university's accreditation but simply urged the chancellor to improve the situation as soon as possible.

In 1929 Bilbo, now convinced that Hume was "temperamentally unfit" to be chancellor, tried again to replace him, but once again the board refused to go along.

Despite pressure to cease his actions against the chancellor—one newspaper editorial said, "Forget it, Theodore"—Bilbo persisted. And by the third year of his term, the governor finally controlled a majority of the board, which oversaw not just Ole Miss but three other schools. He was now in a position to make changes. This time Bilbo decided not just to replace Hume but faculty members as well. The governor had publicly stated that Hume's educational philosophy was outmoded and that the chancellor lacked the vision to turn Ole Miss into the University of Mississippi he envisioned.

Bilbo was willing to put the state's money where his mouth was, recommending that the chancellor's salary be increased from $4,800 to $25,000 in order to attact a leader of national reputation as the University of Wisconsin and the University of Chicago had recently done. Moreover, salaries at other regional universities were more than twice what Ole Miss paid; the universities of Alabama and Tennessee, for example, paid their top administrator $12,000.

With two years of his term already gone, the governor finally got half of what he wanted. Hume was removed in June 1930, but instead of going outside the state for a new chancellor, the board of trustees selected Joseph Powers, who had preceded Hume but had been removed in a power struggle with a previous governor. In one cryptic comment, Bilbo noted that since Hume had gotten his job "by political tactics, he shouldn't kick if he lost it the same way."

Although Powers was as tied to the Mississippi political system as Hume, he had a dramatically different view of the school from his predecessor, one more consonant with Bilbo's. Powers envisioned the university as "a coordinate branch of democratic government out of which may be drawn a body of experts and social minded men of good common sense, ever ready . . . to understand, to analyze and sympathize with the state in its making."

The changes did not end with Powers. When the new chancellor presented his faculty nominations to the board for approval, eighteen of them were rejected. Their replacements, the board minutes showed, were younger and in most cases had superior credentials to those who were removed, an apparent step toward the improvements the Southern Education Association had recommended. The fired dean of the graduate school, for example, did not have a Ph.D. and had been at the university for thirty-seven years. Most of the others dismissed held only baccalaureate degrees, which they had earned at Ole Miss.

Bilbo thought he was moving Mississippi forward, but instead of winning praise, he was pilloried. His detractors labeled the administrative and faculty changes a "purge." The *Jackson Daily News,* for example, decried the "politics" involved in Bilbo's action, contending that even if the new blood at Ole Miss served with "more energy and efficiency" than the old, it was still unnecessary to remove the chancellor and some teachers. Speaking of Hume, the paper said it was "akin to turning a faithful, time-worn horse out of the pasture with a vigorous slap on the rump, and telling him to go elsewhere to seek his grazing." There was also criticism of Bilbo nationally. Most prominent was the *New Republic,* which published a factually inaccurate account, "The Spoils System Enters College," contending that fifty Ole Miss professors had been fired—nearly three times the correct number.

The partisan bickering led by Bilbo opponents was less serious than the reaction of the Southern Education Association, which suspended Ole Miss and three other state schools. The inspector for the organization was a close personal friend of Hume and had spent only a few hours on the campus for his investigation. He declined a request to listen to Chancellor Powers's defense of the institution. The final report did not cite the university for violating any of the association's standards, but the university was suspended because of the "tone of an institution" and "the spirit of administration."

When word of the organization's action reached the Oxford campus, Bilbo was burned in effigy, apparently reflective of a more positive view of Hume than editor Lomax had held. An editorial in the *Mississippian,* now under new leadership, praised the former chancellor for his "iron hand" in guiding Ole Miss, and it likened Bilbo's effort to remove him to the "most stirring case of crass injustice" since Reconstruction.

There was more bad news for the university. The Association of American Law Schools expelled the law school from its membership even though it had made improvements since its previous probation with the help of a $150,000 appropriation from the state legislature. The engineering school also lost its accreditation, and two medical accrediting agencies put the medical school on probation. However, the director of one of them later told Chancellor Powers that "great good will no doubt come out of the whole mess. The school has had a good jolt which should shake it into life."

Perhaps most telling was the treatment Ole Miss got from the National Association of State Universities, which conducted a two-day investigation at the campus and exonerated the university of "many of the criticisms levied against it." It also stated that some well-publicized accounts of the situation—notably the *New Republic* article—were exaggerated and distorted the true picture. The association subsequently declined to censure Ole Miss and criticized the accrediting agencies that had done so.

Not surprisingly, enrollment suffered during this turmoil, given that the critical accrediting organizations threatened not to accept the credentials of Ole Miss students either as transfers or for graduate work at other schools. In the 1929–1930 term, Hume's last while Bilbo was governor, 1,254 students attended the school. Within two years of his ouster, the number had dropped to 728.

By then Bilbo's term had ended. He was succeeded by Martin Sennett Conner, who took office in January 1932 and considered restoring the college's accreditation to be one of his most important missions.

Negotiations between Mississippi leaders and the Southern Education Association ensued, and by December 1932, the organization agreed to restore provisional accreditation to the school. One condition it had required was reinstatement of the administrators and faculty members who had been dismissed by Bilbo—a reflection of the tight bond among educators in the region still loyal to Hume. Accordingly, the trustees, apparently more concerned about the university's immediate reputation than longer-range educational policy, fired Powers and returned Hume to the chancellorship.

As Bilbo left office, he was seen by many as nearly destroying the university in his attempt to change it. But this view lost currency in later reviews of the period. "I believe I was wrong and he was right," admitted one legislator who had opposed Bilbo twenty years earlier. And another conceded that Bilbo had done more than anyone to move the university "on the road to a higher standard."

At the moment of turmoil, however, Hume's return to power was a comforting sign of stability and a reflection of the fact that the controlling white interests of Mississippi had not shared Bilbo's populist vision or the role of Ole Miss in it. Given his standing among like-minded educators in the region, Hume was able to help restore Ole Miss to full accreditation in the Southern Education Association and make sure the law and medical schools regained their standing.

By the beginning of 1935 Hume was sixty-nine; he decided that he had had enough of academic life. He resigned June 30, 1935, amid outpourings of gratitude from those who believed he reestablished "the university's good name" in his final stint as chancellor. His involuntary hiatus as chancellor aside, Hume had ultimately triumphed over Bilbo, keeping Ole Miss tethered to Oxford and secure in the "worthy traditions" he lauded.

In little more than a decade, they would be challenged in ways neither Hume nor Bilbo could have imagined.

3

Climate Control

The Ole Miss students in the immediate post–World War II years were hardly a revolutionary lot. The struggle for democracy overseas had done little to prompt a reassessment of the social caste system in their own state. It rarely, if ever, dawned on them that there was something wrong when a young black neighbor willing to die in his country's fight against Hitler could not come back home and attend his state university in Oxford. They, on the other hand, could look forward to that beautiful first fall day at school when they drove onto the campus, saw the Confederate soldier standing tall to greet them, the sturdy white pillars of the Lyceum in the background gleaming from a fresh coat of paint. There were football games to go to and the parties afterward, most of them joyous celebrations for a victorious team. And in the spring it was always tempting to put off studying for a midafternoon stroll in the Grove, the profusion of greenery providing a welcome relief from the gray winter days.

It was easy to feel buoyant and comfortable, secure in the knowledge that they were going through a prescribed rite of passage at the shrine that Albert Hume had so lovingly protected. These young men and women knew they were making important connections for their professional and personal lives that would ease their path to prosperous futures among the state's elite. They felt that they too had a duty to protect their school and, by extension, the culture that supported it, so it was not surprising that campus leaders in January 1948 declined to join the National Student Association, a suspiciously leftist organization, they believed, with an announced aim they found unacceptable: "the eventual elimination of all forms of discriminatory educational systems anywhere in the United States." "There can be no compromise with segregation," the student government said in a statement widely supported on the campus.

It was the prevailing view in Mississippi. Seven months later the state's political leaders marched out of the Democratic convention in Philadelphia after the party adopted a civil rights plank over their vigorous opposition. They headed to Birmingham, Alabama, to join other unhappy southerners for their own States' Rights Democrats convention, where Strom Thurmond, the governor of South Carolina, and Mississippi's own governor, Fielding Wright, were named the insurgents' presidential and vice-presidential candidates, respectively.

The States' Righters, dubbed Dixiecrats by a clever newspaper editor, used symbols of the Confederacy to promote their cause, adopting "Dixie" as their theme song and the Confederate flag as a rallying point. They looked for votes all over the South, and when they came to Oxford during the fall football weekends, they passed out small Confederate flags for fans to wave during the game. The flag was a resonant symbol for a school celebrating its one hundredth anniversary. One event in particular had rekindled memories of the Civil War and its special significance for the university: a reenactment of the University Greys' charge at Gettysburg, where so many of the young soldiers from Oxford had perished. Waving the rebel flag added one more bond between Ole Miss and the Confederate past. The fact that it was an election year was a political plus. The crowd in the stadium could not only cheer the Rebels on the field. They could also wave their flags and sing "Dixie" for the insurgent politicians representing their cause and their way of life.

The States' Righters carried only four states in 1948, one of them Mississippi—not nearly enough to throw the election into the U.S. House of Representatives as they had hoped. Incumbent Harry Truman won a come-from-behind victory over Republican Thomas E. Dewey and was in position to move forward on the ambitious civil rights agenda he had outlined earlier in the year.

After the election, John Stennis, one of Mississippi's U.S. senators, reassured an Ole Miss audience that there was little prospect of anything happening on these issues in the next congressional session. Southern senators held important positions and could block the reviled Truman legislation, he explained. The senator was correct as far as he went. But he hadn't mentioned the third branch of government: the judiciary. Had he included the courts in his talk, he would have had to tell his audience about lawsuits already underway that were going to affect Ole Miss and every other segregated southern university.

When school started in Oxford in the fall of 1950, Albin Krebs, a senior from Pascagoula, was settling into his duties as editor of the *Mississippian*. He took his writing seriously; he already had been managing editor of the paper and had done well enough that students elected him editor—Ole Miss was that rare school where such positions were filled by election not appointment. He was in two honorary fraternities, one for journalism and the other recognizing his leadership abilities. There was nothing on the surface to suggest he was anything other than a typical, if ambitious, student.

But unlike many of his white fellow students, Krebs had felt the sting of ostracism when he was a young boy in Pascagoula. He was a Catholic in the midst of Protestants, and they made him feel like he was an outsider. His boyhood experiences had shaped his notions of right and wrong, and he carried those ideals with him to Oxford. As editor of the paper, he felt a responsibility to keep up with events that affected the campus, and that included watching the state and national governments.

In June, before his editorship was in full swing, Krebs had noticed two important decisions of the Supreme Court concerning higher education, and he knew they were controversial. It was impossible to miss the drumbeat of criticism across the South when the Court took a significant chunk out of the foundation of segregated education: that seemingly irrevocable notion that "separate but equal" was not only appropriate but constitutional. In one case the justices said that the all-white University of Texas must admit a black man to its law school instead of requiring him to attend a new and obviously inferior law school for blacks. Because the new school did not provide the same educational opportunities as the university, the Court said, the young man was denied equal protection under the law guaranteed by the Fourteenth Amendment to the Constitution. In a second case the justices ruled that the state university in Oklahoma could not force a black graduate student to sit apart from whites at the law school and be separated from his classmates while studying in the library and eating in the cafeteria. These restrictions, the Court said, "impair his ability to study, engage in discussions and exchange views with other students and . . . learn his profession." Citing the Fourteenth Amendment as they did in the Texas case, the justices added that the provision "precludes differences in treatment by the state based on race."

Krebs decided to write about these cases; they dealt with college campuses and segregation, and that was certainly relevant. More important, he agreed with the Court. "Qualified Negro Applicants Should Be Allowed to Enter Schools," said the headline on his editorial. Krebs began the piece by noting that a black-owned newspaper in Jackson reported that it was just a matter of time before Negroes applied to the university's law school. He noted that the reaction to this news ranged from relative equanimity—"well, it won't be as bad as it sounds, if it happens"—to greater hostility—"when the black boys come in, I leave."

Reviewing the legal situation, which also included cases in Louisiana, Tennessee, and Georgia, Krebs surmised that Mississippi officials "will in the end have to admit Negroes to not only Ole Miss but . . . other state supported schools. What's more," he went on, "we believe that qualified Negro applicants should be allowed to enter the School of law and any other professional school that will enable them to better themselves, and thus everyone else in the state." Krebs added that he was sure "a great number of Ole Miss students feel much the same way about the question. We think they believe in the principles of justice for all. . . . We think they believe in the basic principles of the Constitution of the United States."

Hours after the editorial appeared, two hundred students paraded to Krebs's dormitory chanting, "Get rid of Krebs." Then they burned a cross under his window. Another forty-five signed a petition demanding that he be fired and a new editor elected in his place. One Mississippi congressman jumped into the fray, telling news reporters the editorial was "shocking" and "influenced by Communist elements."

The next week a chastened Krebs wrote another editorial, not retracting his statements but absolving the *Mississippian* as a whole for the first one. He said that because he signed the editorial, it was intended to express only his opinion, and he apologized to readers for not making this clear.

The explanation failed to mollify critics. "Why don't you take it and jam it," said one who declined to give a name in a letter to the paper. "You're nothing but a low down, nigger-lovin, small town hick. . . . You should be run right out of the state. Why don't you come right out and say you're on the side of Mr. Stalin and the rest of his stooges. Mister," the letter concluded, "you're a sorry example of Mississippi manhood."

Another critic, "against tearing down any social barriers" between the races, wrote that "anyone who tells you that allowing negroes to enter our schools is not a step toward the mixture of our races is lying or very short-sighted indeed."

A few writers supported Krebs, among them Memphis lawyer Lucian E. Burch. "Your editorial is rational and I think expresses the correct view of the matter," he said. "What is of more importance it took a great deal of courage to write it."

Eight days after the editorial appeared, the student governing body met to consider the petition to get rid of Krebs. After extended discussion, the campus organization voted by a two-to-one margin to ignore it and then passed a resolution recognizing his right to express his opinions in editorials.

Although Krebs remained the editor of the *Mississippian,* his boldness had repercussions for what he hoped would be a newspaper career in the state. Only Hodding Carter, the well-known and admittedly moderate editor of the Greenville *Delta Democrat Times,* and the editor of his small home-town paper would consider hiring him. Krebs also faced continued harassment around the campus—"nigger lover" was the common epithet—even when he attended a football game in his military uniform just before shipping out to Korea. He stayed away from Ole Miss for thirty-three years, returning for the seventy-fifth anniversary of the

Mississippian only at the personal invitation of the chancellor. His career flourished, however. After his stint in the service, he worked for a major Louisiana paper, *Newsweek,* the *New York Herald Tribune,* and then the *New York Times,* where he wrote until he retired.

     William Murphy had solid southern credentials: born and educated in Memphis and a law degree from the University of Virginia. He came to the Ole Miss law school in 1953 to teach constitutional law and labor law, joining the institution that played such a significant role in the state's political life. By 1937, 90 percent of Mississippi lawyers were Ole Miss graduates, and many of them were local and state leaders. As important, the legal system had become an essential tool for maintaining the racial order. Southern courtrooms from Reconstruction on served, in the words of W. E. B. Du Bois, as "instruments for enforcing caste, rather than securing justice."

It was crucial that the young minds of Ole Miss be rigorously trained to preserve the status quo, and most of them were. In a penetrating study of postslavery Mississippi, historian Neil McMillen pointedly described a legal system that "honored white supremacy above the rule of law . . . and spoke eloquently in defense of equity even as it acquiesced in a double standard of justice designed to keep the races separate and unequal." Anyone thought to have questioned that double standard could expect some kind of retribution.

Like law professors at other schools across the country, Bill Murphy paid close attention to the Supreme Court, particularly opinions concerning constitutional law. None was more momentous than the ruling handed down May 17, 1954. *Brown v. Board of Education* on the surface addressed only schools, but in fact it aimed at segregation per se. If the High Court could force public secondary schools to be integrated, then it could force integration in higher education and just about anything else. The *Brown* opinion was brief compared to many other Court opinions, but it was clear. "We conclude unanimously that in the field of public education the doctrine of 'separate but equal' has no place. Separate educational facilities are inherently unequal," said Chief Justice Earl Warren, reading the decision aloud from the bench for emphasis.

Across the South the reaction was swift and angry; in Mississippi it was particularly hostile. James O. Eastland, the state's senior U.S. senator, preached defiance, declaring that the state "will neither abide by nor obey this legislative decision by a political court." The *Clarion Ledger* pronounced May 17 a "black day of tragedy." True to their proud and activist past, Mississippians reacted with more than words. Within two months the first all-white Citizens' Council was formed to preserve segregation and block any attempt to enforce the Supreme Court decision. By year's end Citizens' Councils would spring up in county after Mississippi county and in every other southern state.

Although Murphy could appreciate the emotional aspects of the reaction to *Brown,* he was troubled by the vehemence and the direction the opposition was taking. Outright defiance was not an acceptable approach to a serious issue in a country that prided itself on democratic procedures. Murphy believed he could contribute to the public debate by suggesting from his vantage point as a constitutional law expert how Mississippi could deal with this admittedly wrenching decision in an appropriate manner, so he wrote a detailed response to the opinion that he sent to seventeen southern senators and other individuals around the region, including newspaper editors.

"No state or section of the country, any more than an individual citizen, can reserve to itself the right to disobey valid laws and court decisions because it is in disagreement with them," Murphy said in a frontal attack on Eastland's call for defiance. "The adoption of legal subterfuge in an attempt to evade the decision in the long run will be of no avail."

Murphy then offered proposed federal legislation that he described as "a rational and temperate approach on which men of good will should be able to agree." Its key ingredient was removing jurisdiction of school cases from the federal courts so that the states could take the lead in desegregating their schools. Congress would have the authority to determine if the states were making adequate progress—a forum, Murphy said, "where presumably Southern problems would receive more favorable consideration" than they had at the Supreme Court. Murphy closed by asserting that his idea was "an appropriate and intelligent application of the states' rights principle. The proposal will probably not appeal to either the radicals who demand immediate integration or the radicals who advocate civil disobedience. Surely the great majority of us are in neither group."

The dean of the law school, Robert Farley, thought well enough of Murphy's ideas to pass them on to a special state committee created to deal with the Supreme Court decision, and Farley himself had told a group of local officials that Mississippi could not "outsmart" the Supreme Court. Murphy also received generally favorable responses from the senators. But to many others, his ideas were nothing less than heresy. Most prominent among the critics was William J. Simmons of Jackson, who would soon command great influence throughout Mississippi as one of the chief strategists for the Citizens' Councils. His comments, aimed at both Murphy and Dean Farley, highlighted the resistance taking hold in Mississippi and epitomized the accusations and innuendoes that would ultimately drive these men from the state. "If these two gentlemen are not in favor of racial amalgamation with Negroes through the educational system, let them come out with a public denial," he said. "If they are in favor of Negro amalgamation as their words would indicate, let them say so in plain language, so everyone will know that the NAACP has captured not only the Executive and Judicial branches of government, but the Law School at Ole Miss as well."

"Such attitudes on the part of men in sensitive positions in our state must not go unchallenged," Simmons went on, charging that Murphy's views in particular represented "an open invitation to racial aggression of the most complete nature against the white people of the south and border states."

The governor, attorney general, and other Mississippi leaders are "racking their brains for ways to oppose integration," Simmons said, but at the university, "where our legal talent of tomorrow is being trained, the Dean and Associate professor sabotage these efforts by speech and public letter."

Farley and Murphy survived this contretemps, but Simmons and other Citizens' Council members had long memories. They would not forget the heresy preached by these men, and as pressures in the state increased in the coming years, they would reach back to this episode in the effort to rid Ole Miss of the nonbelievers.

"*Secession from Union*, Slave Auction, Ku Klux Klan to Highlight Dixie Week," said a headline in the *Mississippian* six months after the *Brown* decision. The article went on to embellish these themes, with the chairman of Dixie Week promising students that there would be "enough activities to please the whims of every Southern Belle and Confederate Gentleman." This annual campus ritual suggested that neither Simmons nor other like-minded Mississippians had to worry about integrationist fervor infecting the Ole Miss students despite the views of Krebs, Murphy, or Farley. It left no doubt that the white supremacist mind-set and southern tradition prevailed at the university.

The first day of Dixie Week touched the sacred and the political, beginning with the ceremonial raising of the Rebel flag complete with Drum and Bugle Corps, and then moving to the "assassination of Lincoln in the grill [a popular campus gathering place], secession from the Union, a parade at noon, endoctrination [*sic*] of yankee students [unlike *Confederate, yankee* was not capitalized], a salute at twilight to the Confederate Dead, flag lowering, and an evening pep rally."

The next day featured an appearance by the Klan, followed by the sale of Confederate war bonds and a reenactment of induction into the Confederate army. The highlight of the third day was the slave auction, with Ole Miss cheerleaders—white women—and campus political leaders—white men—being auctioned off to the highest bidder. They were required to obey the commands of their masters (but for only an hour). The rest of the week was devoted to entertainment events that recalled social life on the plantations: a campus-wide dinner, a dance, and a mule race with fraternities, the modern-day equivalent of plantations, competing against one another.

The students gave no thought to the notion that their Dixie Week behavior might be racist and insensitive. It was the same harmless good fun they had always had, the same partying they had heard about from their parents' fond recollections of Oxford.

Ole Miss students may have paid little attention to *Brown*. Not so the board of trustees. Mindful of increasing tensions over race and anxious to avoid any conflicts over the subject on state campuses, the trustees made a preemptive strike nine months after the High Court decision by adopting a policy that required all speakers invited to state schools to "be investigated and approved by the head of the institution involved." The speakers' names also had to be filed with the board.

Although no riots, demonstrations, or even tepid protests for integration had occurred, the trustees were apparently concerned about what young people might hear on Mississippi campuses. At Ole Miss it fell to J. D. Williams, the chancellor since 1946, to clear any future speakers. In his nine years in Oxford, Williams had established himself as an adept promoter of the university, garnering financial support from the legislature and alumni for an ambitious building program that was bringing new libraries and laboratories to the campus and attracting committed teachers.

A native of Kentucky, Williams had come to Oxford after being president of a small college in West Virginia. At his inauguration in the fall of 1946, he had asked one of his mentors, H. L. Donovan, the president of the University of Kentucky, to deliver the major address. Donovan had chosen as his subject academic freedom. "Neither Frankfort, Kentucky, nor Jackson, Mississippi, can control or interfere with what takes place in the classrooms or laboratories at the University of Kentucky or the University of Mississippi, and expect to have an institution that will redound to the glory of the state and the promotion of the welfare of society," he said. The cities he referred to were the state capitals, and he seemed to be warning against political interference in academia by the legislators who served there. Donovan spoke of the "four freedoms" he called essential to the welfare of a school: "freedom to work, freedom to teach, freedom to think, and freedom to write and speak."

It was a noble sentiment offered on a day of optimism for a new administrator, and there had been reason to believe in 1946 that such independence might finally be a reality in Oxford. Two years earlier, with memories of the Bilbo-Hume flap still fresh, Mississippians had adopted a constitutional amendment reordering the college board of trustees once again to keep politics out of education. Under this latest plan, a board of thirteen governed higher education: one trustee designated to oversee a special Ole Miss trust fund and twelve others appointed by the governor from all regions of the state, with confirmation by the state senate. Members served staggered twelve-year terms. In this way no governor could control a majority of the board since governors were not allowed to succeed themselves.

Events outside Mississippi, however, in particular the *Brown* decision and the inexorable march for racial justice that followed, prompted white supremacist leaders to circle their wagons. Diversity of thought, even at universities, was not welcome; the trustees' new speaker investigation policy was evidence of that.

The policy was quickly criticized by the *Mississippian*, which called it "disastrous to our institutions of higher learning in a number of ways." Most important, wrote editor James Autry, "it violates the very objects and purposes of the institutions in that it is a grave intrusion on the fundamental guarantees of free speech and free inquiry upon which the foundation for higher education must rest." In a prescient observation, the editorial added that the screening plan could be "only a wedge, the beginning of thought control which may well lead to censorship of text books and eventually of what is taught in the class room."

Autry was condemned in the Mississippi legislature and summoned for a meeting with the dean of students. Although the dean did not threaten censorship, he asked Autry to back off, telling him his editorial stance was "causing a great deal of trouble for the university" with the legislature, the school's main source of funding.

The campus leadership fraternity, Omicron Delta Kappa, which regularly sponsored campus speakers, sent a petition to the board echoing the newspaper's concerns and calling on the board to rescind the plan. The fraternity had good reason to worry; in the past it had brought an impressive array of speakers to the campus who might not pass muster now, among them Russian leader Alexander Kerensky, British politican Clement Atlee, and Eric Sevareid, the CBS reporter and commentator.

The fraternity's petition concluded with an instructive observation about the students' view of the place and time they were living in: "Many ill-informed persons of the United States consider Mississippi to be one of the most stagnant of the states of the Union. It is believed that, although the [board] resolution expresses great patriotism toward the ideals of the United States, it will be seized upon by accrediting agencies as a limitation of speech and the free interchange of ideas and in the very light of this opinion, burden the University with a reputation of inadequacy."

The board held its ground despite criticism from many quarters. In fact some board members admitted privately that the panel's actions were intended to ward off more draconian measures that might come from the state legislature. On top of that, sympathetic trustees believed the new policy would turn out to be a formality, not an intrusion. Nonetheless, it laid the groundwork for conflict on the state campuses. The first clash between the new policy and a state school came in Oxford, and it would erupt not over some rabble-rousing northern politician but a soft-spoken minister from the Midwest.

Every year since 1939, the university had hosted Religious Emphasis Week. The occasion was used to bring speakers, almost always Christian, to Ole Miss. The young men in fraternities frequently joked about the event, calling it "Be Good to God Week," but they nonetheless participated. Most fraternity members were religious in their own way, even if it was a religion built on southern cultural heritage rather than an unseen, all-powerful deity.

Campus chaplain Will Campbell, whose official title was director of religious life, was in charge of the program for the upcoming event, scheduled for February 19–22, 1956. Planning had begun well in advance. Though he was a Mississippi native, born in rural Amite County, his questioning of the racial status quo made him an iconoclast, even a radical, by southern standards. "Everyone at the university understood that race was not to be discussed," he explained, but he was determined to force the issue. "It seemed to me the annual Religious Emphasis Week was a vehicle to fill the void. If racial justice could not be discussed in the classroom, then it would be proclaimed from the podium of the religious forum." Campbell made sure that those sponsoring the event would "have to select people I knew to be sympathetic to racial justice."

The speakers were chosen by a special committee in October 1955, and one of them was Alvin Kershaw, an Episcopal priest from Ohio who was also an expert on jazz. Kershaw had been on the television quiz show *The Sixty-four Thousand Dollar Question,* where he won $32,000. Because he was a clergyman so knowledgeable about music, his appearance drew considerable attention, as did his announcement on the show that he intended to donate his winnings to certain favorite charities, among them the National Association for the Advancement of Colored People (NAACP).

This did not go over well among white Mississippians, particularly the Citizens' Councils, which made a public objection to Kershaw's speaking on campus. In Ohio, the priest was receiving hostile letters and phone calls, many of them threatening harm if he came to the state.

Campbell and some of the other invitees determined to stand united against the pressure to disinvite the minister. They got support from the campus governing body as well as from students running the *Mississippian,* where an editorial appeared in November 1955 asking in its headline, "If Rev. Kershaw Is Hushed, Where Is Freedom of Speech?" The editorial made clear that the paper was "not endorsing the Rev. Kershaw's views on the NAACP, quite the contrary. However it is the principle of the thing that we object to." The Citizens' Councils, the editorial added, "have neglected to grasp the meaning of a University. Students attend a University to increase their knowledge, gather information through freedom of speech and inquiry and formulate their own opinions. How is this possible when they are coddled like children?"

Pressure against Kershaw's appearance nevertheless continued to build into the new year. One state legislator even drew up a resolution of protest that he presented to the board of trustees. They responded that under the speaker policy it was up to the chancellor to decide what to do about Kershaw.

At first Chancellor Williams was inclined to let the minister come, believing that he had support from the newly elected governor, J. P. Coleman. Williams also hoped to get support from the local clergy on the theory that a church pulpit "should be free." But after meeting with his own Methodist minister, Williams came away discouraged. He had explained the situation and his view of the principle involved, and he hoped for a positive reply from his friend. Instead the bishop simply said, "Chancellor, you do have a problem."

The next disappointment came from Coleman, who had been in office barely a month. Unhappy about the growing opposition to Kershaw's appearance, he backed off from his previous offer of support, telling Williams in a private meeting in Jackson that if he publicly spoke out for the reverend, he would endanger his legislative program just introduced.

To find out more about what Kershaw intended to say at Ole Miss, the chancellor wrote him to ask about the upcoming speech. Though his address would not be about racial issues—it was to be "religion and drama"—Kershaw replied that he would speak about the matter if asked and would respond in whatever detail necessary to explain his support of integration. Editors of the *Mississippian* had also written Kershaw asking about his plans, and the paper printed his answer in the February 3, 1956, issue. It reiterated what he had told Williams: "If I am asked or engaged in discussion I must in the candor any honest question deserves speak from my convictions on segregation."

Not surprisingly, Kershaw's views ran counter to campus sentiment. A *Mississippian* poll in late January of more than two thousand students found that 74 percent favored segregation. Of the 19 percent who supported integration, the vast majority were nonsoutherners, and even they said integration should be gradual.

Early in February, before Religious Emphasis Week began, Williams convened an evening meeting at his residence with twenty-five prominent faculty members. In the early stages, support for Kershaw was still strong, but as the discussion continued and participants raised questions about a backlash against the school, particularly loss of financial support within the state, sentiment began to shift. Around midnight, Chaplain Campbell was summoned. After some preliminary expressions of concern from two of the faculty members, Williams gave Campbell the bottom line: "Will, the man can't come. Whatever it takes, he can't come to the campus. We just can't afford it."

Word of the Kershaw rejection spread quickly, prompting the resignation of sociology professor Morton King, who said he was leaving Ole Miss because the university no longer would defend "the freedoms of thought, inquiry and speech." A government professor at Mississippi State College also resigned in a sympathy protest. The state legislature immediately issued formal praise to the heads of both institutions for accepting the resignations, and Governor Coleman commended the legislature's action, his comments to reporters reflecting the hostile political climate. Professors in state-owned institutions who wanted to be a "sounding board" for the NAACP were not welcome in the state, Coleman said, adding that state-owned institutions belonged "to the people, and the people of Mississippi have the right to demand that teachers expounding against our way of life be ousted."

The retraction of Kershaw's invitation had prompted other invitees, primarily northern ministers, to withdraw from the event in a show of unity they had pledged months earlier. Coleman called them "no friends of Mississippi anyway."

Undaunted, Chancellor Williams determined that he would have Religious Emphasis Week but with local clergymen. "We don't need them," he said of the outside ministers. "We have fine homegrown talent who can speak as well as anyone."

Williams's plan was derailed when Oxford's ministers declined to participate. They said in a statement that "the excitement engendered throughout this controversy would make it difficult to maintain an atmosphere in which real religious values could be given proper consideration."

When Religious Emphasis Week arrived, Campbell set up two chairs in front of the stage in the campus chapel, shined a spotlight on each, and held a silent meditation each day at the hour that had been set aside for speakers. Each morning several hundred students, faculty, and Oxford residents joined him in the observance, which had the approval of university officials.

Campbell stayed on at Ole Miss only a few more months, leaving to take a job with the National Council of Churches. Although technically he was not forced out, Campbell paraphrased an old Chinese saying to describe his departure: "They didn't run us off. They simply turned the bees loose in our house and made us want to go."

The campaign against Kershaw had its effect on campus. Once a free speech issue in the minds of students, the adverse publicity turned it into a racial one, and it became clear that the young men and women were loyal white southerners before they were constitutional purists. Campbell attributed the shift in student sentiment to rising concern in the state about pressures to dismantle segregation. Students could feel this tension when they went home to see their families on weekends, as most did, because there was not much to do in Oxford on a Saturday night. On

Fridays, Campbell had believed he had staunch supporters; by Monday morning, his students, having participated in family discussions, were not so willing to press the reverend's case.

When Chancellor Williams went before the campus senate to talk about the Kershaw incident, he received a standing ovation. If Kershaw had come, Williams said, he "would have spoken on the segregation subject merely for personal conviction, since he has little knowledge of Mississippi's racial problems." In Kershaw's native Ohio, Williams added, the segregation issue is "purely academic." This capitulation seemed reasonable at the time, but it would set a disturbing precedent that would diminish Williams's leadership in future political crises on the campus.

Despite the *Mississippian*'s earlier statements supporting Kershaw, the paper now praised the chancellor for his handling of the matter. An editorial titled "He Didn't Let Us Down" said Williams acted in the best interests of the university. Initially a fight for freedom of expression, the editorial went on, the conflict turned into whether Religious Emphasis Week would be a "publicity circus. . . . How could students enhance their spiritual life," the editorial wondered, "when the garish flash of cameras replaces the fulfilling glow of Christ?" Referring to recent episodes of violence at the University of Alabama over racial issues, the editorial observed, "In Alabama we have seen what fiery publicity can do to a university's reputation."

As later events would prove, these young editors didn't know the half of it.

The Kershaw incident was the beginning of a more sustained challenge to academic freedom at Ole Miss and indicative of a growing intolerance across the state for any deviation from white supremacist orthodoxy. By the fall of 1958, two university alumni, state representative Wilburn Hooker and former representative Edwin White, decided things had gotten so dangerously leftist in Oxford that they had to speak out. With the tacit support of the Citizens' Councils, they went before the board of trustees in September to charge that Chancellor Williams, his rejection of Kershaw notwithstanding, and several faculty members were teaching integration, communism, and socialism, or some combination of the three, thereby subverting the way of life in Mississippi. The board asked for the allegations in writing, and in November Hooker filed a thirty-six-page letter with the trustees chronicling misdeeds he said he had been accumulating since 1952. White had submitted a shorter document a few days before Hooker.

Their charges cut a wide swath through the campus. Among those accused were Will Campbell, for playing Ping-Pong with a Negro in the local YMCA building and then driving "leisurely around the campus"; education professor Roscoe Boyer, for poking fun at a southern drawl and bragging that he was born in the North; and history professor James Silver, former chairman of the department and a faculty member for twenty-two years, for allegedly denigrating the conduct of Confederate authorities. The evidence against Silver, who eight years earlier had been accused of having communist leanings, was a master's thesis written by an Ole Miss student that criticized Confederate officials. The thesis, the accusers said, "could well be the fruit of Dr. Silver's lectures." Silver's own academic credentials were suspect because they were earned at Vanderbilt, "well known for its integrationist sentiments." Silver's defenders noted that he was teaching at Emory University when the thesis was written and that in any event he thought it was poorly done.

Concerns about alleged communists on campus actually predated the Silver charge. In the late 1940s, Ole Miss professors, interviewed for a wide-ranging project on southern politics, expressed reluctance to speak out on many subjects for fear that they might be targeted as subversives. The prevailing sentiment, one said, was that "anyone who disagrees with you is a communist."

Philosophy professor Quinton Lyon was accused of apostasy largely on the ground that his widely used textbook, *The Great Religions,* did not declare Christianity as the only true religion. To help support their case against Lyon, Hooker and White added the following: "At a high school press institute, Lyon gave the invocation, and a high school student, who is an informed Christian, stated that the invocation was odd and strange and that she was unable to understand it." Lyon responded, "When a high school student's report on my prayer . . . is taken as evidence against me, I fear for any basis of discussion."

Also singled out for criticism was Professor Murphy of the law school, whose observations on the *Brown* decision four years earlier had generated controversy.

As part of their general charges against the university's adminstration, White and Hooker also went after the library for how it used a $500 grant to make new acquisitions: "Every book purchased was in favor of integration." As if that were not enough, they charged that the placement of the books in the library showed a bias toward integration. Their evidence was that books favoring integration were in an open browsing room, and books supporting segregation were kept in the library's stacks, requiring a permit to get them. The men said the situation "is plainly a planned and effective method to condition students in favor of integration."

Among White's charges was the claim that Ole Miss was subverting the school's principles. His definition of these principles was telling, ascribing to the university the responsibility for promoting a particular brand of religion and a particular racial and religious orthodoxy. Notably absent was any mention of education. White described the bedrock principles of Ole Miss this way: 1. A belief in God, the accuracy of the Bible, and the immortality of souls. 2. The sovereignty of states and their right, among other powers, to operate public schools and regulate marriage, and the primacy of the Constitution over the Supreme Court. 3. A belief in "the ethnological truth that where races of different color mix with each other socially that inter-marriage inevitably results and that we have the obligation, and the inalienable right to preserve the identity of the white race." 4. The right of private ownership of property and "the right to profitably engage in private enterprise."

That Chancellor Williams later signed a document endorsing these principles was instructive, illustrating both a desire to calm the waters and an apparent agreement with statements that decades later seemed both unduly narrow and outside the traditional scope of a university's mission. Perhaps to emphasize his own southern credentials, Williams also told the board that he had attended only segregated schools and had never taught in anything but a segregated college.

The White and Hooker charges were made public in the summer of 1959, and the board of trustees undertook an investigation of the entire matter. Many Ole Miss alumni came to the defense of Williams and his administration. The largest of the county alumni associations, for example, issued a resolution praising Williams for his "administrative excellence and dedication to academic equality." The *Lexington Advertiser,* admittedly one of the most moderate papers in the state, editorialized against Hooker and White, both Lexington residents, accusing the two men of conducting a "witch hunt" that could damage Ole Miss and other state colleges.

At the end of August, the board publicly reaffirmed its confidence in Williams and dismissed as groundless charges that integration, subversion, and apostasy were being taught at Ole Miss—but not before Williams had signed the statement endorsing White's "principles."

The trustees also said that contrary to other allegations presented, there was no communist cell or NAACP chapter at Ole Miss. Although they paid lip-service to the concept of academic freedom, the trustees made it clear that the board "does not endorse every statement made by every staff member of the University of Mississippi or of other institutions, and may in fact disagree with opinions and views advocated by them from time to time." The trustees deemed it necessary to add this caveat: "It is proclaimed with equal fervor that academic freedom does not mean academic license. With freedom there must be responsiblity for statements, speeches and actions. . . . There is evidence that there have been some tactlessness and imprudence on the part of a very few of the faculty and staff at the University."

White and Hooker appeared to have been rebuffed in their crusade to rid Ole Miss of the alleged heretics, but in a political climate growing ever more edgy over race, the board's statement was not the last word on the school's operations or its personnel.

Although the trustees did not say which faculty members were guilty of "tactlessness and imprudence," law professor Murphy was certainly on their list. The harassment he endured became a case study in pressure to conform and the consequences for failing to do so. It was also a reflection on J. D. Williams. His failure to stand up to Murphy's critics, like the Kershaw incident earlier, helped set precedents for later interference in university affairs that would have devastating consequences.

In one of his major salvos against Murphy, Representative White cited a number of Murphy's writings and alleged activities that he said made him unfit to teach at the school. He first noted Murphy's response immediately following the *Brown* decision, then cited a review that appeared in the December 1957 issue of the *Mississippi Law Journal* critical of a book written by James J. Kilpatrick, who was editor of the *Richmond* (Virginia) *News Leader.* In the book Kilpatrick made a case for state sovereignty and the notion of "interposition," which in advocates' minds allowed states to interpose themselves between the federal government and a particular federal policy. It was seen as a theory of resistance to the *Brown* decision's demand for integration.

Murphy viewed interposition as legal nonsense and state sovereignty "a baseless cause." The fact that ten states had adopted resolutions "purporting to interpose the authority of the state and even nullify the Court's decision" was, he said, "a measure of the anger, emotionalism, and desperation with which much of the white South reacted to [*Brown*]." He added that it was "an almost infallible rule that, whenever a newspaperman expounds on a legal subject, what he says will be unreliable, and this book is no exception." White next cited an article Murphy wrote in the law journal the following March arguing against a political system based on state sovereignty. It was an excerpt from his doctoral dissertation at the Yale Law School and was later published as a book. In it Murphy cited the "disastrous" consequences for the newly independent America under the Articles of Confederation, which preceded the Constitution, and he argued that a state sovereignty system is "inadequate to the needs and aspirations of the American people."

Other portions of the dissertation were scheduled to be published in the law journal, and when some Mississippi lawyers complained about Murphy's arguments and pressured student editors to reject any more of Murphy's writings, Dean Farley stepped in and insisted that the rest of the articles be published as planned.

White also pointed out that Murphy was a member of the American Civil Liberties Union (ACLU), which he said had been investigated by at least three separate legislative bodies. One congressional panel, according to White, asserted that the ACLU was "closely affiliated with the communist movement in the United States. . . . It claims to stand for free speech, free press, and free assembly, but it is quite apparent that the main function of the ACLU is to attempt to protect the communists in their advocacy of force and violence and to overthrow the government." White went on to say that Murphy had been contacted by the executive director of the ACLU to see about finding a lawyer in Mississippi to help a black man who was considering applying to Ole Miss and that Murphy had supplied a name to the director. The lawyer ultimately declined to assist the ACLU.

White closed his presentation on a note of concern for the future of the law school and the state. "Our Governors, Legislators, United States Senators and Congressmen often come from the Ole Miss law School," he said, and few students, after having spent three years under the "subversive influence" at the school, "will have the desire to defend and protect the principles which have made our State great, and without which, it will surely perish."

After presenting his written document, White told the board that Murphy "has not been objective in his teaching of Supreme Court decisions on integration," but has "propagandized and has not presented the point of view and arguments of the South and the majority of Mississippi, as well as the laws and the Constitution of Mississippi."

Early in 1959 Murphy had been warned by one of Williams's assistants that two legislators were preparing allegations against him and some other professors. He was taken aback by the information, completely unaware that he was about to be caught in a highly emotional political vise. The chancellor's messenger asked Murphy to withhold any public reply to Hooker and White. "I will keep quiet if the university will defend me," he told the assistant. But for the record Murphy did write a point-by-point rebuttal of the charges against him, which he sent to Williams and board members.

Murphy was held in high regard by many students and former students, several of whom took the time to write him letters of support. Typical was one from a Jackson lawyer: "Of all the professors I had at the University, you were at the top of the list. . . . Never have I had a better teacher."

Murphy's faculty colleagues supported him, too, sending a formal statement to the board of trustees praising his "learning, ability and high professional reputation" and decrying what they termed "an act of politi-cal interference" in trying to force him out. And more than one hundred law students, nearly the entire student body, signed a petition "to publicly voice our complete faith, trust, and absolute confidence in the teaching ability and integrity of William P. Murphy."

Murphy had been on leave as a visiting professor at Duke University for the 1958–1959 academic year. When he returned to the maelstrom in Oxford, he decided to accept another visiting professorship at the University of Kentucky. He was hoping to stay there permanently, but the professor whose place he took decided to return.

Murphy was expected to come back to Oxford for the following year, and his courses were listed for the summer session of 1961. But the board of trustees, mindful of the continuing hostile political climate, stepped in with unusual action: They approved a summer position for Murphy at a salary of $2,000 but privately ordered university officials not to allow Murphy to teach.

Murphy knew his situation in Oxford was tenuous at best, and he was looking for a job at another university. He was in line for positions at two other southern law schools, but word from Mississippi of the controversy surrounding him derailed his hiring. It felt to him as if the Citizens' Councils wanted to prevent him from teaching anywhere, not just Ole Miss. For a man with a wife and three young children, it was a time of intense worry over such basics as paying the bills and the mortgage. All he could imagine was that his enemies thought of him as "Sampson tearing down their temple."

As things turned out the University of Missouri law school had an unexpected opening in the fall of 1961 for a constitutional law and labor law teacher, Murphy's specialties. He wanted a leave of absence, but the board of trustees, with Williams's acquiescence, balked. They said a leave implied the right to return. If Murphy went to Missouri, he would have to resign. Dean Farley intervened on Murphy's behalf, not only out of loyalty to the professor but also out of concern for the law school. If Murphy were fired, there was a good chance that the Association of American Law Schools, already looking into the Murphy matter, would revoke the school's accreditation.

Farley made a special trip to Jackson to meet with Ross Barnett, now Mississippi's governor, to convince him that Murphy had to be allowed to return to Ole Miss from Missouri if he chose. Barnett acceded to the request. In the meantime, though, still-angry legislators had continued their assault on Murphy. One sponsored a resolution that "respectfully and militantly" requested the board to terminate Murphy's employment, and the senate passed a bill aimed at forcing Murphy's ouster. It prohibited use of state funds to pay individuals who had been members within the previous five years of the Communist party, the ACLU, the NAACP, or any other group declared subversive by the U.S. House of Representatives Un-American Activities Committee. Neither the resolution nor the bill made it through the legislature.

Despite administration promises to defend Murphy publicly against such attacks, nothing had been done. Now he spoke out on his own. "I am not ashamed of my membership in the American Civil Liberties Union," Murphy declared. "It is a lie that the ACLU is any way subversive or unamerican." (In his earlier written rebuttal sent to Williams, Murphy had noted that when he decided to join the ACLU, he asked Hugh Clegg, the Ole Miss director of development and a former FBI agent, if that would cause a problem. Clegg had said it would not.) "As to my teaching," Murphy went on, "it is a lie that I have ever advocated integration in my classes. It is not my job to teach either segregation or integration. I am paid to teach constitutional law, and this includes the Supreme Court's segregation decisions." He concluded with a defiant blast: "I want to make this absolutely clear. I do not intend to give up my membership in the ACLU because of attempted political intimidation. I do not intend to tailor my teaching to satisfy any cult of crackpots, fanatics and wilful ignoramuses." Murphy noted ruefully to one supporter that the state's two major newspapers in Jackson declined to carry his statement even though they had publicized the charges against him.

Hodding Carter, by now one of the most outspoken critics of the rabid segregationists, praised Murphy in an editorial, calling his statement important reading for two groups: "the faint of heart who rather than risk controversy are willing to shut up or alter their thinking" and "that small, vocal ruling clique in Mississippi who are ruthlessly attempting to ram their point of view down our collective throats by whatever means possible." Carter urged more people to speak out against "the odious band of would-be fascists who are currently running amok," a request that went unheeded.

Murphy did come back to Oxford to teach one final semester and then announced he was taking a permanent position at the University of Missouri. He left Ole Miss with nothing but admiration for Farley and complete contempt for Williams. Whenever a controversy arose on campus, the chancellor would tell faculty members, "This is not the ditch to die in." At one meeting Murphy had risen up and asked, "Chancellor, what is the ditch we will die in?"

"When someone tries to get a professor fired for teaching in an area protected by academic freedom," Williams replied.

Murphy believed that ditch had been reached—and many months before. But nobody in the Ole Miss administration had died in it, Murphy thought bitterly to himself; only he had.

They "hit their target and brought him down," wrote Reese Cleghorn in the *Progressive.* "The segregationist extremists lack only the satisfaction of making a public spectacle of the affair." One professor, whom Cleghorn described as "distressed" by the entire episode, worried about the school's future: "If they get away with this one, there will be more. It will come sooner or later. And as a university we already are getting into trouble because we have let a tiger in the gate."

The anonymous professor had picked appropriate imagery to describe the university's future, but he could hardly imagine the tiger that was about to come through the Ole Miss gate.

4

⊱✦⊰

Meredith

James Meredith was many things: husband, father, son, soldier, and, above all, by his own definition, "an American-Mississippi-Negro citizen." He was also determined and deliberate, so there was nothing happenstance about his decision to apply to the University of Mississippi, nothing serendipitous about the day he picked to set the process in motion: January 21, 1961, twenty-four hours after John Kennedy's inauguration. Meredith thought this was a fitting moment to take a bold step for his people. He knew that black votes had played an important part in Kennedy's narrow victory. What's more, Kennedy had promised during the campaign to do something about civil rights, so Meredith reasoned that the new administration owed something to blacks and would have to act if put under pressure by black leaders. He was willing to make sure that pressure would be applied.

Meredith had chosen Ole Miss because it was a symbol of white prestige and power, a haven for the privileged and the finishing school for the sons of the elite. "I always considered myself one of those sons," Meredith explained, fiercely proud of his family's deep roots in the state.

He had prepared for this day carefully and for a long time. His pride of place and sense of belonging to Mississippi had come from his father, the first member of the family to own a piece of land, this in the hill country of the state seventy miles northeast of Jackson. Meredith had been born on that property in an old house at the top of a long, winding driveway that was shielded from neighboring farms, all white owned, by dense woods. "Cap" Meredith, as the senior Meredith was known, ran the household with a firm hand. His son referred to it as a "sovereign state" with its own rules, even in dealing with white Mississippi. Cap instilled in his children a great sense of personal pride. No Meredith, including young "J. H."—the name "James" would come later in life—ever went inside a white person's house because he or she would have had to enter through the back door. And Cap Meredith had taught his children that this was dishonorable. Moreover, no Meredith would work in a white woman's kitchen or take care of her children.

By the time he was a teenager, Meredith understood intellectually that the prevailing white supremacist mind-set in Mississippi meant that he was supposed to be inferior. He could not accept that, and by the time he joined the air force at age eighteen, he considered it his "personal responsibility" to change things. He would later say he believed he was on a "divine mission." It was one of the first things he told his future wife, Mary, when he met her in Gary, Indiana, on one of his military postings.

Meredith believed his years in the air force were an essential tool for his mission. His father had taught order and discipline, and so did the military. He was trained to be a soldier and to fight, and he knew that when he returned home to honor the promise he had made to himself as a teenager, he would be "at war."

Battles take planning, and Meredith wanted to plan the final chapters of his campaign on home soil. While still in Japan with the air force, he and Mary Meredith had decided to come back to the United States and finish their educations. They decided to enroll as full-time students at Jackson State. With his wife's acquiescence, Meredith had picked the school because he wanted to return to Mississippi and because it had just been reorganized to include a liberal arts curriculum. This would give him a chance to take a broad range of courses and to refine his ideas in debates with classmates and professors. He soon became part of a small group of students who were the academic leaders on campus and anxious to force change in their state. By mid-January 1961, Meredith decided he was ready to take on Ole Miss, encouraged by the discussions within the group and driven by the lingering question of one friend: "When are we going to do something?"

Before sending his first application letter to the university, Meredith had written to Thurgood Marshall at the Legal Defense Fund in New York telling the well-known civil rights lawyer of his plans and asking for help. It was the greatest of understatements when Meredith wrote, "I anticipate encountering some type of difficulty with the various agencies here in the state which are against my gaining entrance in the school." He closed his letter with a clear statement of his beliefs and his resolve. He was willing to take on this challenge, he said, for the "interest of and benefit of: (1) my country, (2) my race, (3) my family, and (4) myself. I am familiar with the probable difficulties involved in such a move as I am undertaking and I am fully prepared to pursue it all the way to a degree from the University of Mississippi."

Meredith's long campaign to earn that degree became a battle between the state of Mississippi and the U.S. government when it finally decided to come to his aid. Before he started this extraordinary journey, Meredith had in fact told friends that "only a power struggle between the state and the federal government could make it possible for me or anyone else" to run the gauntlet of Mississippi resistance. Against the president, the U.S. Supreme Court, and finally federal troops, the state was sure to fail, though it would put up an enormous fight. All three branches of the state's government would go to great lengths—off-the-cuff law-making, dubious court orders, and the outright defiance of Governor Ross Barnett—to keep one "American-Mississippi-Negro citizen" out of Ole Miss. It should not have been surprising given that so many of those pulling the levers of power, most significantly Barnett, were themselves products of Ole Miss and absorbed in its mystique as the enclave of white prestige.

On top of that Barnett was different from his predecessors in one important respect. All of them were segregationists, but they had kept their distance from the most rabid white supremacists. Not Barnett. He welcomed them into his administration, giving official license to the worst racial excesses and privileged positions to the purveyors of racial division, Citizens' Council members. William Simmons, the state council leader, became in the words of one pundit, the "prime minister of racial integrity."

The resistance to Meredith's Ole Miss application was slow to develop primarily because school officials didn't know at the outset that he was black. On January 26, 1961, registrar Robert Ellis sent Meredith a short reply to his first letter inviting him to continue the application process. Meredith answered on January 31 and dropped his bombshell in the most polite terms: "I am very pleased with your letter that accompanied the application forms you recently sent me. I sincerely hope that your attitude toward me as a potential member of your student body reflects the attitude of the school and that it will not change upon learning that I am not a white applicant. I am an American-Mississippi-Negro citizen." Meredith expressed the hope that his application would be handled "in a manner that will be complimentary to the University and the state of Mississippi." He added that he was "very hopeful that the complications will be as few as possible."

Instead Meredith's letter set in motion a strategy of delay, diversion, and duplicity by state officials that would postpone his eventual registration by one year and eight months. Two trials, a blizzard of conflicting federal and state court orders, one pronouncement by the Supreme Court of the United States, and the eventual military occupation of Oxford would be required to enroll this determined young man in Ole Miss.

Meredith's January 31 letter also underscored the ripple effects of the racial caste system. He could not comply with the requirement of endorsements from five university alumni, he explained, "because I am a Negro and all graduates of the school are white. Further, I do not know any graduate personally." Meredith instead submitted certificates of good moral character "from Negro citizens of my state."

The requirement of alumni statements had been adopted four months after the 1954 *Brown* decision as one tactic Mississippi leaders used to make sure that the university remained all white. In justifying its new policy, board members had said at the time that the "welfare" of the university "would be better served" if such testimony to good moral character were required. The board had also decided that all applications from blacks would be handled by the trustees rather than by the administrations of the state's colleges and universities—an indication that such applications were as much political as academic matters.

Five men had tried to integrate higher education in Mississippi before Meredith's attempt—two of them seeking admission to the Ole Miss law school, another to graduate school. The fourth man applied to Mississippi Southern College in Hattiesburg. One had been emboldened by the Supreme Court's higher education decisions in 1950 barring outright discrimination against blacks in graduate schools, the others heartened by the High Court ruling in *Brown,* but none proved to be as steadfast in his effort as Meredith.

The first black who wanted to go to the law school was from Ohio, but his application was immediately dismissed because his undergraduate degree came from an unaccredited college in his home state. The Association of American Law Schools required that accredited law schools such as the Ole Miss program require students to have at least two years of undergraduate work at an accredited college.

Charles Dubra thought he could meet that requirement with his overall academic record when he applied to the law school in 1953. He had graduated from Claflin College in South Carolina in 1928, and although the school was not accredited until 1947, Dubra had also earned a master's degree from Boston University in 1946. But over the objection of law school dean Farley, the Ole Miss trustees determined this did not meet the accreditation requirement. Dubra elected not to challenge the decision in court.

Not long after this Medgar Evers, who would go on to be the state's leading civil rights activist, applied to law school but was unable to secure the required letters of recommendation from alumni attesting to his good moral character, a requirement of admission to any state-supported school. Evers did secure letters from two Ole Miss alumni from his home county, only to learn that the board quickly reinterpreted the requirement to mean that the letters had to come from the county in which the applicant resided. The board also increased the number of required letters from two to five. Dean Farley told Evers to consult the board about his application, and although he did so and was given an extension of time to meet the new requirements, he chose not to do so. Instead he became Mississippi field director for the NAACP.

The next attempted integration, this one in 1958, was much more dramatic. Clennon King, an instructor at Alcorn Agricultural and Mechanical College, the school for blacks that had been founded in 1871, wanted to get a graduate degree in history at Ole Miss. He was already controversial in the black community and at Alcorn because he had written newspaper articles defending segregation and had cooperated with the Sovereignty Commission, which had been created after the *Brown* decision as the state's "watchdog for segregation." Concerned that a written application would be found wanting in some way, King told a board of trustees official that he was going to apply at Ole Miss in person on May 16, 1958. The official promptly informed Governor Coleman, who decided to seal off the campus to prevent any violence.

When King arrived in Oxford, highway patrolmen and plainclothes law officers were stationed at every entrance to the school. "We had it fixed to where a rabbit couldn't get through the bushes," Coleman recalled. King was escorted into a room in the Lyceum and left alone there for some time. He feared that he might be in danger and started to shout for help. This was all Coleman needed to take action. He decided King was not mentally stable, ordered him taken off the campus, and sent to be examined by a judge. The judge determined King needed to put in the state mental institution and ordered his committal. But King was judged to be sane by hospital doctors and released. He subsequently left the state.

Back in Oxford, King's application had officially been denied on the ground that he was applying for a doctorate in history and the university offered only a master's degree.

There were tragic consequences for Clyde Kennard, a black Korean War veteran who had spent three years at the University of Chicago but wanted to finish his education in his home state. Although he applied to Mississippi Southern rather than Ole Miss, his fate was instructive.

Kennard's application to Southern was denied. Officials told him in a meeting on the campus that there were "irregularities" in his papers, and they questioned his moral character. Minutes after this meeting, local constables arrested him on dubious charges of reckless driving. Those charges were eventually dismissed, but a more serious charge awaited Kennard: the accusation that he was an accessory to the alleged theft of $25 worth of chicken feed. Kennard was convicted on this charge and given a seven-year prison sentence, wildly out of proportion to the usual punishment for the crime and even more distressing given that there was little evidence against him. He was carted off to the notorious Parchman prison farm. He was released well before his sentence had run, but only because of pressure on Governor Barnett to let him out because he was suffering badly from intestinal cancer. Kennard was near death by the time he was released. He was taken to Chicago for emergency surgery but died shortly after, on July 4, 1963.

These five cases had made clear to Meredith, and any other black thinking of integrating a Mississippi college, that victory would come, if at all, only to a tenacious and patient individual. Meredith also understood that his life might be in danger. "The traditional practice in Mississippi has been to eliminate potential troublemakers before they get a chance to cause trouble," he observed. "Knowing this about my home state I was naturally concerned for my life." But Meredith also knew that at some point his case would attract national attention, and he knew he had to capitalize on public concern for him and his efforts. "The objective," he said, "was to make myself more valuable alive than dead."

Meredith certainly expected resistance to his application. He just didn't know what it would look like. He didn't have to wait long to find out. The school's strategy of duplicitous delay became apparent in a February 4 telegram from registrar Ellis informing Meredith that the university had "found it necessary" to refuse consideration of applications for the second semester that were received after January 25, 1961. "We must advise you not to appear for registration," the telegram said.

The cutoff date was news to Meredith; there had been no word of it in the application materials. It was a transparent move to keep Meredith out, made rather obvious by the fact that the cutoff date was reputed to be January 25 but the telegram was not sent for another ten days. In a later court proceeding, one university official contended that he had ordered the telegram sent "a few days" before January 25, but transmission had been delayed.

As important as the telegram itself was what it represented: a new policy of abrupt rule changes for the sole purpose of keeping Meredith or any other black out of the school. Two more came in short order. On February 7 the board of trustees decided first that transfer students could be accepted "only when the previous program of the transferring college is acceptable to the receiving institution." In other words, Ole Miss could choose which transfer students it wanted, even if, as in Meredith's case, he was seeking to transfer from Jackson State, which was accredited in the state. Then the board barred transfer students who wanted to go from a school on the quarter system to one on the semester system, unless the board made an exception based on special circumstances. It was aimed at Meredith because Jackson State used quarters while Ole Miss went by semesters—nothing more than "a devious piece of nonsense," in the words of one Meredith supporter. Neither change was made public.

Meanwhile, news that some Mississippi black, perhaps more than one, had applied to Ole Miss had leaked out, prompting news stories about the highway patrol's heading to Oxford to keep these individuals out. Asked to confirm the rumors and the reason for the police presence at Ole Miss, Governor Barnett, in office now about a year, was unusually restrained. "It is for the best interests of the state for me not to make a statement," he said. It was one of his few quiet moments in the escalating controversy.

Eight plainclothesmen had stationed themselves in the Lyceum all day on February 7 in case any black had attempted to register for classes. The officers had been given pictures of Meredith so they could cart him off if he tried to break the color line. Two of them saw a dark-skinned man with a thin mustache and started to remove him from the premises, only to be told by a dean that the man was Indian and already a student. The incident made clear that skin color was not the issue for admission to Ole Miss; being an "American-Mississippi-Negro citizen" was.

As he was mulling over his next move, Meredith decided to inform the U.S. Justice Department of his efforts to enter the university. His letter to officials in Washington was a blunt assessment of the racial situation in Mississippi and an explanation of what he wanted from the federal government. "Other Negro citizens have attempted to exercise their rights of citizenship in the past," he wrote, "but during the period of delay, that is, between the time the action is initiated and the would-be time of attainment of the goal, the agencies of the state have eliminated the individual concerned. I do not have any desire to be eliminated." Meredith said he wanted the department to use "the power and influence" of the federal government to ensure compliance with the laws and "to insure the full rights of citizenship for our people."

Although the Kennedy administration was now on official notice of Meredith's plan, it would be more than a year before federal attorneys became involved in the case.

On February 20, two weeks after he had received registrar Ellis's telegram about the application cutoff date, Meredith wrote back that he was "very disappointed" that his application was not being considered for the second semester. Accordingly, he continued, he was resubmitting his application for the summer session, beginning June 8.

The next day Ellis wrote back that the university was unable to accept his application at all and was returning Meredith's ten dollar room deposit.

Meredith sent his reply back two days later along with his room deposit and a reminder to Ellis that he was reapplying for the summer session.

In the meantime, Thurgood Marshall at the Legal Defense Fund had agreed to help Meredith, and by mid-February he had assigned assistant counsel Constance Baker Motley to work with him. She would remain Meredith's principal lawyer throughout his fight with the university.

When nearly a month had gone by and no further word from the university, Meredith wrote to registrar Ellis again, on March 18, asking about the status of his application. Eight days later, on March 26, Meredith wrote another letter, this time inquiring about the number of transfer credits he would receive. He closed by conceding that he was "not a usual applicant" and understood that the process would take time. He repeated his hope that the "entire matter will be handled in a manner complimentary to the University of Mississippi."

By early April Meredith had heard nothing from Ole Miss, though the silence did not mean that his application had been ignored. But the nature of the deliberations among board members and the administration was difficult to know because even at the height of the controversy, when federal judges were issuing contempt orders and troops were mobilizing to descend on Oxford, the official record of the meetings among Ole Miss officials was brief and obscure at best, and no one in authority was saying anything of substance in public. It was clear, however, that the strategy was to find every conceivable way to block Meredith's admission.

On April 12 Meredith wrote to the dean of the liberal arts college, A. B. Lewis, asking him to review his application and tell him if anything more needed to be done. He said he had concluded that Ellis had failed to act "solely because of my race and color." He had not been advised of any deficiencies in his papers, Meredith went on, adding that he wanted "some assurance that my race and color are not the basis for my failure to gain admission to the University."

Finally on May 9 Ellis wrote back to tell Meredith that of the ninety semester hours shown on his transcript, only forty-eight would be accepted by Ole Miss. No further explanation was given. He asked Meredith to tell him whether he still wanted his application to be considered in view of the transfer credit decision.

On May 15 Meredith wrote Ellis that he was applying for the summer session. On the same day he wrote another letter to the director of men's housing seeking a university apartment for himself, his wife, and their infant and enclosing a security deposit of twenty-five dollars.

On the same day, the Ole Miss admissions committee revised the rules for transfer students once again. Following up on the February 7 policy, the board decided that no transfers would be allowed from schools not accredited by the major regional accrediting association. Jackson State had not been—thus another barrier to Meredith's application. Public notice of this change was not given for weeks.

The summer session was set to begin June 8, and by May 21 Meredith had still not heard from registrar Ellis about his application, so he wrote another letter seeking a reply. Finally on May 25, more than four months after Meredith's first letter, Ellis responded: "I regret to inform you, in answer to your recent letter, that your application for admission must be denied." Ellis said Ole Miss could not recognize transfer credits from Jackson State because it was not a member of the regional accrediting organization (this was the new transfer requirement that had been adopted May 15). Furthermore, Ellis said, the application was lacking in other respects, notably the letters of recommendation. "I see no need for mentioning other deficiencies," Ellis wrote, adding that the application file had been closed. He returned the ten dollar fee and the twenty-five dollar room deposit.

On May 31 Meredith, represented by Motley and two other lawyers, took Ole Miss to federal court, suing the board of trustees and top university officials for wrongfully barring his admission. In one sense, however, the university had already won the first round: Officials had delayed Meredith's application so long that he could not attend the summer session without court intervention. Whether such action would be forthcoming was up to federal district judge Sidney C. Mize, and neither Meredith nor his lawyers were optimistic.

A native Mississippian, one-time state Democratic party leader, and a school board member in Gulfport, Mize was a true believer in southern customs and tradition. He would not willingly allow any breach of either, and he would use his courtroom over the next few months to make that clear. The proceedings before him would be anything but a model of efficiency despite Meredith's efforts to meet the university's registration deadlines.

In his complaint against Ole Miss, Meredith charged that the admission requirement of alumni recommendations placed a special burden on blacks and was therefore unconstitutional because all alumni were white. He also contended that contrary to *Brown,* "the policy of Mississippi as clearly understood and interpreted by its officials and residents is that Negroes and whites are educated in separate institutions of higher learning." Meredith asked for a speedy hearing so that he could attend the summer session, and he requested a temporary court order to effect that goal.

Judge Mize had other ideas. He set a hearing on Meredith's request for immediate admission for June 12, four days after the start of the summer session. He started out as though he would move things along, but a few hours after the proceedings got underway, he abruptly called a halt, saying his calendar was too crowded to continue. Mize put off the hearing until July 10, effectively denying Meredith the right to make his case for attending summer school. And there was more. In pretrial maneuvering, he denied Motley's request to take depositions of university personnel, yet he allowed an Ole Miss lawyer to depose Meredith, giving him broad latitude in his questions and ignoring Motley's objections. On July 10 Mize postponed the hearing once again, claiming a conflict with another case already scheduled. The hearing was finally reset for August 10.

During the proceeding, Meredith and his lawyers tried to show that Mississippi had a general policy of segregation. When Motley tried to question registrar Ellis about this issue, Mize cut her off with the comment that such questions were "foreign to the issues here" and would "unduly prolong" the proceedings—a remarkable statement given his own dilatory behavior.

The university sought to focus on Meredith's residence, partly to argue that he did not actually live in the state given his long absence for military service and partly to suggest that he might have violated a voting registration law. There were enough questions about what county he should list as home and where he voted to allow argument on the issue. Ole Miss lawyers seemed to be trying to prove that Meredith was a resident of Gary, Indiana, Detroit, Michigan, and Jackson and Kosciusko, Mississippi. Meredith testified that for purposes of the air force Detroit was home, but his residence was Kosciusko. The lawyer asked why Meredith had registered to vote in Jackson, in Hinds County, rather than in Kosciusko, in Attala County. Wasn't this false voter registration? Meredith replied that he did what the Hinds County clerk told him to, and later the clerk testified that Meredith was qualified to vote in Jackson. The matter seemed to be settled, though not for good.

University lawyers also challenged Meredith's motives in applying to the university, contending that the NAACP put him up to it to force a lawsuit. Registrar Ellis asserted that Meredith was trying to get into Ole Miss "because he was a Negro and not because he wanted to get an education." He called it "insulting" that Meredith would claim he was denied admission because of race, contending that it demonstrated that Meredith was "ready to go off in all directions" with his charge of racial discrimination. It was clear, Ellis said, that Meredith would not be "an acceptable student."

The hearing on the request for court-ordered admission finally ended August 16, but Mize didn't rule until December 12, six months after the first court proceeding and nearly eleven months after Meredith's first letter to Ellis. He denied Meredith's request for immediate entrance to Ole Miss.

Weaving a creative path through the evidence, Mize asserted that "the testimony shows, and I find as a fact, that there was no discrimination against any student, and particularly [Meredith] because of his race or color." Of the January cutoff on accepting applications, Mize said it was justified by overcrowded conditions on the campus, even though the only dormitories that were crowded were for women students and all testimony had been about men students. Mize also took registrar Ellis's testimony about why Meredith was rejected at face value, ruling that it "shows conclusively that he gave no consideration whatsoever to the race or color of the plaintiff." He set January 15, 1962, as the date for a full trial on the merits of Meredith's claims.

Mize made one other finding: that Meredith was a resident of Attala County and that he swore falsely in registering to vote in Hinds County. However, Mize stopped short of determining what effect, if any, this had on Meredith's "moral character" and his suitability for entering Ole Miss.

Motley wasted no time appealing Mize's order, filing papers with the U.S. Court of Appeals for the Fifth Circuit two days after his ruling.

Three circuit judges, Elbert Tuttle, Richard T. Rives, and John Minor Wisdom, promptly heard the appeal, and a month later to the day, on January 12, 1962, they issued their decision. They declined to grant Meredith's motion for a court order requiring his immediate admission and instead ordered a full trial on Meredith's claims to begin promptly. The judges also took the unusual step of reprimanding Mize for his conduct of the hearing and told him how to conduct the upcoming trial.

One passage from the appellate opinion gained immediate attention, becoming the standard description for Mize's courtroom: "This case was tried below and argued here in the eerie atmosphere of never-never land." In a specific slap at Mize, Wisdom, who wrote the opinion, said the panel was taking "judicial notice" that Mississippi "maintains a policy of segregation" and that this was "a plain fact known to everyone." The judges chastised Mize for a "muddy record" that was both incomplete and full of "a welter of irrelevancies" that made a true understanding of the issues virtually impossible.

The appellate panel threw out the requirement of alumni recommendations because it worked a disadvantage to black residents, and they noted that since Mize's ruling, Jackson State had been accredited by the regional college accrediting organization, a development that knocked out one of the main reasons Meredith had been rejected.

When the trial got started on January 24, the atmosphere was tense and the parties testy. Motley immediately objected to the way assistant state attorney general Charles Clark pronounced "Negro," which Motley heard as "Niguh." She told Mize to require state attorneys to pronounce the word "knee-gro," as the *Clarion Ledger* spelled it.

"Although Mr. Clark doesn't enunciate it as well as you, I'm sure he meant no disrespect," Mize said. He denied her request.

Despite the Fifth Circuit's strong language, Mize ignored the court's finding that Mississippi's segregation was "a plain fact known to everyone." Instead, a stream of witnesses from the university contended that race was not an issue at Ole Miss. When Motley tried to pin them down, she had little luck. She asked one of the deans if he had ever seen a black on the campus. He replied that he didn't know because "I don't know the genealogical background of every person I meet." When Vice Chancellor W. A. Bryant was asked if any blacks had ever been admitted since 1941, the year Bryant came to Ole Miss, he said he could not be sure because "I'm not an expert in the field of anthropology." Trustee Tally Riddell told Motley when she asked the same question, "If you'll tell me what you mean by Negro, I'll try to answer it." Only trustee Verner Holmes, a doctor from McComb, gave a straightforward answer to Motley's inquiry: He had never seen or heard of any Negro students at Ole Miss since 1954.

All the witnesses insisted they had never discussed Meredith or Negro admissions generally at any faculty or trustees meetings. Chancellor Williams added this: "To the best of my knowledge no official of the University—and that includes the Chancellor—has the authority to deny the application of a qualified applicant to the University of Mississippi on the basis of race or color."

The big loophole was "qualified," and Ole Miss officials, trustees included, had shown great creativity in finding ways to make sure Meredith was not qualified. The latest was rebutting his recommendations on character from "responsible Negro citizens." An assistant state attorney general had gone to Meredith's home town and visited with the individuals who had signed the affidavits on Meredith's behalf. Each of them had been interviewed before a justice of the peace and a Citizens' Council member. Four of them withdrew their recommendations. In hindsight, they said, they misunderstood what Meredith had wanted, thinking he was seeking a job, not entry into Ole Miss. Of course they would sign retractions: "I could not now certify to his good moral character nor could I recommend him for admission to the University of Mississippi or any other college."

Registrar Ellis repeated the testimony he had given at the previous hearing: Meredith was a "troublemaker," and his "race or color has had no influence on the decisions which I have taken."

Mize apparently agreed with the latter observation. On February 3 he issued his decision: "The proof shows, and I find as a fact, that the University is not a racially segregated institution. . . . Plaintiff [Meredith] was not denied admission because of his race." Mize conceded that Mississippi practiced segregation before the 1954 *Brown* decision, but since then, much had changed and now no custom or policy prevented qualified blacks from attending Ole Miss.

A week later the trustees met and, reviewing the Meredith case to date, proclaimed their full support for registrar Ellis. They found his actions "to be in full accord with the rules and regulations of this Board and the University of Mississippi." To make matters abundantly clear, they ordered Chancellor Williams and Ellis not to admit Meredith.

Meredith appealed Mize's ruling and asked the Fifth Circuit to order his immediate admission while the appeal was pending. Judge Tuttle urged such action, arguing that Meredith was almost certain to win on the merits. In addition, he noted that Meredith would either have to drop out of school or find some way to take courses not leading to graduation to avoid finishing at Jackson State, thus rendering his application to Ole Miss moot. As important, Tuttle argued, another delay would allow even more time for the "rise of massive resistance" to Meredith's admission—a prediction that proved to be correct. The appellate panel nonetheless turned aside Tuttle's suggestions and refused to order Meredith's immediate admission.

Several months later, on June 25, the court did reverse Mize's decision in another biting opinion; it ordered that Meredith be allowed to enter Ole Miss. Referring to Mize's observation of changes in Mississippi since the *Brown* decision, the court said, "This about-face policy, news of which may startle some people in Mississippi, could have been accomplished only by telepathic communication among the University's administrators [and] the Board of Trustees" given that virtually every official denied discussing the subject. Once again the court took judicial notice of the fact that Ole Miss was segregated—"what everybody knows the court must know."

Judge Wisdom continued that a "full review of the record leads inescapably to the conclusion that from the moment the defendants discovered that Meredith was a Negro they engaged in a carefully calculated campaign of delay, harassment, and masterful inactivity. It was a defense designed to discourage and defeat by evasive tactics."

Judge Dozier DeVane filed a dissenting opinion on July 10 that agreed with most of the majority's opinion but would have upheld Mize's refusal to order Meredith's admission because he might become "a troublemaker." DeVane's dissent showed a great sensitivity to the needs of Mississippi whites, less so for law and constitutional principles. "I do not consider that we have the right to ignore what the effect of this decision could be upon the citizens of Mississippi," he wrote, adding that he feared—correctly as it would turn out—that the admission of Meredith would trigger the kind of problems experienced in Little Rock in 1957, when federal troops had to be called in to help integrate Central High School. DeVane said Mize was correct in finding that Meredith "bore all the characteristics of becoming a troublemaker" at Ole Miss, adding that "his entry therein may be nothing short of a catastrophe."

The Fifth Circuit not only ordered Meredith to be admitted, but in the hope of ensuring no further delay, it ordered the board of trustees and "all persons in active concert" with them, including university and state officials, to "act expeditiously" on Meredith's application. Anyone who tried to thwart, obstruct, or otherwise prevent the court order from going into effect would be held in contempt of the Fifth Circuit.

Russell Barrett, a political science professor, had been watching the Meredith case with great interest. A Kansas native who had studied in Australia and at Harvard and had found his way to Ole Miss in 1954 to teach, he had enjoyed his first years in Oxford, staying clear of the problems that had enmeshed a few other teachers. One colleague called him a "gentle academician." But the Meredith challenge had caught his attention, and he began to follow every step closely, rooting for Meredith to win his case and growing increasingly appalled at the forces of resistance arrayed against him. So although he appreciated the strong words of the court order, Barrett doubted they would have the effect the judges had hoped. In every other state, individuals would pay heed to the judiciary. But in Mississippi, he knew, Meredith had reached just another detour.

Judge Wisdom had set July 18, 1962, as the date for transmitting the appeals court order of admission to Judge Mize. But on that same day, another federal appeals judge, Ben Cameron, described as the "most dedicated segregationist on the federal bench," took the extraordinary step of intervening in a case on which he had not previously participated. He ordered a stay of Wisdom's order until the university could seek Supreme Court review of the entire matter.

Like Mize, Cameron had deep ties to the Mississippi power structure, particularly the legal system. He had been a state prosecutor in Meridian and U.S. attorney for the southern district of the state before President Eisenhower selected him for the Fifth Circuit in 1955—the first Republican in fifty years. As Mize had done, Cameron would not willingly stand by and let a century of racial custom go by the wayside.

On July 27, nine days after Cameron first intervened, the court of appeals set aside his stay. On July 28 Cameron issued another stay, and within hours the appeals court set it aside as well. Undaunted, Cameron sought to undo the appeals court's order by issuing a third stay on July 31. The Fifth Circuit promptly responded, issuing an order on August 4 declaring Cameron's actions "unauthorized, erroneous and improvident" and ordering them set aside.

But Cameron persisted, issuing his fourth stay on August 6 and declaring that his colleagues on the court of appeals could not act until the

Supreme Court heard the case. Motley, Meredith's attorney, finally realized that Cameron would not back down, so she filed a petition with Supreme Court justice Hugo Black, who had jurisdiction over Mississippi, among other southern states, to throw out Cameron's stays.

On August 31, the U.S. Justice Department entered the case, filing a friend of the court brief urging Black to support Meredith's petition.

In the meantime, the board of trustees, in consultation with the highest state officials, had their own ideas about how to deal with the escalating crisis. On September 4, the board took the unusual step of divesting university administrators of all authority over Meredith's impending admission and putting board members in charge.

Six days later, September 10, Justice Black acted, throwing out all of Judge Cameron's stays, ordering Meredith to be admitted, and enjoining any official from preventing his registration at Ole Miss. Black added that although he was convinced he had the power to act alone, he consulted with his fellow justices, who all agreed that under the circumstances he was exercising his authority appropriately.

"This is the end of the road for Mississippi," a happy Constance Baker Motley told reporters after the decision. Three days later she would realize her jubilation had been premature.

Although he had paid little heed to the federal appeals courts, Judge Mize was apparently unwilling to buck the Supreme Court. He issued an injunction on September 13 barring the board, the chancellor, the registrar, and anyone who worked for them from interfering with Meredith's admission to Ole Miss.

Emboldened by his coterie of white supremacists, Governor Barnett was not so timid. "We will not surrender to the evil and illegal forces of tyranny," he told a statewide television audience hours after Mize issued his order. "No school will be integrated in Mississippi while I am your governor," he pledged, calling on the doctrine of interposition to create a blockade between the federal court order and state sovereignty. "I speak to you now," he went on, "in the moment of our greatest crisis since the War between the States."

Any state official not willing to go to jail should resign, Barnett said, adding, "We must either submit to the unlawful dictates of the federal government or stand up like men and tell them *NEVER!* We will not drink from the cup of genocide."

Barnett had cited the Tenth Amendment to the Constitution for his interposition proclamation, the same doctrine segregationists had used to protest the *Brown* decision eight years earlier and a concept dismissed as poppycock by a host of legal scholars. As a constitutional theorist, Barnett was on shaky ground. As political theater, he was a hit, winning approval from virtually all white quarters of the state. The few voices of dissent were all but drowned out. One such contrary view came from the little *Pascagoula Chronicle,* which published an editorial, "Governor Reaches Point of No Return." The paper asserted that Mississippians "are mature enough to recognize the inevitable, to accept it and adapt to it with good enough grace. The political faction that rules them is not."

On September 14, the day after the speech, the governor held a three-hour closed-door session with the trustees, who opposed closing the university and pointed out that defying Mize's court order would subject them, and not Barnett, to jail for being in contempt of court. None of this was reported to the public, however; the official word was only that no action was taken, and discussions would continue.

On Sunday, September 16, eight Oxford ministers came together in an effort to calm an increasingly tense situation. They read a joint statement in their churches "solemnly and prayerfully" urging that citizens "act in a manner consistent with the Christian teaching concerning the value and dignity of man." They asked for leadership in maintaining "peace and order among us," urged parishioners to make "every effort to resist the pressures placed upon us by emotionally excited groups and uphold the honor and good name of the University of Mississippi."

The ministers' action was a display of courage given the escalating rhetoric in the opposite direction, fired in no small way by front-page *Clarion Ledger* editorials and daily radio editorials beamed from WLBT-WJDX in Jackson supporting the defiant Barnett. Typical was one on September 14 after Barnett's interposition speech. Calling the governor's remarks "the most historic address that has ever been delivered in the State of Mississippi," the editorial reminded listeners that integration would not come without cooperation from the state. "That cooperation will not be forthcoming in Mississippi. . . . The word of the hour, the word of the day, the word of the year is 'Never.'"

When the board met on September 17, members realized that the crisis was mounting, not abating. Those few counseling some kind of accommodation were outvoted by the diehard Barnett supporters. The moderates—and the term was relative—realized they would have to speak out more forthrightly because the public had been getting only one side: the governor and the people backing him. Verner Holmes, the only trustee who had conceded to Motley that he never saw a black student at Ole Miss, was the first to show a division among the trustees. He told reporters waiting for the latest piece of strategy that he would not vote to close the university and would not be willing to go to jail when such an act would be fruitless.

Trustee Riddell had come to a similar decision after much anguish. Asserting that he was "as opposed to the mixing of the races in our institutions of higher learning as any other man in the state," Riddell said he had also been "taught to believe in law and order and constitutional government," and once the Supreme Court had spoken, that was enough for him. He promised to resist any effort to close the university and told board colleagues that to take such action would "work irreparable injury to more than five thousand students and their parents and the damage to the State of Mississippi will be untold for years to come." In spite of "terrific political pressure, intimidation and threats, I have voted my convictions and have chosen the course which I am convinced is best for our people in the long run."

Riddell insisted that the statement he made to the board be released to the press over the objection of several trustees who wanted to keep information about their Meredith deliberations at a minimum. The official record of one five-hour session during the turmoil was typical: "After further discussion of the Meredith case, the meeting adjourned with no action taken."

The pressure on Riddell had been enormous, so much so that he required hospitalization. There was virtually no one in his community of Quitman who urged him to stand up to Barnett. Instead there were crank calls to his home, at least one death threat because he was "a nigger lover," and a cross was burned on his lawn. His law firm lost business when clients told him they didn't want his services anymore.

Meanwhile in Oxford Chancellor Williams conceded that the Meredith case was out of his hands. "Major decisions concerning policy for all state institutions are made by the Board of Trustees," he told his assistants and inquiring students.

Neither Williams nor his top aides made any public appeal to students for order on the campus. Instead they relied on a strategy of private meetings with student leaders, urging them to circulate on campus and counsel obedience. When the chancellor had tepidly warned that any student who publicly protested against Meredith might be expelled, the *Clarion Ledger* hinted at the consequences. "The governor will watch with a jaundiced eye any attempt to apply punitive action against Mississippi patriots," said one front-page story.

On September 18 in Jackson, the day after Holmes revealed a split among board members, the legislature passed a resolution commending Barnett for his "fearless and courageous stand against political aggression, abuse and misrepresentation designed to disrupt and destroy Southern institutions, traditions and way of living."

The state judiciary got into the act the next day, September 19—one day before fall registration. Acting on behalf of the parents of forty-six students, a county judge issued an order barring Meredith's enrollment, apparently unconcerned about directly contradicting a federal court mandate. A lawyer for the parents said they believed that Meredith's enrollment "would disrupt school operations so as to deprive their children of the right to be educated."

Interviewed by a reporter in Memphis, where he was staying, Meredith was outwardly calm. "Students at the university are the same as those elsewhere," he said. "Negroes are attending other Southern colleges without trouble, and I can't see that Mississippi is any different."

Events on September 20 started early, 12:25 A.M., when a cross fourteen by twenty-seven feet was burned on a street in Oxford between two men's dormitories. Not long after that, legislators finally finished work on their contribution to the stop Meredith crusade: a bill denying admission to any state school to a person "who has a crime of moral turpitude against him" or who had been convicted of any criminal offense or not pardoned. Several crimes were exempted, including drunk driving violations—even manslaughter resulting from driving under the influence—and violations of state fish and game laws. Legislators believed that questions about Meredith's voting residence would amount to a violation of the law, and just as university officials had tailored the rules to keep Meredith out of the school, they hoped they had done the same with their actions.

Hours after this piece of government business, the state judiciary fulfilled their wishes. A local judge in Jackson found Meredith guilty in absentia for false voter registration in Hinds County. Meredith was sentenced to pay a fine of $100 and serve one year in the county jail, an extraordinarily long sentence for the alleged infraction, "but not," Russell Barrett noted back in Oxford, "for a Mississippi Negro."

September 20 was the day Meredith wanted to register in Oxford along with other transfer students. The day before, Attorney General Robert F. Kennedy had sent a long telegram to the board and university officials advising them that he intended to see that the court orders requiring Meredith's admission were carried out. He warned that any effort by the board to prevent university officials from allowing Meredith to enter the school would be considered a violation of the law.

Frustrated by Barnett's inability to present a cogent plan for keeping Meredith out of Ole Miss, hard-line board members decided on the afternoon of September 20 to give the governor full authority to act in all matters pertaining to Meredith. Trustee Holmes recalled ruefully years later that "that was our big mistake."

To supplement his new power, Barnett secured a state court order officially barring the board from registering Meredith. One part of the order made clear what university officials and Mize had tried to deny in federal court a year earlier—that segregation is official Mississippi policy: "It is against the public policy of the State of Mississippi as well as its laws for any colored person to be admitted as a student at said institution."

Barnett flew from Jackson to Oxford the afternoon of September 20 to confront Meredith personally and deny him entry. Meredith and his party of federal officials—Justice Department lawyer John Doar and U.S. marshals—arrived on campus from Memphis, at about 5 P.M. They were met with some boos, a few epithets, chants of "We Want Ross," and the popular Ole Miss "Hoddy Toddy" football cheer:

Hoddy, toddy, God A'mighty
Who in the hell are we,
Flim, flam, bim bam
Ole Miss, by damn

The last three lines had always been considered a declaration of students' pride in themselves and their school, and not a question. They knew who they were.

The group went inside a campus building to meet with Barnett. Meredith told the governor he wanted to be admitted to the school. Barnett read his interposition proclamation and denied him admission. An impassive Meredith left without responding to the jeers that greeted him and his federal protectors.

When Barnett came out, he was greeted with a roar of approval and told the admiring crowd: "The only comment I have to make is that the application of James Meredith has been denied." Meanwhile, on September 20, the federal appeals court issued an injunction barring the prosecution of Meredith under the newly passed moral turpitude law.

The next day Judge Mize cleared university officials of contempt of court in failing to register Meredith because they had been divested of the power to do so. The Justice Department, by now a party to the case on Meredith's behalf, was not satisfied. Department lawyers sought contempt citations against board members and university officials, and a trial before the Fifth Circuit was set for three days later, September 24.

When that day came, the courtroom was full of attorneys because each of the defendants wanted his own counsel. Registrar Ellis made a telling admission on the stand about differences in strategy and about who was in control of events when he said that university officials had been ready to "do exactly what the Court told us to do, and that meant registering Meredith."

Hearing this admission, the NAACP's Motley sought to have Meredith registered "right here and now in open court." Although her request was denied, the court determined that the trustees had acted in contempt of court. Instead of issuing the contempt order, the judges ordered officials to register Meredith the next day, September 25, at the capitol building in Jackson.

On September 25, the board followed the court's instructions, rescinding the power given to Barnett and preparing to allow Meredith to register. Now Barnett stepped in, literally and figuratively. He had issued an executive order barring anyone from interfering with his "official duties," and when Meredith arrived in Jackson to meet with the board, he and Doar, the Justice Department attorney, were met by Barnett with the cocky question, "Which one of you gentlemen is Meredith?" When Doar attempted to hand Barnett the court order requiring Meredith's admission, Barnett read a statement ending, "I do hereby, finally deny you admission to the University of Mississippi."

Meredith expected this rejection, but the day was not without a private moment of satisfaction. Barnett had hoped to come out of the capitol building to announce his victory just as people were leaving work to go home, thereby ensuring himself a good crowd, but his elevator got stuck between floors, and by the time he went outdoors, the crowd had diminished considerably. Meredith quietly smiled at the foul-up, realizing that one of the many black laborers in the building had most likely delayed Barnett's departure by a deft mechanical maneuver. It was the kind of covert support that helped keep him going.

There had been a large crowd to jeer Meredith and Doar when they left the building. State highway patrolmen had to escort them through two thousand hostile Mississippians yelling, "Go home Nigger."

By now events surrounding Meredith were receiving national news coverage, and back in Oxford, the young editors at the *Mississippian* were doing their best to report fast-breaking events to students and faculty. The editor of the paper was Sidna Brower, a senior from Memphis. She had spent the summer preparing to take over the *Mississippian,* now a daily, and the biggest decisions she had had to make were deciding what comic strips to run and how to balance the paper's budget. She never dreamed she would be worrying about whether the school would blow up.

Brower had grown up in a segregated world just like all of her fellow students and thought nothing of it. People were living together "pretty peacefully" as far as she could see, and she did not understand why the voices of resistance were now so prominent. "I never really saw discrimination," she conceded, "but I knew it was there."

As Brower watched events escalate day after day in September, she grew uneasy about the atmosphere. She decided it was her responsibility to speak out against violence and for a spirit of accommodation. Albin Krebs and James Autry, two of her predecessors, had shown courage and grit when they spoke out about social issues, but Brower knew that times were different now—tenser and more dangerous. There probably would be consequences not just for herself but for her family.

Brower's parents had strong ties to Mississippi; her mother was from the state, and her father did much of his business there. In their anger at her calls for patience and common sense, people might retaliate against him, impairing his ability to earn a living. It had happened to others. Her father was reassuring. "Write what you feel is right," he advised.

On September 21, the day after Barnett had first rejected Meredith's application, Brower had written a front-page editorial commending students for "mature behavior." She cited the refusal of one group of students to allow an angry throng to take down the American flag, which flew in the center of the Grove, and replace it with the Confederate flag.

On September 26, after Barnett refused to register Meredith in Jackson, the *Mississippian* featured a bold headline across the front page in inch-high letters: "Barnett Rejects Meredith." Buried underneath in much smaller type was Mize's admission order, which Barnett had so blatantly ignored. "As for the next step," Brower wrote, "there is uncertainty."

By the afternoon of September 26, Mississippians would know the next step: another pas de deux of resistance, this time between Meredith and Lieutenant Governor Paul Johnson. Bad weather had prevented Barnett from arriving from Jackson by plane, and Johnson was already at the school. So accompanied by chief U.S. marshal James P. McShane, Meredith was met at the gates of the university for a third time and denied entry by the lieutenant governor. McShane and Johnson engaged in a shoving match before the Meredith party finally backed off.

None of this hurt Johnson. He knew he was scoring political points for his upcoming gubernatorial campaign and at no cost to Barnett, who could not succeed himself.

After this latest confrontation, the federal judiciary and the Kennedy administration increased the pressure on Mississippi officials. For flouting the court order earlier in the week, Barnett was ordered to appear in New Orleans on September 28 for a contempt of court hearing. And after Johnson's rejection of Meredith at the university entrance, Attorney General Kennedy reaffirmed in Washington that he would do "whatever is necessary"—even sending in federal troops—to make sure the court order requiring Meredith's admission was enforced.

On September 27, the day before Barnett's contempt hearing, the governor and Kennedy had several telephone conversations to try to find a way for Meredith to enter Ole Miss. One of those talks seemed more like a director and actor arguing over a scene than a high-stakes political deal. Barnett wanted to make sure that the marshals surrounding Meredith would pull their guns so it would be clear that the governor was backing down only because of a show of force. "We got a big crowd here," he explained to Kennedy, "and if one pulls his gun and we all turn, it would be very embarrassing. Isn't it possible to have them all pull their guns?" Kennedy balked, but Barnett persisted: "They must all draw their guns. Then they should point their guns at us and then we could step aside."

Kennedy refused to accept this scenario. He wanted assurances from Barnett that state police would make sure there was no violence—assurances he failed to receive. The negotiations produced no agreement.

The effort to enroll Meredith that day was called off when federal officials feared for his safety and headed back to Memphis rather than continue on to Oxford. By midday on September 27, a crowd of well over two thousand had gathered on the campus even though Chancellor Williams had asked students not to assemble in large groups. As the day wore on, the crowd had grown boisterous and seemed more like a mob—too much to handle for the small group of marshals protecting Meredith.

Meanwhile, in Washington Robert Kennedy was making plans to get more federal officers to Memphis to provide protection for Meredith's next admission attempt.

In Memphis Meredith issued a statement reaffirming his "prime objective" of getting an education "to be a useful citizen of my own home state of Mississippi." "It is a matter of fact," he went on, "that the Negroes of

Mississippi are effectively NOT first-class citizens. I feel that every citizen should be a first-class citizen and should be allowed to develop his talents on a free, equal and competitive basis. . . . Certainly to be denied this opportunity is a violation of my rights as a citizen of the United States and the state of Mississippi."

From Dallas came another voice in the controversy siding unexpectedly with Barnett: General Edwin Walker, who had commanded federal troops for the integration of Central High School in Little Rock, had had a change of heart on racial matters. Walker promised that if federal troops came to Ole Miss, "I will be there" to resist, and he called on "10,000 strong from every state in the union" to rally in support of the Mississippi resisters.

Hundreds of angry white southerners would heed his call.

Although the Fifth Circuit had ordered Barnett to appear in New Orleans on September 28 to face the contempt of court charges, the defiant governor chose not to attend the session. The judges were undeterred in their decision to go forward: Barnett was found guilty of civil contempt and given until Tuesday, October 2, to obey the court order. In the meantime he was fined $10,000 a day unless he complied.

Barnett was anything but conciliatory when he appeared in Jackson the next day for the Ole Miss football game against the University of Kentucky. The stadium was a sea of Confederate flags that were waved with special defiance during the playing of the national anthem. To the chants of "We want Ross," Barnett took the field at halftime and incited the crowd. "I love Mississippi. I love her people, our customs" he roared with fist clenched in the air. "I love and respect our heritage." The crowd joined in a song that captured the rebellious spirit of the moment:

Never, Never, Never, No-o-o Never, Never Never
We will not yield an inch of any field,
Fix us another toddy, ain't yieldin' to nobody,
Ross's standin' like Gibraltar, he shall never falter
Ask us what we say, it's to hell with Bobby K
Never shall our emblem go from Colonel Reb to Old Black Joe

The apparent affection for Barnett was quite a turn of events for the governor, who two years earlier had been booed at a football game.

Subsequent invitations to speak on the Ole Miss campus were withdrawn for fear that students, then unimpressed with the man, would be "impolite." But in this spirit of rebellion, he was their hero and their leader, basking in a new-found popularity attributable to the passions of the moment, passions he himself had stoked.

As Barnett was raising his fist in defiance, President Kennedy was taking steps to get the U.S. government more involved. He federalized the state national guard and ordered troops to be sent to Memphis, to be used in Oxford if necessary. And in a series of ultimately fruitless telephone conversations with Barnett, he attempted to resolve what was now regarded as the most serious challenge to federal authority since the Civil War. At 12:01 A.M. on September 30, Kennedy issued a proclamation asserting that Barnett had not provided him with "adequate assurances" that the federal court order admitting Meredith would be obeyed and obeyed peacefully and therefore commanding "all persons" engaged in obstructing the order "to cease and desist."

Initial plans during that hectic Sunday called for Meredith to make his fourth attempt to enter the university on Monday, October 1. But those plans changed, largely in response to Barnett's determination that having Meredith arrive on Sunday afternoon would be less dangerous. University officials, prepared for the inevitable, had been putting their own plans in place to ensure a peaceful arrival for Meredith on Monday. They were not notified of the change to Sunday until the last minute. They pleaded with Kennedy's representatives for more time but were rebuffed.

The agreement called for Meredith to come onto the campus around 5:30 P.M. A little later President Kennedy would make a special presidential address on the conflict.

Surrounded by twenty-four federal marshals, Meredith finally arrived on the campus and was escorted to his dormitory, Baxter Hall. Within an hour, a riot broke out in front of the Lyceum, where besieged federal marshals tried to hold off an advancing and increasingly belligerent crowd—many of them nonstudents who had streamed into Oxford at General Walker's urging. By now the general was on campus, urging the rioters on from his post near the monument to the Confederate war dead. "I want to compliment you on the protest you make tonight," he said as the mob prepared to charge the Lyceum.

Around 7:30 P.M., well after Meredith was on campus, Barnett went on statewide television to preach what amounted to defiant acquiescence. He urged Mississippians to avoid violence and to preserve the peace, but then he seemed to undercut this very plea with a slap at the federal government and another appeal to white Mississippi pride: "Surrounded on all sides by the armed forces and oppressive power of the United States of America, my courage and my convictions do not waver. My heart still says, 'Never,' but my calm judgment abhors the bloodshed that would follow." He ended on anything but a conciliatory note: "Mississippi will continue to fight the Meredith case and all similar cases through the courts to restore the sovereignty of the state and constitutional government."

By the time President Kennedy went on television a short time later, the campus was awash in gunshots and flames and then shrouded in tear gas, fired as a protective measure by the outnumbered marshals. Already in the television studio and unaware of the riot, Kennedy looked out at his audience and urged Mississippians to comply peacefully with federal law. "The eyes of the nation and all the world are upon you and upon all of us," he said. "And the honor of your university—and your state—are in the balance."

While all this was going on Brower and other student leaders, including Trent Lott, a senior from Pascagoula (later a congressman and then majority leader of the U.S. Senate), were in the student union building meeting with university officials, who were urging the students to fan out and speak against the violence. Brower headed back to the *Mississippian* office amid the melee, dodging rocks tossed by rioters as she made her way through the Grove. Gunshots were in the air as federal troops, including the Mississippi National Guard, began arriving from Memphis to put down the insurrection. For one of the guard commanders, whose jeep was hit by gunfire, bricks, and large piece of lumber, it was "absolute hell" trying to get to the Lyceum to help the besieged marshals. He sustained three broken bones in his left arm when he raised it to ward off a brick hurled through the window.

By morning the campus looked like a war zone: smoke from smoldering fires billowing in the air, the burned-out hulks of cars overturned at curbsides, shards of glass from the many broken windows strewn over the grass, and the irritating stench of tear gas permeating everything. Bullet holes in the red bricks of the beloved Lyceum were testimony to this latest civil war.

On September 20, the U.S. border patrol car that had been used to ferry Meredith back and forth to the university on his admission attempts had been spotless, not a mark on it. Now it was battered almost beyond use—bullet holes in the sides, the windows smashed out, and seats unusable without a protective blanket.

There were dozens of national news reporters on the scene writing for their newspapers or broadcasting for their television stations; the front-page story in the *Mississippian,* under the headline "Chancellor Issues Plea," was as descriptive as any others: "Students started out yesterday by shouting slogans of pride in Mississippi and ended up with nothing to be proud of. Last night the restraint and simple boisterousness that had marked most of the demonstrations in the Meredith situation degenerated into unrestrained hatred and violence." In her editorial titled "Violence Will Not Help," Brower appealed for peace. Throwing rocks, bottles, and eggs at federal marshals helps no one, she wrote, and endangers students' ability to finish their education. The Civil War is over, she reminded her readers, adding, "Whatever your beliefs you are a citizen of the United States of America and of the State of Mississippi and should preserve the harmony of both governments."

Also in the paper was a plea from Williams for order. He urged students to avoid congregating in large groups, to identify "agitators" to campus police, and to "cooperate fully" with them. It was a plea that was too little too late in the minds of some faculty who had urged the administration to speak earlier and more strongly about disciplinary action against any demonstrating students.

By midday on October 1, it was known that two men were dead: French news reporter Paul Guihard, shot between the shoulder blades by an unknown assassin, and Ray Gunter, a maintenance man felled by a stray bullet. Among those injured were 166 marshals and 40 soldiers; 200 individuals, including Walker, had been arrested.

Meredith formally registered as more than sixteen thousand federal troops streamed into Oxford to set up camp. Escorted by federal marshals, Meredith went to his sparsely attended first class, on American history. Many other classes were cancelled, the *Mississippian* noted, because "there was too much tear gas in the area."

Later in the day, Barnett was on the telephone to the Justice Department trying to unintegrate Ole Miss. Looking for Robert Kennedy, he instead reached one of his top assistants, Burke Marshall. Couldn't Meredith be taken off the campus? Barnett asked. Mississippi would even pay his expenses at an out-of-state school. "He would be happier, everybody would be happier," Barnett said.

"Governor," Marshall replied, "he wanted to go to the university, and the court gave him the order and there is nothing we can do about that."

As he was escorted to his registration early on October 1, Meredith remained quiet and unemotional in the face of the turmoil around him. Asked by news reporters if he were happy now that he had enrolled, he quietly replied, "This is not a happy day."

Given all that had happened and how long it had taken to reach this moment, Meredith's observation was understandable. But if it was not a happy day in Oxford, for Ole Miss it was, without doubt, a new one.

5

Picking Up and Moving On

James Meredith's arrival in Oxford had precipitated a tug-of-war between the past and the future.

A few days into October, the first underground resistance fliers appeared, setting a venemous tone for Meredith's first days on campus. "Ignore the nigger with vigor," one handbill instructed, promising retribution against those who befriended him. Another flier showed a fierce-looking bulldog, teeth bared, ready to bite a caricature of a black dressed as if he were in a minstrel show. The caption said "Sic 'em WHITE FOLKS."

This was the "meanness" and "severity" that Willie Morris knew was so deeply entrenched in his homeland. When the "tenderness" and "nobility" that made him proud to be a Mississippian would emerge was anyone's guess. There were nascent signs when two hundred prominent businessmen gathered in Jackson on October 2 to plead for a "sane approach" to the tense situation. The *Wall Street Journal* deemed the meeting important enough that it ran a story on the front page. Reporter Neil Maxwell provided some context. It was "the first time any sizable group of whites in Mississippi have committed themselves to work publicly for law and order," he noted. "These white leaders' stand might not seem a bold step in most states but in Mississippi it is extraordinary. With responsible business and professional elements keeping quiet until now, the public stage has been occupied by extreme and highly vocal segregation leaders and their political allies." When Governor Barnett preached defiance and threatened to arrest and jail federal officials, Maxwell went on, "no influential voice of moderation was heard in reply here."

After the meeting, W. H. Billy Mounger, a prominent young businessman, made a courageous move: He went on television with a call for an end to violence and urged obedience to federal laws. He apologized for not doing so sooner. Although his plea did not fall completely on deaf ears, hopes for an end to racial hostilities were just that—hopes. For the moment, meanness and severity had the upper hand.

Back in Oxford, diehard resisters had formed themselves into the Rebel Underground. Their first newsletter, a nine-paragraph flier with a waving rebel flag in the upper lefthand corner, explained that the underground was made up of students "who resent the Negro, James Meredith being forced into our University by federal might." His admission, they said, was "only the beginning of organized aggression to bring about Negro political domination and racial amalgamation throughout the South. . . . We will never accept integration at this or any other institution. . . . Beware of marshals posing as students," the flier concluded. It was a reflection of the hostile and suspicious atmosphere and a reminder that although Ole Miss was a university campus, it now resembled an armed camp. Students and teachers had to pass through checkpoints on their way to class and thread their way through jeeps parked around school buildings. James Meredith never went anywhere without an escort of U.S. marshals.

"Soldiers requesting ID cards now replace the welcoming signs that decked the entrances to the University," the *Mississippian* observed. A doctor in Jackson, unhappy about the state of affairs, had a stamp made up for his correspondence: MAILED IN OCCUPIED MISSISSIPPI.

There were few things more important at Ole Miss than football, and an immediate issue after the September 30 riot was what to do about the next week's homecoming football game. University officials wanted to keep the game in Oxford as a signal that life was returning to normal, but federal officials intervened and insisted that the game be played in

Jackson. Although a few hundred of the marshals were being withdrawn from the campus—and Meredith's escort was reduced from six marshals to three—federal law authorities said the situation was still too tense, and they were not willing to risk the turmoil that might result from exuberant football fans. After all, two weeks earlier Barnett had inflamed an already agitated crowd with his halftime remarks.

Robert Kennedy was concerned enough about the atmosphere on campus that he called Chancellor Williams the day before the game to complain about an apparent failure to discipline students who continued to cause trouble. He was particularly unhappy about the treatment of Meredith, reminding Williams of the young man's plight: "Today Mr. Meredith goes through the hallway of the campus and he is booed and hissed and obscenities shouted at him . . . is anyone going to do anything?"

"We are going to, but Mr. Attorney General, you do not realize that we have thousands of people in Mississippi who will come here at the defense of these people [anyone disciplined] at the first opportunity," Williams replied, trying to make Kennedy understand the delicate situation. "We're doing everything we can. You take 4,800 students who have come from homes and communities that are not in sympathy at all with what we are having to do. You can't handle people by the thousands when we can't get the support we need. The marshals were doing their duty, but the student body now have grown resentful. I regret every one of these incidents," Williams added, "and it's a matter of humiliation and embarrassment to me."

In the days before Meredith's admission, several Oxford clergymen had appealed to their congregations for calm and common sense. A week after the riot they returned to that message, ignoring the continuing cries for resistance to lead a "day of repentance." The Reverend Duncan Gray, Jr., of Oxford's St. Peter's Episcopal Church was particularly pointed in his remarks. Ross Barnett was a "living symbol of lawlessness," he said, and Mississippians had been "deceived and misled by their political leaders" that integration would never come. "Is it any wonder, then, that violence erupts when the issue becomes real, rather than academic, within the borders of our state?"

The blame went beyond the politicians. Over at the First Presbyterian Church, Reverend Murphey C. Wilds, in a sermon echoed across the city, said everyone should repent for those who turned to violence and "for all who remained silent when we should have spoken."

A similar message was coming from the Ole Miss faculty. Just after the riot, a group of professors drafted a statement not only deploring what had taken place but also defending the marshals' actions. In a courageous move given the hostile climate, they refuted the politicians' charge that the marshals had caused the melee. The accusation, they said, "is not only unfair and reprehensible but is almost completely false. . . . Some news media in Mississippi have entertained irresponsible and secondhand stories in distortion of facts and have thereby helped to provide a general state of confusion, alarm, and misdirected wrath." The statement was signed by sixty-four faculty members, including two former deans, nine department chairmen, and four former department chairs. Although he did not sign the statement, Bob Farley, dean of the law school, said publicly that any student who jeered or taunted Meredith or took part in the riot should be expelled.

In the immediate aftermath, telegrams and letters of praise to the professors, including one from President Kennedy, were balanced out by hate calls, usually late at night and filled with vulgarities. Most came from supporters of the Citizens' Council, which had circulated a list of resolution signers for its members' convenience.

Although he was constantly surrounded by federal marshals and regularly harassed by students, Meredith was determined to be the one who defined his experience at Ole Miss, so it should not have surprised anyone when he stepped forward on the tenth day of his studies to criticize the army for keeping black soldiers away from Oxford and essentially resegregating the units on duty there. (Army Secretary Cyrus Vance conceded that black soldiers had not been used on patrols on the campus "in order to avoid unnecessary incidents.") "Negro soldiers were purged from the ranks 100 years ago," Meredith said in a statement. "And today, 1962, this is an intolerable act. My conscience would not allow me to go on observing the situation without at least letting the Negro soldiers know that I did not like them being dishonored." A short time later, black soldiers were back on the campus patrol.

When Meredith went to eat in the cafeteria after releasing his statement, he was nearly hit by a rock tossed through one of the building's windows.

In his short time on campus, Meredith's dining arrangements had already become symbolic—a way for people to show what side they were on by shunning him or joining him. When one group of professors pointedly sat with him over lunch, it was worthy of a front-page picture in many newspapers across the country. The *New York Times* caption explained that the professors "refused to reveal their names," but the picture was clear enough to see who was eating with Meredith, and the reaction was immediate, particularly for the lone woman at the table, Lucy Turnbull, a professor of classical archaeology. Family and friends called immediately with about the same message: "Get out of there before they kill you." The harassing telephone calls from segregationists were similar, but with one notable change: "Get out of there before *we* kill you."

"It had to cross your mind as you greeted Meredith that somebody might be taking a bead on you," Turnbull admitted, recalling one incident when someone lobbed a cherry bomb at her feet as she was walking down the hall to one of her classes. "But you can't just spend time under the bed."

By the third week in October, tensions on the campus seemed to be easing. The army sent thirty-five hundred troops home, leaving only two companies of military police and supporting personnel in the area—about five hundred men. But the apparent calm was both tentative and short-lived.

On October 24 the second issue of the Rebel Underground newsletter appeared, encouraging students to form into groups in every dormitory and sorority and fraternity house. "Our primary objective is to encourage James Meredith to transfer to some college where he would be welcome," the flier said. "There are many Yankee colleges which would eulogize him and make him 'Tar Baby' of the campus." This issue also went after Russell Barrett, who ate breakfast now and then with Meredith. The underground called him a communist and an "honorary nigger," and it referred to the federal marshals as the "KKK"—"Kennedy's Koon Keepers."

Barrett responded by meeting Meredith for coffee. He wore his World War II ribbons on his jacket lapel alongside the "honorary nigger" card that had been sent to him.

The verbal harassment aimed at Meredith was minor compared to another outburst that occurred on October 29, just as university officials were trying to relax controls over students who lived in Baxter Hall, Meredith's dorm. As if to sabotage this effort, groups of students, aided by outside supporters, had stockpiled a large supply of firecrackers and cherry bombs. When Meredith and his marshals' escort left the cafeteria, they let loose with a barrage. The marshals and military police eventually dispersed the crowd but not before they were pelted by eggs and bottles from fleeing students. The disturbance prompted Deputy Attorney General Nicholas Katzenbach to come to Oxford on October 30 to talk with administrators about the discipline problem. His presence on campus apparently did nothing to deter student resisters. Not long after he arrived, a bottle was thrown through the window of a car Meredith was riding in, and a marshal was slightly injured.

Concerned faculty members now took matters into their own hands, organizing into patrols to walk around the campus and discourage further incidents. There was some talk of deputizing the teachers, but they rejected that idea. "You can't police at night and be a professor by day," one professor told authorities. "It was enough just to let the few trouble-makers on the campus know that they would be observed and probably recognized." In the *Mississippian,* Sidna Brower wrote an editorial chiding the administration for its failure to maintain order. "It is disgusting to see such demonstrations permitted, especially when the rules are supposedly enforced," she wrote. "Why should students be suspended for yelling 'We want panties' when they are allowed to throw rocks and yell profane and obscene comments at members of the United States Army?"

Chancellor Williams took more aggressive steps on November 1, summoning all male students—though he specifically asked Meredith not to attend—for a lecture on discipline. "If there are any who cannot support the establishment of peaceful and orderly conditions, be advised that I am prepared to see us part company," he told them. He added that the university was ready to take "swift and drastic disciplinary action, including expulsion from the university."

Williams made good on his word; five students who were involved in the October 29 incident were expelled.

The day before this meeting with students, Williams had given a speech to civic clubs in Greenville. He reminded his audience that despite the extraordinary turmoil, the university had remained open, with most of its students still dedicated to pursuing their education—what to him was the most critical fact of the previous month. Although 144 students had withdrawn—about 100 more than usual for the first month of school—Williams said that "approximately ninety-eight of every one hundred students who came to us have stuck with us." This, he insisted, was "a wonderful demonstration of loyalty."

The chancellor's firm stand seemed to bode well for continued calm in the rest of the semester, but a different and more subtle kind of resistance was still at work, fueled by a new anti-Meredith circular distributed on campus in early November. This one was styled "Rebel Resistance." Its key point was a call for complete ostracization of Meredith: "Let no student speak to him, and let his attempt to 'make friends' fall upon cold, unfriendly faces. In addition the students should banish from their midst ANY white student" who violated this directive.

Students seemed to take the message seriously. Meredith realized in early November that classmates who once said hello to him had stopped, and even the number of faculty who had made a point of having coffee with him had diminished. Meredith didn't really care that so many did not accept him, but he was bothered by the fact that students who wanted to be friendly were either afraid or unwilling to do so. "Sympathy doesn't mean much unless it is demonstrated where it can be seen," he told Barrett during one of their visits.

A group of students decided to have supper with Meredith one fall evening, and for two of them the price of the kind gesture was high. They returned to their dormitory room to find it in shambles—books, records, and clothing scattered all over and next to the door the standard epithet printed crudely with black shoe polish: "Nigger Lovers."

There was no official administration response to the vandalism. Some officials had said privately that the students had asked for it by eating with Meredith, and anyway, their room was not that badly damaged. No one was ever disciplined in the incident, and several of the group that had eaten with Meredith that one time eventually transferred to other schools.

By mid-November a different kind of protest was brewing, this one against *Mississippian* editor Brower. Her alleged offense was failing to represent the student body in the editorials she wrote. Calling for calm, criticizing demonstrators, and taking the administration to task for being too tame on student discipline was not the right message, her detractors said. It was an ironic moment for the young editor, for as this protest was brewing she had been nominated for a Pulitzer Prize. (She didn't win.)

The controversy was an indication of the deep feelings the Meredith issue provoked and a reminder of the relatively narrow bounds for debate that existed. Brower's problems were also reflective of Mississippi's strictly ordered society, where "place" covered gender as well as skin color. White women were to be protected, sheltered, and revered. Translated into campus life this meant, among other things, a curfew for female students and a dress code. Young women on their way from the dormitory or sorority house to their tennis classes, for example, were not permitted to cross the campus in shorts. They had to wear a coat lest their bare legs show. Yet these same young women were expected to put themselves on display as potential beauty queens. Even in the midst of campus turmoil, there was time to track the progress of various coeds in their pageants, and the *Mississippian* regularly announced the "campus cutie," which featured a picture of a young woman in a fetching pose. Women perceived to be too outspoken, as Brower was, or otherwise out of the "campus cutie" mold were suspect. It also didn't help Brower that she was from Memphis, and thus an outsider.

The *Mississippian* had gained notoriety not simply because of the riot over Meredith but because the *New York Times,* among other papers, had printed Brower's post-riot plea for peace. In the weeks that followed, the paper was full of more out-of-state letters than most college newspapers receive. In fact Brower got so much mail she had to take it home to Memphis on weekends to read through it. She worried, only half-jokingly, that if she were stopped for speeding on her way through northern

Mississippi, some highway patrolman would see the letters, know who she was, and give her trouble.

Brower's critics charged that she had been "brainwashed" by federal officials who told her what to write. "I most certainly have not been brainwashed nor have I received pressure from anyone," she retorted. "I simply, but firmly, believe in writing what I feel is right. However," she went on, "it is sad, indeed, when supposedly educated people must be reminded that rioting and violence do not help any cause but bring humiliation to all concerned."

Brower also denied that she had printed only letters in her support, pointing to one that called her a traitor similar to the infamous Tokyo Rose of World War II. Most of the critical letters, she added, could not be printed because they were either obscene or full of profanity or unsigned, violating the paper's policy of printing letters only if the writer was identified.

Although Brower had worried about repercussions to her father's business, none occurred. Her parents nevertheless regularly received hate calls throughout the fall, and one of her uncles—her mother's brother who lived in Mississippi—publicly denounced Brower, perhaps the most painful moment in a period that had many.

Brower had even taken some knocks from her sorority sisters. One young woman, whose room was at the top of the front stairs of the Kappa Kappa Gamma house, spat at Brower as she came back home one night after her newspaper work was done. Instead of provoking a confrontation, Brower simply used the back stairs until the hostile atmosphere eased. The Kappa Kappa Gamma president did step in, calling a meeting to announce her support for Brower and telling the rest of the women she expected them to do the same.

George Monroe was one of the prime movers behind an effort to censure Brower for her editorials. A native of Newton, about sixty-five miles east of Jackson, Monroe had been interested in politics since he was a child, even working for Senator Eastland as a page before going to college. He was admittedly conservative and worried that the way of life he had known would be irrevocably changed by an overly aggressive federal government. He wanted to do what he could to prevent that.

Once at Ole Miss he became a leader of the Patriotic American Youth, a kind of college-aged Citizens' Council, and a member of the campus senate. He had drafted a resolution calling for censure of Brower to make clear that the student governing body did not agree with her editorials. There was not any specific piece but rather several taken together that amounted to a "culmination of agitation." What particularly galled Monroe was Brower's failure to talk about what in his view were violations of the students' civil rights by federal marshals. His own dorm had been hit with tear gas for no good reason that he could see, and it made him mad.

Brower had a right to say what she wanted but "within reason," Monroe asserted. "And I would defend her right to say what she wanted if she worked for her own private paper." But she was elected editor "by the student body and is paid by the student body and taxpayers of Mississippi. I feel she should be loyal to their feelings."

After a ten-day struggle within the senate, the students finally approved a compromise resolution: reprimanding Brower but not censuring her. What apparently helped forge the compromise was the concern that the word *censure* might be confused with *censor,* which was not the senate's intent.

Some of Brower's supporters thought they had won a victory, but Russell Barrett astutely observed that the outside world would miss the nuance and see this as punishment for someone who dared speak out. The *New York Times* seemed to prove him right, headlining its story on the subject, "Mississippi Student Group Denounces Editor."

The faculty was quick to respond to the reprimand, passing a resolution commending Brower for her "unwavering determination to follow a constructive editorial policy." The resolution added that she had "significantly contributed to the preservation of the University's integrity."

In this difficult moment the university got one piece of good news: It had not lost its accreditation. The Southern Association of Colleges and Schools instead criticized Governor Barnett for interfering in university operations and put Ole Miss under special observation to prevent such interference again. It also called on the Ole Miss administration to maintain discipline and a "climate conducive to intellectual pursuits."

Students left for the Christmas holiday with the campus in an uneasy state. There had been continuing rumors that Meredith might not come back, maybe could not come back because he was going to fail—rumors that were untrue. And there was still the presence of the underground resisters, who had put out another pamphlet in December promising, "We are prepared to resist integration from now on, if necessary. . . . *SEGREGATION IS INEVITABLE.* It is human nature and one of God's laws." The flyer ended by wishing all those who refused to accept the "coon" a "White Christmas."

Given this latest missive, the prank that greeted Meredith as he prepared to leave for the holidays was not surprising: Someone left a dead raccoon on top of his car. The *Jackson Daily News* printed the picture with this ominous though accurate caption: "Dead Coon on Meredith's Car."

To make it abundantly clear that he was attending Ole Miss as his own man and on his own terms, Meredith announced early in 1963 that he might not return to the campus for the second semester of his senior year. In a news conference at his dorm, Meredith said he would not come back to Oxford "unless very definite and positive changes are made to make my situation more conducive to learning." He did not elaborate, but he went on to describe his efforts as part of "a war, a bitter war for the 'equality of opportunity' for our citizens. The enemy is determined, resourceful and unprincipled. There are no rules of war for which he has respect. Some standard must be set."

Most of the students who watched his statement did so silently; a few yelled, "Goodbye James," and shouted that he just wanted to get publicity.

Meredith's statement prompted an immediate reaction from Robert Kennedy, who urged state and university officials to make it possible for Meredith to continue his studies at Ole Miss. He added that if Meredith left because of the "extreme racial intolerance" focused on him, it would be a reflection not only on the university and the state. "That this should occur anywhere in the United States is a reflection on all of us."

Sidna Brower struck a much different note in her editorial the day after Meredith spoke. She argued that much of the hostility to his presence had abated and that the campus had essentially returned to normal. She closed by asking a pointed question: "What then was James Meredith's purpose in entering Ole Miss?"

Brower proved to be overly optimistic in her assessment of campus calm. "Meanness and severity" were still winning out over "tenderness and nobility." Two days after Meredith's news conference, one of the white students who had befriended him was injured by a soft drink bottle hurled through the transom of his dormitory room. But anti-Meredith sentiment got even more intense the next day, January 10. More than four hundred students, some of them shouting "Go home, you nigger," converged on the cafeteria to heckle Meredith while he tried to eat dinner. Not content with interrupting his meal, they followed him to the library, disrupting his efforts to study for upcoming exams. Campus police finally broke up the demonstration and took a few of the participants into custody.

Three days later, on January 13, Meredith got another taste of student ill will: One of his car tires was slashed. He told news reporters he thought the increase in the harassment was partly the result of a new issue of the Rebel Underground newsletter and of disagreements between university officials and the Justice Department over student discipline. The latest issue declared its dedication to "unceasing resistance to racial amalgamation" and said it was grateful for the students who refused to "accept Kennedy's four million dollar coon"—apparently a reference to how much the fight over his admission cost but a figure that was greatly overstated. Federal authorities said the October 1962 melee cost the government about $2.7 million, which included all of the military's expenses; the state's tab was $344,000.

A few days later the Underground circulated a more vicious issue. This one called Chancellor Williams "a LIAR," "a quisling," and "an example of Soviet type government at its worst" for suspending a student for demonstrating against Meredith. The flier said the student did nothing wrong by yelling "nigger at a coon" for this is what blacks "have been called (and are) in this area for centuries." The issue also took aim at Brower, referring to her as "a vicious wench" and advocating physical reprisals against her because "you were in a position to betray a tradition and you did so."

The Underground had thought Meredith was on his way out of Oxford—resisters boasted of "separating the coon from the curriculum." But he disappointed them by announcing January 30 from Jackson that he would return to school. Meredith chose to make his statement at a news conference to answer all questions at once, hoping to forestall a crush of reporters hounding him for their individual stories. True to his mercurial nature, Meredith was determined to deliver the information the way he wanted. He toyed with the audience when he said that after much deliberation, he had concluded that "the Negro should not return to the University of Mississippi." A white radio reporter burst into applause. "However," Meredith went on, "I have decided that I, J. H. Meredith, will register for the second semester." There were signs, he said, that "give me hope that I will be able to go to school in the future under adequate if not ideal conditions." In response to a question, Meredith said it was significant that President Kennedy had said publicly he hoped Meredith would continue at Ole Miss. "I think it was very important and very necessary that the president should make his position clear."

It had been obvious to anyone who knew Meredith that he was no ordinary individual. He made no secret of the fact that he considered himself on a mission to take on Ole Miss and the white supremacist mind-set in the state, and such strong beliefs helped propel him forward in these difficult days. His unusual phraseology in his remarks hinted at another means of surviving this pressure-filled time: finding a way to preserve the distinction in some deeply personal way between Meredith "the Negro"—a symbol—and Meredith the person. There was an additional benefit. He was sending a signal to other Mississippi blacks that it was a flesh and blood human being who was going to school in Oxford and that they, too, should aspire to do the same.

Meredith's second semester proved to be an improvement over the first, but it was hardly the kind of school experience any white student was having. He was still the target of scurrilous attacks by the Underground, which published a few more issues in the year, as were professors who supported him, particularly Barrett and Jim Silver of the history department.

For Meredith improvement was a relative term. It was ten months before he could walk down a hall or across the campus without someone calling him "nigger," and he continued to be distressed at the campaign of ostracizing him—not so much that he minded being ignored but because of the consequences for those whites who sought to break this informal code. "If a white student sits down and drinks a cup of coffee with me or walks with me across the campus, he is subjected to unhampered intimidation and harassment," he observed. "I have been denied my privileges all along, but these whites have not been." What was most troubling about this, he said, was that it "sets back the Negro, because anytime you move backward, the person already down suffers more."

One young woman who had the temerity to sit next to him in class was a case in point. For this the Underground accused her of ignoring the color line by "playing hands with the coon." Noting that Meredith was married, the flier added, "We ask the help of every Rebel who may know some nice single coon to put him in touch with [the student]. . . . She needs help." Then it printed her Oxford address and that of her family in Jackson. University officials did nothing to reduce the harassment she encountered, and she subsequently left school.

Meredith had been asked to write about his experiences for *Look* magazine and did so in a candid piece that appeared in the April 9, 1963, issue. "Most of the time, I am perhaps the most segregated Negro in the world," he wrote. Because there were so many unusual things about his stay in Oxford, Meredith conceded "that I seriously doubt that I am in a true sense a student of the university. I'm inclined to go along with diehard segregationists on this point."

But Meredith also knew that he was paving the way for others much younger than he, a point brought home to him virtually every day on the campus. "It was always a heartbreaking sight to see young Negro boys and girls who should have been in junior high or high school wiping the tables and carrying trays for white students," he explained. Because of what he was enduring, some of them would be motivated to return to school and then have the chance to go to college. The most irrefutable sign of his success would be his graduation, but that was four months away. In the meantime, other events on campus reflected how his presence had shaped the atmosphere.

Sidna Brower's term as *Mississippian* editor was coming to an end, and the election of her successor prompted much debate. (After her graduation, Brower continued on in journalism, having won a fellowship that took her to London. She returned to the United States to continue her career at a variety of papers, and then moved into public affairs. In the spring of 1995, she was deputy director of the New Jersey Council on

Affordable Housing.) The leading candidates were two staff members, Ed Williams, who was managing editor and a junior, and John Corlew, the news editor, also a junior. Williams described himself as "middle-of-the-road"; Corlew presented himself as the "conservative" *Mississippian* candidate. Although he didn't mention that Brower and Williams, who was from Missouri, were out-of-staters, Corlew told fellow students that "being from Mississippi, I feel my views will be fairly representative of the thinking of the campus."

Corlew easily beat Williams, racking up one of the biggest margins of victory in *Mississippian* history. In his own mind, Corlew didn't think of himself as that different from Brower—he supported her calls for calm and common sense—but he acknowledged feeling that Mississippi had been singled out unfairly. This came through in one of his first editorials as editor elect, titled, "Discrimination?" He took critics to task for arguing that the state discriminated against blacks. He pointed out that spending on black schools and teachers had increased and that enrollment at black colleges had increased more than it had at white schools. "If this is discrimination, we need more of it. Mississippi doesn't retard Negro progress. Give us a chance."

Years later Corlew conceded that his editorial failed to point out that the gains he cited were almost uniformly the result of federal pressure and that much of the increased expenditures had likely been federal money. But back then, he recalled, "you wanted to say something to defend yourself."

More vivid evidence of the conservative tide on campus was the scathing letter written to the *Mississippian* by Brad Lawrence, recently elected vice president of the student body. He was answering Meredith's *Look* article, and his words reflected the deep and continuing resentment at Meredith's presence. "There is no organized ostracism campaign against Meredith," Lawrence contended. "He has been ostracized because almost every individual at Ole Miss has been repulsed by his presence. . . . Meredith is naturally avoided by thinking people," he went on, "because of the element he represents." Not only that, Meredith had set back blacks' progress in the state "many years and has made their lives more difficult by engendering white bitterness and resentment." Lawrence's letter prompted many responses, a good number of them critical. But the fear of retribution still existed; some appeared with "name withheld for obvious reasons."

Ray Kerciu, an assistant professor of art, found out the price for dissent in art as well as speech. An exhibition of his work was put up in the spring in the campus Fine Arts Center. Among the selections were provocative renderings of the Confederate flag to reflect the recent turmoil. One had the words "SOVEREIGN STATE OF MISSISSIPPI" on it, with the S's backward. Another image of the flag included epithets and slogans from the Rebel Underground, bumper stickers, and actual comments from rioters: "Impeach JFK," "Back Ross," "Kennedy's Koon Keepers," and "Would you want your daughter to marry one?"

Citizens' Council members immediately protested the exhibition, and quickly the university ordered the exhibition taken down. "Certain paintings have been taken by many viewers as indicating a slighting attitude toward the Confederate flag itself and all that it may mean to southerners," said an official school statement. While insisting that Ole Miss administrators were not trying to curb Kerciu's artistic freedom, the statement said that Kerciu was asked to remove the works because "these paintings have given distress and offense to many."

Kerciu retorted that his artistic convictions not only had been questioned but "in fact violated." Several students picketed the arts center in protest. Another took a different tack, filing criminal charges against Kerciu on the grounds that his paintings were "obscene and indecent" and a "desecration of the Confederate flag." The charges were subsequently dropped for lack of sufficient evidence.

In one of her final editorials, Brower took critics to task, walking boldly on sacred ground: "If anyone violated the sanctity of the flag of the Confederacy, a nation which no longer exists except in the minds of men, the villain was the one who rioted on the night of September 30, 1962," she wrote. "For on that night, all principles for which the fair and genteel Southerners have stood were sacrificed in a bloody battle over the admission of a Negro to the University of Mississippi." She argued that art was the same as the written word and posed a pointed question: "Should not the artist have the same right to make known his personal feelings concerning an issue with pictures, as the writer can express himself with words? Or will the University of Mississippi suppress this freedom of expression because it does not adhere to the principles of certain groups? Is Ole Miss truly a University?"

Brower had posed a provocative question. Another was whether the campus was ready for a second black student. Cleve McDowell, a twenty-one-year-old graduate of Jackson State, would find out soon. He wanted to go to law school, and although he was qualified, McDowell nonetheless had to file a lawsuit to gain admission. On June 4, Judge Mize, the same judge who had presided over the Meredith litigation, ordered him admitted. The next day McDowell arrived on the campus to begin his studies.

Governor Barnett had been threatening to resist once again. Instead, he appeared on television in Jackson to announce that "it would be unwise and futile for the state of Mississippi to enter into a physical or shooting combat with the United States Army." But he reiterated his past refusals to guarantee the safety of black students, contending that it was the responsibility of the federal government. And he repeated for his staunchest followers his adamant opposition to integration: "We will oppose, on all occasions and at every opportunity . . . all dictatorial powers and police which seek to change our school system, our customs, our heritage, our way of life."

McDowell ended up being Meredith's roommate. Meredith had been living alone because he was denied the right to bring his wife and son on campus to live in married student housing. In his written explanation of the denial, Chancellor Williams told the board of trustees that the administration did not want to make an uneasy atmosphere any worse. "The other students cannot be compelled to accept this or any other student as a member of the University community," Williams wrote, "nor can they be forced to accept his family. The presence of the family on the campus could readily occasion the aggravation of existing tensions."

The ease of McDowell's entry to Ole Miss was a deceptively calm counterpoint to the eruption of violence that came just five days after he started classes. Late in the evening of June 11, Medgar Evers, the NAACP leader, was shot in the back and killed as he was walking from his car to the door of his Jackson home. Meredith, one of Evers's close friends, was outraged and anguished. He had always thought he would be the one to take a bullet, not Evers. He blamed the murder on "the governors of the Southern states and their defiant actions" and "the blind courts and prejudiced juries" for creating an atmosphere that made such killings possible. Roy Wilkins, the head of the NAACP, echoed these words when he told mourners, "The killer must have felt that he had, if not immunity, then certainly a protection for whatever he chose to do, no matter how dastardly." (Byron de la Beckwith was eventually convicted in 1993 of killing Evers after two previous mistrials.)

The violence in Jackson did not deter federal authorities in Oxford from continuing to wind down their operations. On June 12, the day after Evers was slain, the army contingent guarding McDowell and Meredith was removed from the campus to an outlying post. All of the troops would be gone from the city by July 24.

In one of his occasional pieces of analysis for the *New York Times,* Claude Sitton, the paper's senior reporter in the South, captured in a few words the import of what Meredith had done. The violence in the last year had convinced many Mississippians that the strategy of resistance and defiance was harmful to the state's overall economic and social health, Sitton wrote. "Mr. Meredith's continued presence at the university served as an irritating symbol of its futility."

Nothing would make that clearer than his graduation, an obvious sign that he not only had broken down a barrier but had passed through to the other side. He and Ross Barnett would now be fellow alumni. The diehard resisters were not willing to back off even in this final hour, however. Several anti-Meredith members of the board of trustees—those appointed by Barnett—sought to prevent him from getting a diploma. They were outvoted, but just barely, by a majority appointed by previous governors.

The local paper, the *Oxford Eagle,* was dumbfounded that this minority of trustees would even try such a thing. "We could hardly believe that they thought the state would really benefit from such a vote," the editorial steamed, pointedly noting that denying Meredith his diploma would have meant a sure loss of accreditation. The names of the six trustees who voted to let Meredith graduate were printed in case readers wanted to "convey your vote of thanks to the six men who saved Mississippi by their stand on this issue."

The scene on August 18 in the Grove was the complete opposite of the one that had greeted Meredith eleven months earlier: calm, order, and good feeling. Meredith and his family had arrived in a caravan of cars bringing several members of his family and friends. They were escorted by two carloads of marshals to ensure their safe passage from Kosciusko to Oxford.

As he marched with his classmates past the Lyceum Building—the bullet holes from the previous September night still visible—and into the Grove, Meredith saw living proof of what he had accomplished: the presence of some fifty blacks sitting freely and without fear amid the white audience. He was struck by the scene. Equally striking was the moment Meredith's name was called and he stepped forward to receive a handshake and a diploma from Chancellor Williams. Sitting in the audience, Russell Barrett realized that the handshake looked no different from that extended to thousands of other Ole Miss seniors, and he thought to himself how easy it all could be. But by now Barrett understood that a century and a half of a rigid racial orthodoxy would not be swept away overnight or even in eleven months.

The good feeling surrounding the graduation ceremony was tempered by the realization that more than 20 percent of the faculty was leaving. Chancellor Williams conceded that this was about twice the normal turnover, but he insisted that the university would not suffer and that new and equally qualified professors would be coming to Oxford. Some of the professors spoke publicly about their decision to leave. Dr. Samuel F. Clark of the chemistry department offered one of the sharper explanations for his departure. Declaring that Ole Miss was an institution "for which I have and still feel a deep affection," Clark said he was leaving nonetheless because of "the serious loss of academic freedom to faculty and students and the breakdown of moral and professional responsibility on the part of the university's administrative officers." A professor who had invited Meredith over to his house for dinner on occasion decided to leave because of the repercussions for his family. The most cruel was directed at his youngest daughter during the Christmas celebration at her school. Each of the children bought a gift for another child after drawing names out of a hat. The gifts were opened one by one in front of the whole class. When she opened hers, a black doll was inside with a card attached that read "Nigger Lover."

One of the departures was forced by the university—that of law dean Farley, who years earlier had encouraged Medgar Evers to come to the Ole Miss law school, had stood up for beleaguered professor William Murphy three years earlier, had spoken out against defiance of the federal government, and had suggested expelling students for demonstrating after the September 30 riot. Farley had reached the mandatory retirement age of sixty-five, and although it was customary for deans to stay on as teachers—and Farley wanted to—he was told that he would not be approved. He told friends not to make a fight.

Criticized since 1954 as an integrationist, Farley had a ready retort: "You've got to teach what the law is. You've got at least to give the students all the various views. Certainly you can't have a law school that tries to cover up the law you don't like." Farley retired to Florida, where he taught law classes at the state university.

"Abandoning him is the most shameful act I have known on this campus," one colleague remarked.

Farley's departure boded ill for other outspoken professors, particularly Jim Silver. His day of reckoning with Mississippi's resisters would not be far off.

Many on the campus breathed a sigh of relief when the fall semester of 1963 got off to a smooth start. Cleve McDowell was proceeding with his legal education, and while there was no physical resistance to his presence, the outward calm masked underlying tensions. He had taken over Meredith's dorm room, but all the white students had moved off the floor, and he was subjected daily to low-level verbal harassment as he went back and forth across the campus. More disturbing and potentially dangerous were the difficulties McDowell occasionally had driving between Oxford and his home in Drew, a small town in the Mississippi Delta.

Despite the possible dangers, McDowell's family were solidly behind him even though there had been repercussions. The most difficult were the economic ones, when the McDowells' credit was cut off at stores where they had shopped for years, and there was the usual stream of hate calls. Fortunately there was no violence, primarily because the family lived in the middle of the black community, and being surrounded by friends deterred the night riders, who preferred to harass and intimidate those who lived in more isolated settings.

Because McDowell had bought Meredith's car, which was recognized because of all the publicity in the previous year, he was easy to spot. Some drivers periodically tried to force him off the road or drove in a way that threw gravel onto his windshield. McDowell was understandably concerned that some of his tormentors might step up their activities when the fall semester began. He was even more concerned when he realized there would be no more federal marshals on the campus.

A more private and considerably younger racial pioneer than Meredith, McDowell tried to deal with his concerns on his own. Meredith likely would have called a news conference to lay out the problem and put pressure on the university and government officials to protect him. McDowell bought a gun to carry in his car. (University regulations prohibited guns on campus, and students were required to sign cards stating they would abide by the rule.) One friendly clergyman in whom he had confided counseled McDowell to get rid of the weapon, but he ignored the advice. In the meantime, someone in the Citizens' Council learned McDowell had bought the gun and tipped off local authorities.

On September 23, a Monday morning, McDowell was running late for class because he had stopped at the U.S. attorney's office in Oxford to ask for a resumption of federal protection. Anxious not to miss too much class time, McDowell parked in a no-parking zone. Fearing that his car might be ticketed and searched, he took the small gun with him and put it in his jacket pocket. As he ran up the stairs to the classroom, he dropped his sunglasses. As he stooped to pick them up, the gun fell out. The Lafayette County sheriff, alerted by two law students, was there to arrest McDowell when he emerged from class.

Later that day, university officials suspended him. The next day the student judicial council recommended his expulsion, and by the afternoon university officials made that a reality. Ironically the only interview McDowell had granted since his admission was printed in the *Missis-*

sippian the very day of his suspension. He chose his words carefully, especially when asked about the atmosphere at the school. He said the attitude toward him "hasn't necessarily been friendly. . . . The students don't have to speak to me or recognize me as such," he added, "but they certainly can't ignore me."

Hodding Carter's paper, the *Delta Democrat Times,* soberly reported that "the University of Mississippi today returned to 'all white' status." Over in Jackson, the *Daily News* was more gleeful: "McDowell Expulsion Erases Only Mixing Blot in State."

Bill Champion, a young law professor, was surprised that McDowell felt he needed a gun. Champion hadn't seen any overt acts directed against the young man. Such were the markedly differing perceptions of life on campus for the lone black student.

Russell Barrett had better understood McDowell's mind-set, and he was so chagrined by what had happened that he wrote a trenchant letter to Burke Marshall, head of the Justice Department's civil rights division. The withdrawal of federal marshals was a grave error, he said. "I would emphasize that we at this University are a long way from the time when an unguarded and unadvised Negro can hope to attend the University successfully. Even if there were no physical danger to the student, there is still the nagging isolation from regular human contacts and the presence of an administration which is at best neutral. The purposeful 'man with a mission' such as Meredith may make it," he went on, "but the young man such as McDowell who 'only wants an education' will not make it."

McDowell went to court to appeal his expulsion, contending that other white students had been found with guns on campus but had not been tossed out of school. His appeal was unsuccessful. He spent the next few years working for the NAACP in Mississippi and other parts of the country and then eventually resumed his law studies at Texas Southern University. He was admitted to practice in Mississippi in 1971.

McDowell saw a silver lining to his expulsion from Ole Miss. "The cold-blooded reality is that I probably would have been killed. It [the expulsion] probably saved my life. Only historically when you look back do you really realize how much danger you were in," McDowell went on, adding that he remained convinced that it was a mistake for the federal government to have left the campus after Meredith graduated. "No state level people were going to help. In effect you were on your own."

Like Russell Barrett, Jim Silver, the history professor, had been deeply troubled by the McDowell incident. He considered it another downward spiral for a place he had loved and had devoted all of his professional life to. Though Silver was not a native southerner—he was born in New York—he had lived in the South for forty-four years, twenty-eight of them in Mississippi. He was fond of pointing out that his wife was from Alabama and an Ole Miss graduate, and his two daughters were eligible for membership in the United Daughters of the Confederacy. He was no carpetbagger and no modern-day scalawag. But he did like to challenge his students to think hard and to question everything around them, particularly the racial caste system that shaped so much of their daily lives. Many like Albin Krebs considered him their mentor and the best thing about being at Ole Miss.

Although Silver had had many opportunities to teach elsewhere over the years, he had turned them down. And after each visiting professorship in such places as New England, the West Coast, and Scotland, he was always glad to return home. "Hell, I like it here," he told one newspaper reporter, ticking off the choice places to go fishing, the proximity of a good golf course and tennis court, and "convivial companions" for bridge and poker. But as he watched the lethal consequences of Mississippi's stubborn resistance, he could no longer keep silent.

As outgoing president of the Southern Historical Association in the fall of 1963, it was his duty to address the group's annual meeting. He decided to tell his fellow historians—some nine hundred in all—about the last few years in Mississippi. His theme was that the state was a closed society.

The "totalitarian society of Mississippi imposes on all of its people acceptance of an obedience to an official orthodoxy almost identical with the pro-slavery philosophy," Silver asserted. "Mississippi is the way it is not because of its views on the Negro—here it is simply the South exaggerated—but because of its closed society; its refusal to allow freedom of inquiry, to tolerate 'error of opinion.'" The effect on the state was that the "totalitarian society" had "eliminated the ordinary processes by which change is challenged. Through its police power, coercion and force prevail instead of accommodation and the result is social paralysis. Thus the Mississippian who prides himself on his individuality in reality lives in a climate where non-conformity is forbidden and where the white man is not free, where he does not dare to express a deviating opinion without looking over his shoulder."

The speech gained much national attention: *Newsweek* magazine profiled Silver in its November 18, 1963, issue; *Life* would do the same a few months later. It also incensed several trustees and legislators, who wanted Silver dismissed from the faculty. Typical was U.S. Representative John Bell Williams, who said it was time for the state to "fumigate some of our college staffs and get those who will teach Americanism and not foreign ideologies." Taking direct aim at Silver, he added, "The time has come to call the bluff of anyone who cusses a state which has fed him for 28 years and get rid of him." Brad Lawrence, who had responded so caustically to Meredith's *Look* article, used his platform as vice president of the student body to criticize Silver as "bitter" and "unable to convince the young people of Mississippi to accept his theories of centralized government and racial integration."

In Jackson, one legislator demanded Silver's dismissal, pledging to take any action necessary short of violence to force Silver off the faculty. Another sponsored a bill to prevent Silver from speaking about certain activities and to clamp down on his "degrading activities." Such actions would boost Silver's reputation among northern sympathizers, he conceded, but this state senator said that didn't matter. It was "better that he get national fame than for us to receive social death," adding that the legislature should fire Silver if the university would not.

The trustees did not shirk their duty. They created a committee to gather evidence to fire Silver even though he had been a tenured professor of history since 1936. Formal charges were drawn up accusing him of making "provocative and inflammatory speeches calculated to increase racial tension and provoke racial violence." The charges were mailed to Silver in late April, a month after the legislators threatened to take matters into their own hands.

By this time the controversy over Silver had become the subject of public discussion. He had many vocal supporters within the university community. Two student honor societies passed a joint resolution defending academic freedom and calling "reprehensible" any attempt to curb a professor's academic pursuits. Former Silver students wrote board members expressing their support for Silver in the strongest of terms. One said Silver "did more for my education at Ole Miss than all the other professors combined. He was and is one of the rare men who make a college education worth all the time and expense."

Silver had already retained legal counsel, and as his lawyers were preparing responses to the board's charges, he in effect made the entire matter moot. In a move similar to the one William Murphy had made four years earlier, Silver took a leave of absence to be a visiting professor at Notre Dame. He left before the trustees finally resolved the charges against him. He would never return to Oxford to teach.

Early in 1964 Silver had expanded his provocative speech into a book. *Mississippi: The Closed Society* was officially published on June 22, 1964. The timing was both fortuitous and tragic. June was the beginning of the Freedom Summer project in Mississippi, the full-scale effort by civil rights groups to register Mississippi blacks to vote, so attention was naturally going to be focused on the state. On June 21, the day before the book's release, three civil rights workers were reported missing, and for the next six weeks, until James Chaney, Andrew Goodman, and Mickey Schwerner were found shot dead and buried in an earthen dam near Philadelphia in Neshoba County, the nation was caught up in the drama of their disappearance.

Closed Society hit the best-seller lists in good part, Silver acknowledged, because of the widespread anxiety over events in Mississippi.

Silver's departure from Ole Miss coincided with the arrival of the school's third black student, Cleveland Donald, Jr., an eighteen-year-old from Jackson. He had spent his first year at Tougaloo College in the capital city and was entering Ole Miss as a sophomore. His arrival on campus was peaceful but not entirely voluntary on the university's part. Like Meredith and McDowell before him, Donald had to go to court for an order requiring Ole Miss to admit him, and although his wait was shorter than Meredith's, it still took four months of legal maneuvering before a federal judge finally ordered Ole Miss officials to let him in. The judge also took the unusual step of ordering Donald not to participate in any civil rights activities or "engage in any publicity program by civil rights groups." The order referred to an affidavit Donald had signed stating that it was "not my desire to to attend the University of Mississippi to obtain publicity for myself or for any group."

Donald stuck to this line when he enrolled June 11. Pressed by reporters to talk about his registration, Donald said only, "I have come for an education and have decided to hold no press conferences. He told the reporters "to just stay away. . . . Maybe in three or four years I'll be ready."

Donald's arrival on campus had been uneventful, a possible sign that the climate was changing. The state had a new governor, Paul Johnson, Jr. As Barnett's lieutenant, he had established his segregationist credentials by barring Meredith on one of his unsuccessful attempts to enter the campus, and he trumpeted his pro-segregation stand louder than his opponents. One campaign slogan, "Stand tall with Paul," was an allusion to the Oxford business. But in his inaugural address on January 21, 1964, Johnson stuck a different tone, edging toward the nobility of Willie Morris's equation: "While I am governor, hate, prejudice, and ignorance will not lead Mississippi. If we must fight it will not be a rearguard defense of yesterday. It will be an all out assault on our share of tomorrow."

The message was encouraging, even courageous given the time and the place, but reality was another thing. Yesterday still loomed larger than tomorrow. At Ole Miss the quiet that greeted Donald's arrival was deceptive, just as it had been a year earlier for McDowell. The surface adjustment covered over unease, discomfort, and in some cases outright resistance to the notion of integration. This was made all too apparent by the violence heaped on the civil rights workers who had come to be part of Freedom Summer, not just Goodman, Schwerner, and Chaney, who had been murdered, but the dozens who were beaten and regularly harassed.

On the Ole Miss campus federal marshals were gone, so Donald, fearing the worst, set up his own security device. He installed a button under his window that was connected electronically to a red light in front of his dormitory. Campus police were stationed across the street twenty-four hours a day in his first year watching for the light to go on.

During the summer, state legislators had been busy passing laws intended to keep a tight rein on the "invaders," as they were called by many. The board of trustees also wanted to maintain control over the campuses under its jurisdiction. And when members learned that some of the civil rights workers had visited Ole Miss at the invitation of two faculty members, they responded promptly with a resolution that said in pertinent parts that some of those in the "invasion" belonged to communist groups bent on overthrowing the government and that "a concerted effort should be made by all Americans" and particularly those on college campuses "to avoid these dangerous movements and to support conservative constitutional government."

Julien R. Tatum, the chairman of the sociology department who had approved the visit of the civil rights workers, gave Chancellor Williams a three-page, single-spaced report defending their appearance on the campus. He described it as a perfect opportunity for students to understand "a view that was quite likely foreign to their own." It would have been "unthinkable," Tatum added, for the civil rights workers to have "come and gone without the opportunity of Mississippi students hearing from them why they came, why they did not devote time to race relations in their own states and what they were doing here."

But typical of the angry letters that came into the chancellor's office was one from state representative Ben Owen. It is, he wrote, "surely disgusting to waste our students' time with such trash. I have a lot of alcoholic, illiterate Negro farm hands down on my place . . . who could add more to an Ole Miss sociology class than these enlightened philanthropies from the up-country . . . Ditto for my very neat and attractive maid who had seven children by four different husbands and literally is an extremely clean and neat young employee."

Following the lead of the legislature, the board adopted new rules restricting the use of college facilities to students, faculty, staff, and alumni—in effect barring all but a handful of blacks from these buildings. The rules were invoked for the first time at Ole Miss for the football game against Memphis State, which had black players. (The bar to Mississippi teams playing against schools with integrated squads had come down a year earlier, but not without a fight, when Mississippi State was allowed to compete against integrated teams in the National Collegiate

Athletic Association basketball tournament.) Under these rules parents of the black football players from Memphis State were not allowed to eat in the Ole Miss commons. White cafeteria workers were deputized to arrest any blacks who attempted to use the dining facilities on the day of the game. Although black families were turned away from the cafeteria, they left without incident and the Ole Miss–Memphis State game went on without any problems.

This might have looked like a victory for the resisters, but the more significant point was that an integrated team came onto the Ole Miss campus, played its game and left, and life went on. However grudgingly, Mississippi was facing the future. The federal government would see to it with pressure on those who stood in the way. Washington's tenacious effort to find the killers of Goodman, Schwerner, and Chaney provided one stark piece of evidence. Seven Ku Klux Klansmen were later tried, convicted, and sentenced to prison, a first in Mississippi for a civil rights–related killing. Passage of the 1964 Civil Rights Act, opening up public spaces and accommodations to blacks, had been more proof that the once-rigid social order was crumbling. By August, federal attorneys, white and black, were in the state doing advance work for hearings on the next item on the civil rights agenda: voting. Because of the public accommodations law, they were able to eat as a group in any restaurant they wanted. They chose the Admiral Benbow Inn in Jackson for their first meal and were served without incident. As he watched the lawyers file out, one patron captured the prevailing mood of many unhappy but resigned whites when he told his wife, "Well, dear, I guess this is something we'll just have to get used to."

That seemed to be the message over in Oxford, despite some bumpy times. In the fall of 1964, another black student, Irvin Walker, was admitted as a freshman without having first to obtain a court order. He participated in freshman activities without interference, and when he got into a brief fight with a white student who insulted him, the fracas was covered in the *Mississippian* without a great deal of fanfare. On the other hand, a funeral wreath was hung anonymously on Walker's door, and neither his family nor Cleveland Donald's family could eat in the Ole Miss cafeteria because of the trustees' directive. Moreover, many of Walker's white classmates never spoke to him in his entire four years on campus.

One senior administrator bluntly admitted to *Ebony* magazine that integration in the fullest sense was yet to be achieved. While some whites "have approached Negroes, often at the risk of cutting themselves off from their own families," he explained, "generally a Negro at Ole Miss, even today, has to have something deep down inside."

Nonetheless, the arrival of more black students after Walker was not considered newsworthy. And equally important, black students started gaining admission by twos or threes, not just one at a time. Though other southern universities were admitting blacks at a faster pace, at Ole Miss, *Ebony* observed, "even leisurely integration amounts to a miracle."

There seemed to be a change in the tone of public discourse on the campus early in 1965. In February, state treasurer William Winter, one of Mississippi's most moderate politicians, came to Ole Miss to speak. "We can no longer deal in the romantic details as we would like them to be," Winter said. "We have to be willing to face the hard facts as we find them." This was going to take new leaders, Winter went on, "willing to say frankly that we do our state no service when we consider defiance of the laws of this nation." He went even further, condemning the "facile demagogues" who preached "gloom and doom" and who would "hoodwink our people into believing that our state is going to crack up unless we keep everything just the way it has been for the last century." On the contrary, Winter said, "we are going to crack up and fall out of the running unless we do take into account and make adjustments for these changes."

The *Mississippian* wrote approvingly of Winter's speech, noting that Governor Johnson and other senior politicians had recently delivered similar messages. Finally, the editorial said, Mississippi leaders were realizing that "the people who are doing the most harm to Mississippi are not out-of-state agitators, not biased journalists, not left-wing television commentators. The people who are doing the most to drag Mississippi down are Mississippians who think they don't have to obey the laws they don't like; Mississippians who attempt to live in a dream world of moonlight, moonshine and magnolia blossoms; Mississippians who burn churches; Mississippians who refuse to recognize the fact that two-fifths of the population in this state is non-white."

Ed Williams, by now editor of the paper, took heart in the development, believing the turn of events was peculiarly southern. "Southerners, black and white, have had a lot of experience picking up and moving on," he said. "We are not incapable of dealing with reality when faced with it. People have a way of accepting change when it is not presented as an option."

But Williams also understood that change was slow—sometimes two steps forward and one step back. An incident early in the spring of 1965 involving visitors from predominantly black Tougaloo college in Jackson was a reminder that admitting blacks to Ole Miss was one thing; accepting black and white social relationships was another.

An integrated group of students from Tougaloo accompanied by a white professor from the school had come to Oxford to participate in the annual Southern Literary Festival, the first time blacks had officially been admitted since the festival's creation in 1937. The decision to seat the Tougaloo representatives had been a difficult one. At one point officials threatened to cancel the program over the issue, and one of the professors working on the program threatened to resign if it was. But the board of trustees allowed the event to go forward.

The concerns about this integrated meeting turned out to be well founded. Near the end of the first day, nearly five hundred Ole Miss students gathered near the dorm where the black men from Tougaloo were staying. They created their own version of the well-known "2-4-6-8" sports cheer, reversing it to say: "8-6-4-2-send them back to Tougaloo." To the whites in the party they shouted, "We don't want nigger lovers at Ole Miss."

As darkness settled, the crowd became unruly, throwing rocks, bottles, and firecrackers toward the protesters. Campus police eventually broke up the demonstration but not before the car driven by the Tougaloo professor was severely damaged, windows smashed, tires deflated, and the gas tank filled with sugar. As a final gesture someone had painted "nigger" across one side in bright orange.

Echoing the views of Sidna Brower three years earlier, the *Mississippian* was quick to condemn the demonstrators. "Ole Miss students have again succeeded in endangering the future of Ole Miss," an editorial began. "Ole Miss is known to many people only as the riot school. To them, disturbance equals a riot, if the disturbance occurs at Ole Miss." This only tarnishes the school's reputation and endangers its much-needed financial support, the paper said. "The handful of students who organized the demonstrations last night may have been working to close the doors of Ole Miss. And they probably don't even understand."

The incident also prompted the reappearance of the Rebel Underground, which blamed the incident on the Tougaloo visitors for violating racial taboos by kissing in public, holding hands, and hugging each other. This was little more than "an obvious attempt to violate the social and moral standards that we have known all our lives," the Underground said, insisting that the demonstrators were simply "protesting an open and flagrant violation of our long established social behavior patterns."

Ed Williams was called over to the university administration building to talk to officials concerned that the wire services had overstated the number of demonstrators. He was dumbfounded by the questions he was asked. "You people are troubled over the impression of a news story," he told one administrator. "The reality is you had a riot. You ought to be worried about that."

The Southern Literary Festival was a single incident that illustrated how much change could come and how fast. The experience of the law school in this trying period illustrated the point more broadly.

Joshua M. Morse III had replaced Bob Farley in 1963. His credentials suggested that he was a safe choice. He came from an old Mississippi family, had practiced law for fifteen years in the state, and after he joined the law faculty, he had declined to back Farley and other Ole Miss professors in public protest against the state's handling of the Meredith matter. But when he became dean, Morse surprised his supporters. He went to Yale in 1963 for a year of graduate work, charmed his northern colleagues with his storytelling ability, and returned with some new Yale-trained teachers for the school. A year and a half later he helped persuade the Ford Foundation to give him nearly $500,000. A good part of the money was used for scholarships for white and black students, a move the *Clarion Ledger* condemned as a "sell-out . . . to voluntarily negroize Ole Miss." And some of the money was used to hire more instructors from Yale.

The dean's pitch to the foundation had been telling—candid if you agreed with him, condescending if you did not. "This law school can be tremendously influential of the political thought and action of the state of Mississippi," he told the grantors. "Many of the problems which plague the University of Mississippi and our state stem from a provincial outlook. Our students are accustomed to examine every question in light of its impact on Mississippi culture rather than taking a broader view."

Impressed by the legal activism in such an unusual place, *Time* trumpeted the "new mood at Ole Miss." One of the incoming Yale graduates said he felt as if he was "in the Peace Corps except we're given much more responsibility," a comparison that did not set well with the state's legal establishment. Nor did the comment of Yale law dean Louis Pollack: "The law school is at the threshold of becoming a focus for the kind of thinking that can bring Mississippi into the 20th century." Pollack was one of more than a dozen part-time teachers from Ivy League law schools who came to Oxford for two-week lectures. The students dubbed these the "jet-set" courses.

Of the new full-time courses under Morse's reign, the most noteworthy was the one on civil rights. It was put together after nineteen students petitioned Morse for the class, and the first enrollment was so great that participation had to be limited to third-year students. Although there was the usual grousing from conservative whites, Morse said things had changed and "we don't pay any attention to it." He might have added, "at least not yet."

One of the first Yale graduates to arrive had been Michael Horowitz. He quickly learned the political and racial facts of life. Anxious to get the *New York Times* on a daily basis instead of waiting two weeks for the library copy, he approached university officials about working out an arrangement between the newspaper and the school. He thought they'd be happy to get the paper so promptly. Absolutely not, he was told. Ole Miss would not be part of any special arrangement for bringing in the *Times,* considered too leftist by many Mississippians.

In his contracts class, Horowitz gave students an unusual assignment: He asked them to write a sonnet, explaining that if they could handle the discipline of the poetry form, they could handle the constraints of legal writing. Word of Horowitz's teaching method got out, and not long after that assignment was given, he was denounced on the floor of the legislature in Jackson for teaching poetry in a law class. Horowitz also figured in Byron de la Beckwith's run for state office. Among his campaign pledges was to "fire the Jew professor."

Determined that the four black students in his class would not be isolated in his room, Horowitz assigned seats alphabetically. One of the four, Reuben Anderson, was in the front row. One day in the winter of 1966, a photographer from *Ebony* came into the classroom to shoot pictures for a story on the university. Several of the white students tried to duck out of the camera's way or covered their faces with books. Horowitz later apologized to the students for the intrusion, explaining that he considered the classroom private and had not known the photographer was coming. If any of the white students took heat at home for sitting next to a black, he said, they could blame it on him. Then he told them, "You might want to buy a copy of *Ebony* and hold on to it. Because fifteen years from now you might want to say you were a friend of Reuben Anderson."

Anderson went on to become the first black to serve on the Mississippi Supreme Court.

Ole Miss had given Anderson a good legal education but little else. The isolation he experienced was the same that Meredith had experienced three and a half years earlier. Some classmates and some professors— though not the ones from Yale—never spoke to him once during his entire time there. Indeed the difference between the northern-trained professors and the veterans on the Ole Miss faculty was striking. Anderson was completely ignored by some of these older men; the younger men from Yale, along with Dean Morse, went out of their way to be helpful. When Anderson had financial difficulties, Morse found scholarship money for him. Horowitz lent him his car because he didn't have one on campus.

Another of the Yale-educated teachers was Walter Dellinger, a native southerner, from Charlotte, North Carolina, and he was impressed with Morse's desire to train black lawyers in Mississippi. He, too, thought that was a worthy and important goal, and he was impressed that by his second year in Oxford, only historically black Howard University in Washington had more black law students than Ole Miss. Dellinger also believed that as a white southerner, he had a better chance of reaching the young white men and sprinkling of women in his classes than a northerner would. Morse thought so too, which is why he asked Dellinger to teach constitutional law and the course in civil rights. Better to hear a discussion of *Brown v. Board of Education* and an exposition on social justice with a North Carolina accent than in the northern cadence of a Mike Horowitz.

Dellinger thought it was useful for his students to hear outside speakers, so he invited Aaron Henry, head of the state NAACP, to address his class. This did not go over well with David Clark, one of the most conservative students in the school.

Clark had grown up in Jackson in a family close to Ross Barnett. In fact Barnett had taught him in Sunday school and had been impressed enough with the young man that he got him a job as a page in the legislature. During the Meredith crisis, Clark had a ringside seat for one of the many dramatic moments of that time, flying up to Oxford in the governor's plane for one of Barnett's confrontations with Meredith. Clark was sure the state was about to fight a second civil war, and he wanted to be part of it, ready to defend his home and way of life as his ancestors had.

When Henry came to the law school class, Clark was caught in a dilemma. He wanted to hear what the man had to say—and Dellinger had made class attendance a requirement—but he couldn't stomach the thought of being in the same room with a black man who would be in a position of authority—a position superior to him. He told Dellinger he wanted to pull his chair into the hallway and listen to Henry through the open door, an ironic reversal of M. B. Mayfield's covert art lessons sixteen years earlier. Aaron thought the scene was hilarious and did not object, nor did Dellinger, and neither man objected when Clark refused to address Henry directly. When he asked a question, he put it to Dellinger, who then relayed it to Henry, sending back the response the same way.

Dellinger knew that even though he was a native southerner, he was suspect because of his Yale credentials. When he learned that his classes were being surreptitiously taped and sent to the Citizens' Councils and Sovereignty Commission, he announced that no one needed to hide his equipment. Tape in the open, he said. His lectures on American constitutional law would be good for the conservatives to hear.

All the Yale-trained teachers considered themselves lucky to be teaching at Ole Miss, believing they were in the forefront of something special and exciting. And although many of their students felt the same way, referring to it as the school's "golden era," not every student was happy with the influx from Yale. Clark looked at every class as "a battleground," and Trent Lott resented what he felt was the patronizing, condescending attitude of the outsiders, "leading us poor, barefoot Mississippi boys out of the wilderness." In his mind, they had an unintended result: creating a generation of thoughtful conservatives. "We had to develop our minds to combat the junk they were heaping on us," he said, referring to too many lectures he thought were laced with "socialism."

One of the by-products of a provocative faculty was an active law student association, and early in 1966 this group asked Robert Kennedy to speak on the campus. To some in the state, this invitation was worse than heresy; it verged on treason. One segregationist group immediately announced plans to disrupt the event, scheduled for March, and tried—unsuccessfully—to get the legislature to pass a resolution deploring the invitation. One member of the board of trustees called the gesture "an affront" and demanded that it be rescinded. His colleagues declined to go along with that suggestion.

The vituperative debate between the February announcement of Kennedy's speech and his actual presentation on March 18 reflected the continuing racial tensions in the state. Russell Barrett took note of this in remarks he made at predominantly black Rust College five weeks before Kennedy's speech. Mississippi, he told listeners, is "emotionally and socially many miles from that point at which a person can work openly and honestly and even moderately for racial justice without some risk of verbal or physical attack against him as a person." He cited a recent bombing in Hattiesburg as evidence. And he reminded listeners that although Congress had passed the tough Voting Rights Act just six months earlier, there was no guarantee it would be enforced properly in Mississippi without constant federal pressure. Although local registrars grudgingly were accepting black voters, "we still cannot say that the welcome mat is really out everywhere." But Barrett did concede that the 1965 voting law and the landmark Civil Rights Act passed the year before were altering prevailing racial sentiments. Those who once lit Molotov cocktails, he noted, were now willing instead to light a few candles.

That Mississippians could even entertain the idea of a speech by Robert Kennedy at Ole Miss was little short of remarkable. He was "a man with a prominent name, radical views, high placed friends and powerful enemies—and nowhere are those enemies more numerous than in the state of Mississippi," noted *Mississippian* editor Gene Fair. "Nowhere is Kennedy remembered more bitterly than at the University of Mississippi."

By the time Kennedy arrived in Oxford, the biggest issue was where he would speak: at a relatively small hall or the coliseum, where several thousand could hear him. The university had been reluctant to allow the latter because of security concerns, but in the end officials relented. His speech went off without a hitch Friday afternoon, March 18. One newspaper reported that a man who was "once the object of general hatred" in the state was greeted with "brimming cordiality." More than five thousand students, faculty, and visitors cheered the senator during his speech and question-and-answer session. And although there had been threats to his safety, no one "laid a hand on him except in admiration."

Kennedy was calm and conciliatory in his remarks, appealing to the audience for greater understanding between North and South. "I come here not to discuss old issues," he said, "but new problems, not to revive old differences but to share new responsibilities, not to the heart of the South, but to the Southern part of the United States of America." "You have no problem the nation does not have," he went on. "You share no hope that is not shared by your fellow students and young people across this country. You carry no burden that they too do not carry."

During the question session, Kennedy responded candidly about the conversation with Ross Barnett in the days before Meredith's entry. He made them laugh as he recounted how many marshals Barnett said should draw their guns before the governor retreated. The students greeted this information with roars of laughter.

Barnett was not amused. "Every time Bobby Kennedy spoke of anything concerning me at Ole Miss he either twisted statements or willfully misrepresented the facts," he thundered in a speech three days after Kennedy's appearance. "It ill becomes a man who never tried a lawsuit in his life" but who was attorney general and used thousands of troops "and spent approximately six million dollars to put one unqualified student in

Ole Miss to return to the scene of this crime and discuss any phase of the infamous affair." (The Meredith episode was by now completely past history for Barnett. Ten months earlier, on May 5, 1965, a federal appeals court dismissed the contempt proceedings it had instituted against him and Paul Johnson for their actions in the fall of 1962. Neither paid a penny in fines or served a day in jail for their refusal to obey the court orders requiring Meredith's admission.)

A short article in the *Mississippian* on June 16, at the start of the summer session, seemed to be a fitting coda to spring events. The story noted that more than thirty blacks had registered for the summer session. "The registration attracted no attention," the paper said, "a marked contrast to the events occurring when James Meredith broke the color barrier here in 1962," barely four years earlier. Indeed, anyone who had dodged a brick in the Grove on that awful September night or choked on tear gas would have been hard pressed to believe that registration went so smoothly or that Robert Kennedy would have been welcomed so warmly on the campus.

Among those thirty summer students was the first black woman, who was beginning her sophomore year. Her name was Verna Bailey, and she was from Jackson, the daughter of Sam Bailey, a successful businessman who was president of the local branch of the NAACP and vice president of the state organization. Bailey had grown up with the civil rights movement, and she made her decision to go to Ole Miss knowing it would not be easy. Two things were driving her: Ole Miss would offer her a good education, and she could help widen the path James Meredith had started. She felt especially strong about that point. Meredith had been a guest in the Baileys' home during his ordeal, coming not only for a good meal but for spiritual sustenance as well. More than once family members and other guests would tell him, "James, be brave. James, be strong."

Bailey's first days on campus showed that southern chivalry had its limits. It was less important that she was a young woman than that she was black. When she went into the cafeteria to get her first meal, she was greeted with hisses and shouts of, "Here comes the nigger, here comes the nigger." Students threw food at her when she went to get her tray from the cafeteria line.

Although she had a private telephone in her dorm room—and she lived alone—the number got out. The harassing calls were mostly from young white men who told her, "Nigger bitches don't belong here. Nigger bitches belong in the cotton fields."

Bailey managed to toss off the insults and cope with an isolation that was a marked departure from her high school years. She had been a star academically and a leader in a number of social activities at the school, and she had never lacked for friends. On the bleakest days in Oxford, she thought that perhaps the warm and loving atmosphere of her childhood had given her the strength to deal with the harsh environment in Oxford. She reached the breaking point only once, in the last semester of her senior year, when she had thought the worst was over and real racial progress had been made. It was in her philosophy class, and she was sitting near a white football player, who would later go on to play professionally.

"You know," he told the teacher and his white classmates, "I would really like for Verna to fan me with a palm and serve me mint juleps."

Bailey ran out of the classroom to her dorm and called her mother in tears. "They hate me," she sobbed. "I just don't understand it."

She knew she could finish out the semester—only a month or so was left. But Bailey knew that if she had had to go through another full year in Oxford, she would have transferred. She graduated in the spring of 1968 with the bachelor of arts degree from the University of Mississippi that she had set out to get.

Early in his tenure Josh Morse had blithely dismissed opposition to what he and his Yale-trained teachers were doing at the law school, but by 1968, pressure to put a halt to "Yale-at-Oxford," as one magazine called it, was building. It was not a good sign when M. M. Roberts, one of the most conservative members of the board of trustees, said, "I'm embarrassed by my law school."

The list of grievances from Roberts and other power brokers was long: the invitations to Kennedy and Henry, professors' signing a petition opposing the war in Vietnam, helping with a lawsuit challenging the board's policy on outside speakers, helping professors invalidate a requirement to list their organization memberships, and too much participation in a legal services program for poor residents in northern Mississippi. It was this last item that unleashed the opponents after the federally funded program, which was operated by the law school, filed a school desegregation suit in Holly Springs, a small town north of Oxford.

The state bar had previously tried to kill the program by passing restrictive regulations, and it had made its displeasure clear to Morse. He was not allowed to speak at an annual bar meeting, something that every law dean in recent memory had done. One legislator even suggested that a law should be passed "that a professor at the university Law School would not sue the state of Mississippi or the University of Mississippi."

Finally enough pressure was brought to bear on university officials to remove the legal services program from the law school. Law professors were told they had to make a choice: teach at Ole Miss or be a legal services lawyer. They could not do both. When three teachers ignored the warning, they were taken off the payroll, and their summer school classes were canceled. They sued immediately, alleging that their civil liberties had been violated, and eventually prevailed in a federal appeals court.

Other teachers, including Morse himself, were denied the general raise given to the rest of the university faculty; in Morse's case, he was not given a raise for three years. On top of that he was told that the law school's share of Ole Miss funding would be cut, a move he believed was clearly designed to force him out.

"The great experiment at the law school is almost dead," Professor Michael Trister, one of the Yale recruits, told *Time.* Morse thought so too. By 1969 he felt he had lost control over the curriculum and lost the ability to recruit the kind of teachers he wanted. He left to become dean of the Florida State University law school in Tallahassee.

As if to signal that one period of transition was over, J. D. Williams had announced on January 19, 1967, that he was retiring at the end of the year. He would step down just two months after the fifth anniversary of Meredith's admission to the school. The Meredith affair would be an indelible mark on his career, but he could take credit for keeping the university open in its most troubled time. He had seen a great deal of "picking up and moving on"—the literal kind, when students and professors (some of the latter involuntarily) left, and the spiritual kind, as the university community, with admitted fits and starts, tried to leave the past behind.

It would be up to Williams's successor, Porter Fortune, a former dean at the University of Southern Mississippi and more recently executive secretary of the National Exchange Clubs, to steer the university into the next decade. Racial conflict would continue to be a constant on the campus, only now the growing number of black students would have the clout to help determine the resolution.

6

⊰⊱

An Awakening

Anxious to capitalize on election year interest in the fall of 1968, the Ole Miss Young Democrats invited Charles Evers, the civil rights activist and brother of Medgar, to speak to students a month before the vote. The invitation should not have surprised anyone. The Democrats were what passed for radicals at the school. They were the only integrated group on the campus. On top of that they were formally affiliated with the national party, which had just chosen the ebulliently liberal Hubert Humphrey as its presidential candidate and Maine senator Edmund Muskie as his running mate, politicians not in sync with most of Mississippi's white voters.

The founder of the Oxford chapter, Bob Boyd, was an iconoclastic young man from Greenville and perhaps the only white who could boast of being thrown out of a white-owned eatery in Oxford. He had had the temerity to take a black friend to one of the popular barbecue places, infuriating the owner, who chased Boyd out at knifepoint. "The law says I have to serve that nigger," he yelled. "But I don't have to serve you." Boyd could only chuckle at logic that, however twisted, at least showed some appreciation for recently enacted federal civil rights laws.

Boyd considered it his mission to raise the political consciousness of Ole Miss students he thought were too apathetic—most of them, in his view. One of his fellow Democrats, David Molpus, had often complained that their classmates were "not into rebelling against what their parents thought. And they knew what their parents thought." The *New York Times* went further, writing in one article that the "easy going, disengaged campus" was "little more than a party school attended by the empty-headed offspring of planters and bankers." The reporter expressed his surprise that students were not interested in the issues that had so engaged other campuses, notably the war in Vietnam, "free love and abortion." One undergraduate, only slightly sarcastically, told him that most students "wouldn't even know what those things meant."

Raising political issues on campus was a tall order for the Young Democrats, but by the fall of 1968 they had become a vibrant if small force at the university, a haven for politically moderate whites and the few politically active black students. It was like a second home to Molpus, a young white man who came from the small Delta town of Belzoni.

The admissions department that let Molpus in, and Tommy Turner, the board of trustees member from Belzoni who helped get him financial aid, could not have known how events in Molpus's early life shaped his thinking. If they had, they might have told him to go elsewhere. Turner would say as much in a bitter note after one fight over campus policy: "You should go to Berkeley, California, where all bearded idiots go."

Molpus had been deeply affected by what happened to his father, the Reverend Chester Molpus, for twenty-two years pastor of Belzoni's Baptist church. Like virtually all other whites, Reverend Molpus had never seriously questioned the racial order, but when his friend, the Reverend George Lee, Belzoni's leading black minister, was shot to death in 1955 for persisting in his voter registration efforts, Molpus knew something was wrong. He was hardly a firebrand, but over the next several years he began to speak out about prejudice and discrimination, sharpening his message as race became a major topic of debate. Church elders were unhappy; ultrasegregationists were angry. Hate calls to his home became more frequent. The minister learned not to turn on his car before checking the hood—a precaution to make sure no one had put a bomb in the engine.

There were also repercussions for David, whose friends let him know what they and their parents thought. "We've got nothing against you or your family," his friends insisted. "But we don't want to go to school with niggers. Got that straight?"

The race issue finally came to a head in the church when the deacons wanted to pass a resolution that barred blacks from worshipping there. Molpus found that unconscionable and told the congregation that a vote for the resolution was a vote for his resignation. The tally was not unanimous in favor, but it was overwhelming. Reverend Molpus and his wife were soon on their way out of Belzoni.

This was October 1964, and David was two months into his junior year in high school. He wanted to stay in Belzoni for the rest of the year and then join his family in Kentucky, where they had moved, for his senior year, but not one member of the church offered to take David in. Finally, the band director, a bachelor with some extra space in his house, let David stay with him until the school year was over.

On the day Reverend and Mrs. Molpus left, not a single person from the church had come to say good-bye. It hurt David as much as it did his parents.

By the time he finished his senior year at a Louisville, Kentucky, high school, Molpus was convinced he wanted to go to Ole Miss despite painful memories of the last days in Belzoni. His reason was rooted largely in the admiration he had for his father's courage and his affection for his home state. "I belong here," he told himself. He thought that by returning and going to Ole Miss, he could help create a new Mississippi. "Who is going to change Mississippi," he reasoned, "if Mississippians don't?" So it was no surprise that Molpus would be in the thick of conflict over race and politics almost as soon as he got to the campus. And it was also no surprise that there was a premium to be paid for speaking out, just as there had been in Belzoni.

Following in his older brother's footsteps, Molpus had joined Kappa Alpha, a fraternity that personified the Old South in its rituals and traditions. It was well known that one of the keys to a successful social life at Ole Miss was to be in a sorority or fraternity. They were at the center of most campus activities, and Molpus wanted to have as much fun as any other student. But he had not checked his budding political activism at the fraternity house door. Irritated by an article in the *Mississippian* criticizing Russell Barrett and law dean Morse, Molpus fired off a reply, asserting that the university was "fortunate" to have "such progressive and courageous men" who "will help bring Mississippi into the 20th Century." Why had Mississippi "turned its back on the United States of America and the federal government?" he asked. "Why must Ole Miss follow in the manner prescribed by Ross Barnett?"

The letter did not go over well at the Kappa Alpha house. The officers told Molpus he was bringing disrepute on the fraternity and had two choices: change or keep his mouth shut. Molpus chose to leave, and he put his energies into the Young Democrats. He knew before inviting Evers to speak in October 1968 that he would have to work within a speaker screening policy put in place by the board of trustees. The controversial policy was an outgrowth of the board's concern that outside speakers might come on campus and incite students to demonstrate. They had been angry about Aaron Henry's presentation at the law school the previous year and another at Mississippi State, and to keep tighter control over campus guests, they now required the names of any speaker to be given to each trustee before an invitation was even tendered. This amounted to giving members an individual veto.

Earlier in 1968 the board had gone even further with a regulation that barred outside organizations from holding any kind of political or sectarian meeting on the campuses of state-supported schools. It was driven by fears that the rising opposition to the Vietnam War would bring the same kind of violence and rebellion that had hit other campuses around the country, even though there was no sign of militant protest at Ole Miss.

As required under the speaker policy, Molpus and his program chairman, Danny Cupit, a law student who had been an active Young Democrat at Mississippi State, had submitted their request to have Evers speak a week before the proposed October address. Hearing nothing for a day or two, they assumed all was well and went ahead with their plans. When they tried to get confirmation two days before the event that everything was all right, they got only evasive responses. Finally, the day before the speech, Molpus and Cupit met with administration officials and were told that Evers would not be permitted to speak after all. The school had not had enough time to contact board members, they said, and to do so by telephone would be inappropriate—even though the board had handled other matters this way. On top of that, the administration said Evers could be barred because his address would be "political" in nature.

Molpus and Cupit immediately went to court, and the federal judge in Oxford ordered the university to let Evers speak. A marshal served the papers on Chancellor Fortune less than an hour before Evers was to begin.

The speech, a plea for allegiance to the national Democratic party, went off without a hitch. Afterward Fortune, who had been in office barely ten months, tried to minimize the conflict. He said his original denial was simply a matter of timing dictated by the constraints of board policy. If Evers were to be invited again with enough lead time, he said, "it will be my recommendation that Mr. Evers be allowed to appear."

That was Fortune's public statement. His chief enforcer, George Street, took a much harder line. Though his title was director of development, Street was much more than the chief fund raiser for Ole Miss. He had been part of the university administration since the late forties, starting right after he finished law school. He knew so much about the school's operations that regardless of his title, he played a major role in carrying out his superiors' policy, often having a hand in setting it. On the speaker issue—and he considered himself "the official determiner of who was eligible and who was not"—he believed the university could block whomever it wanted to. In his mind, freedom of speech meant the ability to say something, not the right to say it in a particular forum to a specific audience. These outside speakers "could speak in downtown Oxford," Street insisted. "We didn't have to honor them with the university setting."

The periodic fights over outside speakers served to keep a current of agitation running through the campus. Molpus knew the majority of white students wanted no part of the provocative activities sponsored by the Young Democrats, but he took satisfaction in knowing that his group was at least making them wrestle with issues beyond after-class parties and weekend entertainment.

Watching from the sidelines, the black students were realizing they needed to be better organized if they were going to improve their lives at Ole Miss. They numbered about one hundred now and were clearly a highly motivated group of individuals. None of them had taken lightly the decision to come to Ole Miss; many were the first in their families to attend college at all, and there was particular pride in taking on the flagship of the state higher education system. It was true that the admission door was now open to them, but it was not yet clear just how far, and even less clear what awaited on the other side. While Stokely Carmichael, the volatile black activist, would drop in on the state and incite the crowd to action with his calls for black power, these young Mississippians were hoping to derive their power from an education and the contacts they could make at the jewel of Mississippi's university system. They wanted to fit in—easier said than done on a campus that was still an enclave of white privilege.

The reaction on campus to the assassination of Martin Luther King, Jr., helped highlight the point when the university refused the black students' request to fly the American flag at half-mast. Eugene McLemore was nearing the end of his first year in law school when King was murdered. As soon as the news made its way through the campus, McLemore and a handful of other black students went to the *Mississippian* office to make sure their views were known. McLemore spoke first: "If Dr. King's tactics will not work, we must find new methods with which to express ourselves in order to gain our equality. Now is the time for all blacks to assess their situation." McLemore didn't mean it as a threat but as a statement of fact.

Taking a lead was nothing new for the twenty-six-year-old. He had grown up in Walls, Mississippi, a town so small it had no traffic light. He and his older brother, Leslie, were the first blacks from Walls to go to college and to graduate. Eugene had attended Mississippi Valley State, where he was president of the student body, and then decided to pursue a graduate degree in political science at Atlanta University.

Part way through his course work, McLemore decided to go to law school and settled on Ole Miss. It was a decision that came from the heart rather than the mind, for there were other schools that would have been more hospitable to a young black man, but McLemore had a deep sense of home, and Mississippi was home. He wanted to come back.

John Donald, who had also gone to the *Mississippian* that night to talk about King, had more direct ties to the school. He had already done his undergraduate work there, and as the younger brother of Cleveland, the third black to enter the school, he could claim the beginnings of a family tradition. He was even more pointed in his comments than McLemore. "We live in a hypocritical society," he asserted. "Blacks are dying in Vietnam for the dream of American freedom when it actually doesn't exist at all. . . . The system is against the Negro," he went on. "We have been oppressed in every possible way, and now it is time for us to do something about it."

Aware of the rioting and protests going on in other cities and the tensions right there on campus, Chancellor Fortune decided to close the university a few days early for the traditional spring break. Although the administration was worried about counterreaction from white ultraconservatives who might accuse the university of "worshipping" King, Street had reasoned that it would be easier to deflect this kind of protest than a demonstration on campus by angry blacks. When classes started up again later in April, Fortune laid down the law before an assembly of students: The administration would not tolerate any disruptions, and any student intending to foment disturbances "does not belong on this campus." The chancellor did not name any names, but the message was clear: Protest for whatever reason would not be tolerated.

The black students let the moment pass without more than their statements and private memorials, but it highlighted their sense of separateness from most of the whites on campus.

In the meantime, the "Several Black Students," as they called themselves, sent Chancellor Fortune a memo titled, "Bigotry, Bias and Racial Prejudice." The opening paragraph was blunt, charging that at the university "there prevails an atmosphere of bigotry, bias, and prejudice because the faculty, staff, administration, diverse officers, officials, teachers and workers facilitate and substantiate said atmosphere." The memo spelled out the students' self-styled demands in detail. One asked that the black students be granted a charter to form themselves into a Black Student Union that would be treated like other organizations on the campus. Another asked that Negro History Week be recognized at Ole Miss, as it had been at so many other institutions since 1926.

In February 1969 the university did meet the second request, instituting the first Negro history celebration, which featured a display of black history in the library, a display of black art in the Fine Arts Center, and two addresses, "Black Identity" and "Development and Trends in Black Thought." The professors presenting these talks had been invited from other schools—evidence that there was no one on the Ole Miss faculty qualified to impart this information.

The Several Black Students considered the creation of Negro History Week to be a step in the right direction, but it was a small part of their concerns. The petition sent to Fortune nearly a year earlier had spoken of more concrete changes: more black students, the addition of black faculty and counselors, the recruitment of blacks for the athletic teams, and an improved atmosphere on the campus. It was irritating to keep hearing epithets as they walked through the campus and hardly pleasant to feel the hostility when they went to eat at the student cafeteria. They were tired of the condescension from some of their professors and outright rudeness from others. They developed their own group warning system, passing along tips to one another about which teachers to avoid.

On March 7, 1969, black student leaders again presented their concerns and grievances to Fortune. A week later a group of thirty marched peacefully to his house and sat on the front steps for a half-hour until he came out to talk to them. It was not an action they took lightly. They knew that the future of an aggressive, activist black in Mississippi could be uncertain. Reverend Lee in Belzoni, Medgar Evers, and James Chaney already had paid the ultimate price. James Meredith had survived with the ubiquitous presence of the federal government. These young men and women waiting patiently at Fortune's door believed things had changed enough so that they could step forward without fear of harm. Besides, there was some safety in numbers.

When Fortune finally appeared, the students wanted to know if he could do anything to meet their concerns—or, they inquired, should they go directly to the board of trustees? Fortune said he could handle some of the items they had mentioned and promised to set up a formal meeting with them later. The evening ended peacefully.

From the students' perspective, it was a modest but important first step. To George Street it was a warning that things could get out of control, and he was determined not to let that happen. He had a direct line to the governor's office that allowed him to get the highway patrol to

Oxford whenever he deemed it necessary. Before the demonstration at Fortune's house had ended, fifteen cars of patrolmen had come on campus, parked on a nearby street waiting to be summoned. It was part of Street's strategy to keep order by having force at the ready, but on this night none was necessary.

Street's military service in the mid-forties had been good training in such preparedness, but his childhood and adolescence as a white in rural Mississippi had not prepared him as well to understand the evolving racial dynamics at Ole Miss. Street had been dumbfounded when he heard that Meredith had applied to the university. He had seen how the ugly opposition to Autherine Lucy had thwarted her attempt to integrate the University of Alabama in 1956, and he never imagined anyone would try the same thing in Mississippi, let alone the university of all places. Yet during the Meredith imbroglio, Street was at the center of the action, escorting Lieutenant Governor Paul Johnson around when he came to block one of Meredith's attempted registrations and then helping Meredith get through the process when he was finally allowed in.

Street had never thought there was anything wrong with Mississippi's racial order, and six years after Meredith he was still perplexed when he had to confront black students who were aggressive, even "militant" in his view. He couldn't fathom what fueled the anger, and years later he would admit, "I didn't see it coming."

By the end of March, Street was involved in more amicable discussions with black leaders about getting their informal organization of black students officially chartered. When that was finally accomplished, Chancellor Fortune spoke to the group. He acknowledged their concern for a greater black presence on campus—students, athletes, teachers, counselors, security officers—but he was candid in his assessment of the future. "I cannot in all honesty promise immediate effective implementation of programs in these areas," conceding in so many words that it was often difficult to sell blacks on Ole Miss. "We have no procedure by which we can insist that any individual cast his lot with us," he told them. But he promised to keep "the lines of communication open."

A spokesman for the black students pronounced the group satisfied with Fortune's presentation but cautioned that they would be watching to see "if the chancellor means what he says." Their disappointment with him would be manifestly apparent in less than a year.

Although the formation of the Black Student Union (BSU) was an important step for the black students, there was a downside for left-leaning whites: They had hoped to maintain a strong coalition with their black classmates given their agreement on a number of political issues, but the BSU wanted to go forward on its own. Molpus could understand this wish for independence, but he was hurt by the exclusion. The hurt turned to irritation when the BSU flexed its muscle against its supposed allies in the Young Democrats. The group had invited Julian Bond, the controversial black Georgia legislator, to speak on the campus and had sold a number of tickets for the event, but they had not consulted black student leaders, who were miffed about the oversight. They told Bond not to come. He honored their wishes, leaving Molpus and his group in the lurch and nearly broke.

Bond had chosen not to speak on campus, but in the meantime there were more problems over the outside speaker issue. One set of board regulations had been thrown out by a federal court as "unconstitutionally vague," so in early 1969 the trustees were drafting new ones. In this period of review, however, university officials had been given authority to seek a federal court order to block any speaker they deemed inappropriate. And that is exactly what they did in the case of Dr. Earle Reynolds, a Quaker antiwar activist who had been invited to address a political science class and a law class.

Reynolds already had a profile that caused concern to Fortune and Street: delivering medical supplies to civilians in Hanoi and Saigon and interfering with military weapons testing by sailing his yacht into the test grounds. He had been convicted of crimes in both instances, though the convictions were overturned.

The administration was already on edge over protests about the war and the presence of the Reserve Officers Training Corps on campus—Street had forced three student war protesters to leave school—and no one wanted to take a chance on a speaker like Reynolds. Street considered him the kind of individual who gave men like him heart attacks: "They were against the system, and I was the system, not the system for evil purposes but to keep the ship running."

When Street told Fortune of the plans to have Reynolds speak, the chancellor immediately decided that M. M. Roberts, the president of the board, needed to be informed, setting in motion a fast-paced day of travel around the state that left no doubt how seriously the administration feared any breach of the peace. Roberts wanted to see Street in person, so Street raced out to the Oxford airport and took the university's plane down to Hattiesburg, where Roberts had an office. After brief discussion, Roberts drew up the necessary legal papers to stop the speech, and Street flew back to Oxford. There he took another plane over to Ackerman, the home of federal judge J. P. Coleman, the former governor who had kept Clennon King from being the first black at Ole Miss, to ask Coleman to sign an injunction barring the speech. The highway patrol had been alerted that Street was coming, and as soon as the plane landed, officers provided an escort straight to the judge's office.

In a hasty proceeding, Coleman took testimony from Street about the possible dangers of a speech by Reynolds and then signed the papers. The patrol escorted Street back to the airport, and by the time he landed in Oxford a federal marshal was waiting for him at the Lyceum to get the order and serve it on Reynolds.

Although the officials had hurried through the proceedings as fast they could, they were not fast enough to get everything accomplished before Reynolds arrived on campus. He had already started his lecture by the time the marshal was on his way, but this did not deter the officer. He marched into the classroom and stopped Reynolds in midsentence. Students and teachers alike were flabbergasted, but no one interfered. Reynolds left quietly. He finished his lecture later that day at the Earth, a counterculture gathering place run by the Wesley Foundation and frequented by Young Democrats like Molpus and Danny Cupit and some of the black students.

Faculty members were outraged. Several of them complained publicly about the effort to stifle political speech, and the local chapter of the Association of American University Professors, which had spoken out so strongly during the Meredith imbroglio, did so again, accusing the university of a "flagrant violation" of its own stated principles about academic freedom. The injunction was "an unjustifiable invasion of the classroom teacher," and far from damaging, Reynolds's speech would have given students a chance to hear his views and promote robust discussion. What's more, the professors said, the administration's actions were counterproductive, prompting the dissent they seemed so interested in curbing.

Street blew off the statement as so much hot air; he was used to such protestations. Board chairman Roberts was equally unmoved, convinced he was doing the right thing to keep control of the campuses under his jurisdiction. By this time, Roberts, now seventy-four, was a fixture in Mississippi. He was one of the better-known lawyers in the state and had received numerous honors in his forty-three years of practice. He was a product of the Ole Miss law school, class of 1926, and years later, when he was sixty-eight, he had earned a doctorate in educational administration from the University of Southern Mississippi. He had virtually hand-picked Fortune, who had been a dean at Southern, to run Ole Miss.

Appointed by Barnett, Roberts was among the most conservative board members. He opposed Meredith's admission—"over my dead body," he had said. Later he had helped force the departure from the law school of professors he thought were too liberal.

He was unapologetic for his views and where they came from. "As I've gone along through the years and looked back I've said to myself really that I am a racist. Every time I read a definition I say, 'Well that's me.' I have no apologies for it, though," he said in one of his more notorious speeches. "It's me. And maybe that's the reason why we have some of the problems we have—because of how I feel about certain things that have come out of my childhood long ago, but it's my philosophy. Many of you don't share that philosophy, and that doesn't bother me," he added, "and I hope it doesn't bother you that I don't share yours."

But differing philosophies did bother Roberts. He was, after all, the architect of a policy that would keep speakers who did not share his views off state campuses. And he was not at all happy about an integrated student body, let alone an integrated faculty. "That's a thing that's destructive," he argued, and anyone who advocated "full-time Negro faculty" is "a stupid idiot."

Roberts didn't mince words. During a fight to block Charles Evers from speaking at Mississippi State, he fired off an angry letter to fellow board members after one court proceeding. Noting that the Young Democrats, who had invited Evers, were going to hold a luncheon for him before he spoke, Roberts wrote, "I know they enjoyed it. I hope he smelled like Negroes usually do." The gasp in Mississippi political circles, where at least the racial rhetoric had tempered, was nearly audible.

Roberts's comments brought criticism from many student quarters. At one time or another, several groups, including the Young Democrats and the Ole Miss leadership fraternity, Omicron Delta Kappa, passed resolutions calling for his resignation. Molpus even had bumper stickers printed up that said in big red letters, "Roberts Must Go."

Roberts was running the board with tight control, leading a group of men who were, like most of Fortune's staff, uniquely ill equipped to guide Ole Miss through its continuing transition. All of them were white, all were in their sixties or seventies, and all had known only a certain way of life and particular roles for the men, the women, the whites, and the blacks in it. Their watchwords seemed to be "don't knuckle under," and "nip every protest in the bud," all in all a recipe for conflict.

The power and control of white men like Roberts reinforced the views of the Ole Miss black students that their efforts to push for change in Oxford were not going to be easy. By now they had a tremendous sense of solidarity. The plain fact of being black bound them together, overriding differences in background and interests. It was now the end of 1969, and the students' meeting with Fortune almost nine months earlier seemed like a distant memory. Not much had happened that they could see. The defiant words of Roberts notwithstanding, they were chafing for action as 1970 began, encouraged by the influx of new black students over the preceding two years that swelled their ranks to roughly two hundred.

These young Mississippians had come to Ole Miss with determination and dedication, like their white classmates wanting above all to secure a stable and productive future. They came as anything but dissidents. But their frustrations at trying to fit into this citadel of white supremacy was turning them into angry young men and women ready to fight battles they had never dreamed of as children. Their aspirations ran headlong into the university's century-old culture and traditions, and it was the latter that would eventually give way.

Sam Givhan had grown up east of Oxford in the little town of Pontotoc. He was twelve when Meredith had broken the color line at Ole Miss, and the event was fixed in his memory. Some of the federal troops had gone by his house on their way over to the university. And he recalled the mixed reaction to Meredith at his church: some congregants proud of his courage, others thinking it was a foolish risk that might backfire for all blacks in the state. The reaction in the white community was standard: nearly universal condemnation. Givhan had made up his own mind about Meredith: He was doing something that was right. Meredith's experience became more personal when Givhan decided to step out of the racial routine in Pontotoc and spend his senior year at the all-white high school. In theory families were given freedom of choice in selecting a school, but in reality it was little more than a legitimate way to maintain segregation. No black families had chosen to send their children to a white school, and no white families wanted to send their children to black schools.

One day during the summer before Givhan's senior year, after he had filled out the form to transfer to the white high school, the principal at his old school came to talk to him. He asked the young man to think carefully about changing schools, telling him that although he was a good student, he would likely be behind in all of his courses because the white children had had better preparation.

As a seventeen year old, it was confusing to have a man he had looked up to deliberately tell him to lower his goals. By the time he turned forty, he would consider what the man had said to be reprehensible. But young Givhan persevered, steeling himself against the hostile atmosphere he faced every day. Most of the school year he felt as though he was someone with a contagious disease; few of his white classmates had anything to do with him. But he felt he had stood up and done something important, and he had succeeded academically.

He was determined to go to college even though the family (he was the tenth of twelve children) had suffered a blow midway through his senior year when his mother died of cancer. Givhan knew he didn't want to be too far away from home, and Oxford was only thirty miles away. He was thinking about becoming a doctor, and Ole Miss had the only medical school in the state, so the university seemed like a good idea. His senior year in high school and the years of segregated living in Pontotoc before that made him feel prepared to live as an outsider at Ole Miss, but he underestimated how the university's unforgiving atmosphere could turn his ambition into anger.

Mary Thompson's decision to go to Ole Miss seemed a more natural one. She lived just outside Oxford, and her mother was on the university's housekeeping staff. Mary herself had worked in the cafeteria on the food line and had seen black students coming in and out to get their meals. Sometimes they would come over to the local black high school to visit with students, where they were always the center of attention. And there was a particular allure for the girls when the college men came by. So in Thompson's mind if there was a place for them at Ole Miss, there was one for her too.

Unlike Sam Givhan, Thompson had made a choice to stay in her all-black high school for her senior year. She and a large group of friends made the decision collectively so they could graduate as a class, even though under the law they could have integrated the white school. Her classes at the university would be her first with white students. She was determined to have a "positive experience," and told herself over and over, "I'm going to make it work." By her sophomore year, that would require a greater effort than she had ever imagined.

Donald Cole didn't so much come to Ole Miss as Ole Miss came to him. He had never imagined going to Oxford. The memories of 1962 were too vivid, especially the pictures of young white men with hateful looks on their faces as Meredith sought admission. But those had been the thoughts of a twelve year old. By the time he graduated from his all-black high school in Jackson, Cole had a more open mind, and one of his counselors, aware that the university was looking for black students, put together a trip to the campus for some of the seniors. It was quite a couple of days, from the four-hour taxi ride up to the campus to the presentations that were made by Ole Miss officials who were putting their best foot forward.

Cole was hooked before he was on his way home to Jackson, impressed by his cordial hosts and even more so by the beautiful buildings and well-stocked libraries and labs. There was nothing like that at any black school he had ever seen. When Cole told his parents he was going to Ole Miss, they were happy and proud that he was willing to take such a bold step. They also reminded him that his mission was to get an education, not to buck the system.

Cole was optimistic about going to class with whites for the first time and believed completely a saying he had heard about the university: "Ole Miss, where everybody speaks." So he arrived in Oxford in the fall of 1968 with a smile and the same positive outlook Mary Thompson had brought with her.

It was a chemistry class that first semester that made Cole realize he was different from most of his fellow students. He noticed that when he took a seat in the lecture hall, there was no one in his row and no one in front or in back of him, and in fact few whites had spoken to him when he nodded hello to them. It was a rude awakening, one that made him realize he had been naive. Over the next several months, fueled by late night talks with fellow black classmates, he became more militant, ready to take on the "system" if the "system" would not respond to him. "There were questions nobody seemed to be able to answer," he told friends, "and no one in the administration seemed even to have a desire to answer them."

Kenneth Mayfield came to Ole Miss from Okolona, a town about fifty miles southeast of Oxford. His father had died when he was young, and he felt he had grown up early, worrying about his five siblings and his mother. Just before his junior year in high school in the fall of 1966, Mayfield had the chance to go to Okalona's white high school and had filled out the forms to do so, as had his older brother. But his mother asked them not to. The Ku Klux Klan was still active in the area, spray-painting signs in the county to make sure residents knew they were still around. With no adult man in the house, Mrs. Mayfield was fearful.

The Mayfield brothers acceded to their mother's wishes and stayed at the all-black high school. When it came to college, however, Kenneth struck out more boldly. What interested him in Ole Miss was the fact that no other black from Okalona had gone there since the school accepted blacks. A few had gone to Mississippi State for graduate school, but he would be the first to go to Oxford. He was expecting to keep pretty much to himself and decided that as long as he was not physically attacked, he could deal with any harassment that came his way.

Mayfield resolved to study hard. He had been told over and over again while growing up that blacks were inferior to whites, and part of him secretly believed it. But another part of him was convinced that if he worked assiduously, he could make up any difference. Within a few weeks of classes Mayfield could see that he was as smart as or smarter than many of his white classmates, and by the end of his freshman year, after rap sessions with his black classmates, he was angry at what he considered Mississippi "brainwashing."

Givhan, Thompson, Cole, and Mayfield, like their fellow black classmates, had entered Ole Miss to learn, not to rebel. But eight years after Meredith, they were still pioneers, and they still had a heavy underbrush of racial animus to clear away before they felt comfortable at the university. So when two BSU members, Jesse Dent and Brian Nichols, gave a long interview to the *Mississippian* in February 1970 about the student group's aims, the harshness of their rhetoric was not surprising. "A bunch of small-minded individuals . . . a bunch of ignorant people" was what Nichols called the board of trustees, and Dent contended that to bring change, "any organizations, not just the Black Student Union, should keep the administration in a state of alarm at all times."

This warning shot did not escape Street's attention. He considered it his job to monitor everything any potential dissident might do, and the BSU certainly fit in that category. But neither he nor anyone else in the administration was prepared for the flare-up that occurred on February 24. They hadn't realized the depth of frustration among the students or their disbelief at Fortune's contention that "there is very little I can do."

If Ole Miss had its own traditions, the black students realized they had some of their own to draw on, going back to 1960 when college students in North Carolina staged the first sit-ins at lunch counters to break the race barrier. Black college students had been in the forefront of the Freedom Rides to integrate bus stations in southern states and had played important roles in later civil rights activities, particularly the 1964 Freedom Summer in Mississippi. More recently black students at both predominantly black colleges and largely white institutions were raising their voices, sometimes militantly, to demand changes that would make these campuses more responsive to their needs and concerns. Confrontations, some of them bloody, had broken out at schools around the country as administrators sought to meet dissent with a strong show of force.

Closest to home for the Ole Miss students, blacks at Mississippi Valley State had risen up to protest administration policies and to demand change. They had orchestrated a massive boycott of classes to make their point, and 889 students had been arrested, the largest mass arrest ever recorded at a college campus. When the *New York Times* sent a reporter to do a story about the school, he noted that Mississippi Valley was "embarrassingly short on students" because so many had been jailed and not allowed to return. Many of the black students in Oxford now wore pins saying, "Ole Miss blacks support MVSC students."

By this time Mayfield was no longer the bookish loner from Okalona. Nicknamed "Hawk," he was emerging as one of the leaders along with John Donald. He had adopted a look that seemed to match his more aggressive personality: a large beret (in the style of the Black Panthers) that drooped down to one shoulder, a long goatee, sunglasses worn day and night, dashiki, jeans, and combat boots. It was his way of sending a message that he was in rebellion, and he wanted that message to be clear every time he stepped out of his dorm room.

On the afternoon of February 24, Mayfield was among those who responded to Donald's call to meet in front of the cafeteria before it opened to protest one of the dignitary slights that was a continual thorn in the side of the black students: Few, if any, whites would eat with them in public, and those who did often were harassed by other white students. Donald wanted to make sure at least forty or so BSU members were on hand so that one person was at every table. As soon as the white students came in, they would have no choice, if they wanted to stay inside, but to sit with a black student.

They had missed one table though. And when a white student came in and sat at that one, one of the blacks went over to join him. "Don't you sit at this table," he hissed, loudly enough for the other blacks to hear, so a few of them took their chairs and surrounded him. Obviously flustered, the white student got up, put his plate of food on the conveyor belt to the kitchen, and left.

Mayfield chuckled in satisfaction. He and his friends had wanted to make a point and make somebody angry, and they had accomplished their mission.

Donald wanted to talk about strategy, and Mayfield decided it would be good to hear some political speeches and maybe a little music. He went back to his dorm to pick up his little stereo and came back with James Brown's "I'm Black and I'm Proud" and some Eldridge Cleaver speeches. The combination of Brown's infectious music and Cleaver's obscenity-laced calls to action was powerful, taking the group to a fever pitch. One of them went to the campus bookstore to buy a Confederate flag, and within minutes after he returned, it was on fire.

Someone in the group decided it would be appropriate to file formal charges against the university, so they all walked over to the campus security office to fill out individual complaints against the university, each writing "racism" on the line that asked what the nature of their grievance was.

From there the group walked to Chancellor Fortune's house, stood at his door, and shouted their complaints until he finally came out. He spoke to the group calmly but promised them nothing. Standing with his classmates at Fortune's door, Cole thought the chancellor spoke in too many platitudes and did not answer the students' questions. Mary Thompson didn't think they were being taken seriously.

The students finally dispersed when word came that fully armed highway patrolmen were watching everything from the third floor of a nearby classroom building. Street was taking no chances.

The next day, February 25, the black students met again to discuss their concerns and strategy. They realized that Up with People, an integrated musical group with a quasi-religious message, was scheduled to perform in Fulton Chapel. The news media were going to cover the concert, and the university had put out the welcome mat. BSU members thought they should present another dimension of life at Ole Miss, and doing so during the concert would be a good way to get their grievances heard.

Over in the Lyceum, Street was on high alert, and with good reason. He had plenty of other campuses to look at for examples of how unrest could escalate into violence: San Francisco State, Columbia University, the University of Wisconsin, and, closer to home, Duke University in North Carolina. The Mississippi highway patrol had been on the campus for more than a day, and before the concert began, patrolmen were nearby at the Alumni House waiting to be summoned.

Around 8 P.M., the black students, numbering nearly a hundred, started their march over to the concert, chanting, "What're you going to do? Do it to them?" Once inside they made their way up the aisles, and those in the front went on stage while Up with People was singing, ironically, "What Color Is God's Skin?"

Mayfield grabbed a microphone and shouted, "Well, he sure ain't white."

After some more shouting and jostling for mikes, which sound engineers tried to turn off, some of the students gave the black power salute: a raised fist in the air. One student read a list of demands from the BSU, and within minutes the group was on its way out the door.

Some in the audience thought the entire episode was part of the program; most sat in stunned silence. Watching it all was Patsy Brumfield, news editor of the *Mississippian* doubling as a photographer. She had been over at the paper's office trying to finish the next day's edition when the phone rang alerting the staff that blacks were marching on the chapel. She and a colleague got into a car and drove the few minutes over to the chapel just as the last of the black students was going in the door. She fell in line behind them and then made her way to the orchestra rail, snapping pictures the entire time.

Brumfield had never been so scared—not afraid that she would be harmed but afraid because she had never before seen anything so radical. She was too young to have been at Oxford in 1962 to witness a real riot, and although she had read about it and seen pictures, it was not the same as watching individuals rise up in unison and disturb the peace.

Coming from McComb, which had had its share of bombings and violence, Brumfield knew something about civil rights protests, but she had not really grasped the meaning of it all. Up to this moment she had thought of her world, including Ole Miss, as peopled by "good little southern children," white and black. She could hardly believe what she was seeing, but the adrenaline was flowing so fast that she didn't take time to stop and think. She just kept shooting pictures and trying to take in as much as she could.

Brumfield followed the black students out of Fulton Chapel and saw that there was only one way for them to go: straight into paddy wagons and police cars that would take them to jail. The lawmen had surrounded the chapel, their weapons pointed at the unarmed students as they filed out. Mary Thompson saw only that the guns were pointed at her. In her mind she had engaged in a peaceful protest. To come out and see highway patrolmen in full riot gear everywhere she looked was a complete shock. So were the details of being arrested, especially the fingerprinting and the mug shots.

Crammed in his cell with a dozen or so other young men, Givhan felt he was caught in some kind of psychic bind. If he stepped out of line from the administration's perspective, he would pay a severe penalty, yet if he did nothing, would things get any better? On top of that was an assault on dignity he had never before experienced. Givhan had grown up with some sense of personal privacy in his modest home. In jail there was none of that, not even a separate bathroom. He had never seen a piece of plumbing like the one in his cell: commode and water fountain attached as one piece.

By morning he realized that his biggest decision was whether to stay at Ole Miss or leave for friendlier surroundings. Mary Thompson reacted differently. While it was hard to go from a jail cell back to class, she was determined to do so. Otherwise it would have been "giving in," she told herself. "It would have been defeat."

All in all, sixty-one blacks had been arrested outside Fulton Chapel. Another eighteen were arrested for trespassing at a building near Fulton, and ten more were arrested at Fortune's house. Eugene McLemore was among them. He had not gone to Fulton Chapel but arrived there just as the first group was being taken to jail. He decided it was important to head over to the chancellor's residence to protest.

As he was being led to a police car, McLemore saw one of his fellow law students, Nausead Stewart, the first black whose grades entitled her to join the *Law Journal*. She had been studying in the library, unaware of the demonstration. But when she saw McLemore being led to a police car, she inquired what was going on. Told of what had happened, she handed her books to a passerby and told the nearest police officer to arrest her too. There was no doubt in her mind it was the right thing to do. She considered it an act of solidarity.

By this time the Lafayette County jail was full, and Street had to make a decision. He was not about to release those in custody, so he told the patrol to send them to Parchman Penitentiary, the state's maximum-security facility. It was a tactic that had been used a year earlier by administrators at Delta State College, who ordered fifty-two protesting blacks to the prison for disturbing the peace.

When word got out that some of the students were on their way to Parchman, a shot of alarm went through the campus. Faculty members complained of an overreaction; David Molpus immediately got on the phone trying to raise money to bail the students out.

By the next day, everyone had been released, and the students who had been sent to Parchman returned unharmed. But the administration's action had left no doubt how seriously officials would treat any obvious show of dissent.

Now that everyone was free on bail, the issue on campus was punishment. The main story in the February 26 *Mississippian* described the events of the previous evening under a five-column picture—Brumfield's work—of several black students on stage, right arms raised in fists. Also on the page was a short editorial critical of the BSU and revealing a gulf in perception of campus life between whites and blacks. "If students have some specific gripes, they should be taken to the student government or some authority, who can look into it; but causing disruption is no good," wrote editor George Fair in a piece headlined ". . . Finally Gone Too Far." "People have been bending over backward trying to give students a fair shake with their 'rights', but when these 'rights' start infringing upon others' 'rights', and causing disorder, it's time to call a halt."

Later in the day Molpus convened a gathering in the Grove to talk about what had happened. Nearly all of the students who showed up were white, many of them wanting to ask the few blacks in attendance what was really going on. Law professor John Robbin Bradley told the group that administration officials had been advised not to arrest the black students, but, he said, the police "were just looking for an opportunity to arrest them." Bradley added that the black students needed to know that "we want to see what can be done about their demands, some of which are quite reasonable."

In the meantime, Lieutenant Governor Charles Sullivan, already planning to run for governor the next year, announced from Jackson that every student found guilty of participating in the disturbance at Ole Miss should be expelled. There was no need to wait for any court adjudication of guilt or innocence, he said. The university should be free to enforce its own regulations against the students.

BSU president Donald issued an immediate retort, asserting that there had been no violence at Ole Miss and that the Fulton Chapel protest "has been simply an act to dramatize our demands." What's more, Sullivan's statement was nothing more than "a threat to harass black people to succumb to the racist practices of the administration. We feel that our needs are of such urgency that we cannot sit idly by and be apathetic and complacent any longer."

That evening Donald and McLemore were invited to address the faculty senate, which had called a special session to deal with the crisis. Their presentations at the long and contentious meeting gave professors first-hand evidence of the black students' frustrations. Two years earlier, Donald explained, black students had drawn up a list of requests for Chancellor Fortune seeking ways to improve their lives on campus. Although he accepted the list of proposals, Fortune promised nothing and in fact, Donald said, nothing happened. After several months, they gave the list of proposals to the chancellor again. To emphasize their seriousness, the students went peacefully to his house and waited to speak with him. He promised a meeting, which subsequently occurred. But once again nothing was done: no black studies course, no black full-time faculty, no black athletes, no minority counselors. A third time the proposals were sent to Fortune, and still there was nothing but rhetoric in return. The Fulton Chapel protest, Donald said, was an act of "desperation" to get the administration's attention.

McLemore interjected to express his distress at the law school's failure to hire a black teaching candidate whose law degree and doctorate from Harvard and memberships in two state bars were considered insufficient. "Maybe a little disturbance is needed around here to make people think," said McLemore.

Some of the professors in the room could only smile at McLemore's observation, for it reminded them of one of the founding fathers. Thomas Jefferson had once said, "A little rebellion now and then is a good thing."

McLemore also related one of his experiences as a black man at Ole Miss, using the resonant example of football. Every time he went to a game, McLemore told them, he had to contend with someone shouting, "What are you doing here today, nigger?" Had Givhan been invited to the meeting, he would have added one more thing about Ole Miss, blacks, and football. It had galled him from his first month in Oxford to listen to white students shout racial epithets and watch them litter the stands with their refreshments, knowing that by morning it was an all-black grounds crew that would have the place looking spic and span and ready for the next game. And he would have reminded them of the times he and his black dormmates were nearly scalded when one of the white boys deliberately flushed the toilet while they were showering—just one of the small harassments they endured on a regular basis. The administration did not seem to take these issues seriously, McLemore went on. He hoped the faculty would. "It's on your shoulders now," he told them. "Professors at the University of Mississippi have been quiet too long. Stand up."

McLemore's comments rang true to John Bradley, who had been upset about the arrests from the moment he heard about them. Bradley had been at the law school since 1966, intrigued by the chance to teach under Josh Morse. He liked what the dean had been trying to do with the curriculum and the faculty and considered Ole Miss on the cutting edge.

Although the handful of Yale-trained professors had gotten plenty of attention, most of the faculty was, like Bradley, from Mississippi. He was from the delta town of Inverness. He couldn't pinpoint the moment he started to question the segregation he had once taken for granted, but by the time he started to teach law, he had come to believe that part of the university's mission was to educate all people "and social change was necessary to educate all the people."

When McLemore told the professors they needed to "stand up," Bradley agreed. He thought it was time for the faculty senate to go on record with its views, so he proposed a motion recommending that the university use its influence to have criminal charges dropped against the black students who were arrested at Fulton Chapel and that no disciplinary action be taken by the university against these students.

The motion precipitated immediate opposition from other faculty members, who thought it was both hasty and unwise. They didn't know all the facts, they said, and one added that he was "appalled" that a law professor would suggest such action instead of letting a court of law determine the outcome. Most seemed to share that sentiment. Bradley's motion was eventually rejected by nearly a two-to-one margin. But the faculty senate did agree to a resolution stating that it recognized that black students "have urgent, legitimate grievances" and urged the university to "address itself to them immediately."

Fortune, however, was more concerned about disciplinary matters than responding to the demands the students had made. On March 2 he told a meeting of the entire faculty that he would "move vigorously against those whose actions would subvert the orderly process of the university and usurp the rights of others in the university community." He intended for those arrested to be brought before the student judicial council, and if that group found students guilty of violating campus regulations, Fortune would mete out the punishment.

In a slap at the faculty senate, the larger group of professors pointedly agreed to a resolution expressing "confidence and full support of the chancellor and our complete cooperation."

The faculty senate met again that night, and Bradley tried once more to pass his motion on the discipline issue. What the students had done in Fulton Chapel was less disruptive than many other actions by university students, he said. Furthermore, the students should not be penalized for expressing their views and making legitimate demands. Moreover, such an action by the administration could be a good-faith gesture toward the students that would help ease tensions.

Bradley prevailed this time, after his resolution was watered down to say that although the faculty did not condone all of the activities of the black students, it recommended that the university "give serious consideration to using its influence to have criminal charges dropped" against those arrested. With no hesitation the senate agreed to establish five com-

The University of Mississippi faculty circa 1872.

The monument to the Confederate War dead was erected in 1906 by a local chapter of the United Daughters of the Confederacy. It stands at one end of the Grove and faces the Lyceum.

Football at Ole Miss is a near-sacred activity. This is the first team, fielded in 1893, by Dr. A. L. Bondurant, back row, far left in the white uniform.

Old South pageantry has long been a part of university celebrations. For decades, one week a year was designated "Dixie Week" and in the fifties and early sixties featured such activities as slave auctions and a re-enactment of Confederate enlistment. In 1956 students dressed up in nineteenth-century garb to commemorate the past.

The Rebel flag was first introduced as a spirit symbol for the Ole Miss Rebels football team in 1948, coinciding with the "Dixiecrats" defection from the Democratic party that year over civil rights issues. A tradition was established of cheerleaders carrying the flag onto the field as the band played "Dixie" and then tossing bundles of small flags into the stands for Ole Miss fans.

A typical Saturday afternoon at the Ole Miss football stadium, circa 1965.

7

8

Along with waving the Confederate flag and singing "Dixie," the Ole Miss students created a mascot, Colonel Rebel, to help cheer on the athletic teams. Here is the colonel in 1962 caricature and dressed up for a 1982 football game.

On January 21, 1961, the day after John Kennedy was sworn in as president, James Meredith sent a letter to Ole Miss registrar Robert Ellis, seeking an application to the school. Twenty-one months later, after protracted litigation that went all the way to the Supreme Court, Meredith was finally admitted to the school on September 30, 1962. He is shown here October 1 registering for class as Ellis looks on.

Meredith's arrival on the campus precipitated a riot that left two dead and brought thousands of federal troops to the campus. Here an angry student shouts insults at U.S. marshals as state highway patrolmen look on.

Two U.S. marshals wearing gas masks and carrying tear-gas guns detain two rioting students. The marshal at right is carrying a folded Confederate flag taken from one of the students.

The morning of October 1 these three burned out cars make the Grove look more like a war zone than a college campus.

Three professors, by design partially hidden from the news photographer, join Meredith for coffee at the Ole Miss cafeteria. Already subject to harassment for befriending Meredith, they refused to give their names.

On August 18, 1963 a smiling Meredith accepts his degree in political science from Chancellor J. D. Williams.

Cleve McDowell was the second black student to enroll at Ole Miss, starting law school in the summer of 1963. He was expelled three-and-a-half months later for carrying a small gun, which he had obtained out of fear for his safety.

By 1970 there were approximately two-hundred black students on campus. By this time they had formed the Black Student Union to provide both a social network and a means of presenting their concerns to Chancellor Porter Fortune about campus life. In mid-February 1970 many of the students felt that their complaints had not been taken seriously by the administration, so they decided to interrupt a concert in Fulton Chapel to read their demands aloud. Eight of the students, some of them pictured here, were suspended from school as a result of the protest. But their demonstration prompted university officials to step up their efforts to integrate more facets of the campus.

16

17

Coolidge Ball, who joined the Ole Miss basketball team in 1970, became the first black athlete at the school. His senior year he was named captain of the team and had been selected to the all-conference team three years in a row.

18

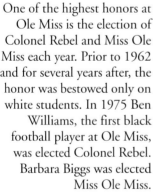

One of the highest honors at Ole Miss is the election of Colonel Rebel and Miss Ole Miss each year. Prior to 1962 and for several years after, the honor was bestowed only on white students. In 1975 Ben Williams, the first black football player at Ole Miss, was elected Colonel Rebel. Barbara Biggs was elected Miss Ole Miss.

In 1982 John Hawkins became the first black student elected to the cheerleading squad. He refused to wave the Rebel flag at football games, breaking with a long tradition.

Hawkins's decision prompted the Ku Klux Klan to demonstrate in support of the flag. Pictures of their protest were included in the 1983 yearbook, which was published in April. Angry black students threatened to burn their annuals prompting a large group of white students to demonstrate at the Lyceum on April 18.

On April 20 Chancellor Fortune announced that the Confederate flag would no longer be used as an unofficial symbol of the university. After the announcement, which was made to a group of news reporters, history professor David Sansing read the chancellor's statement to students.

Ole Miss students between classes in October 1996.

24

Homecoming 1996.

25

mittees to look into each of the black students' grievances, a move that eventually would bear fruit.

Russell Barrett, who had been so outspoken during the Meredith crisis, took the occasion to write Fortune a memo urging him to be lenient with the black protesters. Reminding Fortune of his own hostile treatment for befriending Meredith, he told him, "If you can find it in your heart to forget some profanity and personal indignity—I have taken many threats against my life and destruction of my property—you may find that a 'soft answer turneth away wrath.'"

The debate over discipline dominated the campus over the next few weeks, and the *Mississippian's* editorial pages were full of letters on the issue. When Fair had become editor, he wanted to make sure the paper represented a variety of views, so in the fall of 1969, he had instituted a sort of point-counterpoint, with one avowedly conservative writer sharing editorial space with the much more liberal Molpus and Danny Cupit.

On March 11, Molpus and Cupit weighed in with their opinion, reminding readers that in 1962, when Ole Miss students joined the destructive riot over Meredith, politicians, including Charles Sullivan, "had no words of condemnation" for their behavior. As for Porter Fortune, Molpus and Cupit said his pledge to deal harshly with the black students seemed to be "grossly inconsistent" when compared to the university's response to other disruptions. They pointed in particular to the one thousand students who had rioted on the campus and in downtown Oxford to protest a referendum on the sale of beer. "Property was destroyed, profane language was abundant, and disrespect for law enforcement officials was not rare." Most students escaped punishment. Those who did got little more than a slap on the wrist. The same went for students involved in panty raids, which disrupted traffic and generally brought havoc to the campus. Few students have ever been disciplined, they wrote, "and none of them have ever been hauled off to Parchman."

In short, they concluded, Ole Miss had a double standard in dealing with white and black students: tolerance for one, "complete intolerance" for the other.

Their column generated a number of critical letters. Typical was one that drew a strong distinction between a panty raid—"simply fun," said the writer—and the Fulton Chapel disruption, which the writer contended was the "intentional use of physical force as a means of influencing university policy."

The American Association of University Professors chapter also entered the debate, criticizing the black students for some of their behavior (in particular swearing at the chancellor) and condemning the university's decision to send some of the students to Parchman. More pointedly, the group condemned the "general indifference" by most whites to the "well being of the black student at this university." They were treated as "an unwelcome guest," and this view, the professors said, "pretends to deny the frustrations that led the black students to angry demonstrations." The professors recommended the dropping of criminal charges and leniency in disciplining the students. Like Molpus and Cupit, they said the punishment should reflect past punishment for white students, which did not include time at the Lafayette County jail and certainly not at Parchman.

As part of its effort to give the racial conflict an airing, the *Mississippian* devoted several pages of the March 6 issue to listing the BSU's twenty-seven demands along with a discussion of them with BSU leaders. The demands included the requests for a black studies program, black instructors throughout the curriculum, an end to discrimination in employing students at campus jobs, recruiting black athletes, more scholarship funds for black students, and the employment of a black barber in the campus barbershop.

The request for a black studies program had perplexed many of the white students, who could not understand why a separate program was needed. The BSU told *Mississippian* editors the following: "Blacks have been reading white history all along. We know your history, why can't you know ours?. . . When we begin to look at each other as Americans, then books will be able to tell the combined story."

While the debate over punishment was going on, the university disciplinary process was moving along. Those arrested had been brought before the student judicial council to hear the charges against them and make their own statements. Kenneth Mayfield figured he knew what the outcome would be before he said the first word. He felt as hostile toward the white students sitting in judgment as they seemed to feel toward him. He was determined to go through this process on his own terms—no sense of contrition, no giving in to outside pressure. So while it might have been politic to dress in a less provocative way, Mayfield would have none of it. The beret, the sunglasses, and the dashiki would stay. The standard dress for most young white men was khakis, button-down shirts, and loafers.

Mayfield had also composed a poem as part of his testimony, "To Be Born Black." "To be born black in Nat Turner's day was to be a nigger," it began, with an allusion to the leader of a slave rebellion. "It was to be looked at by the white man as a low animal and not a bit bigger." The final stanza declared that to be born black in Nat Turner's day "was to be refused an education, denied freedom of religion and staunchly hated."

Donald had told the faculty senate he was prepared to go to jail if necessary. Mayfield hadn't thought that far ahead, but he never believed that he would face serious punishment. He assumed that at some point in the process, probably in a courtroom, he would be exonerated. So when he received a letter March 16 on the first phase of punishment, he was not surprised. He was even proud. The student judicial council had recommended that he and seven others, including John Donald and Donald Cole, be suspended from Ole Miss immediately until January 1971. Another forty-five, including Givhan, should be put on probation. Although Thompson was among the first taken to jail, she escaped any sanction.

The eight given the harshest penalty had been chosen largely because they were the most easily identified from the pictures taken—Street called Patsy Brumfield "my star witness." Mayfield was not sure that was completely accurate. He felt that he and Donald in particular had been singled out because they were considered more militant than some of the others. On the other hand, one of the young women, Oxford native Linnie Liggins, had been an assistant to a professor and was known as quiet, even shy, and a serious student. Street had been there when she was taken to jail, completely unable to understand why she had deliberately put herself in jeopardy.

"You don't have to do this," said a family friend who had come to take her home.

"You're wrong," she replied. "I do have to do this."

Street stood in disbelief as he watched the police take her away.

Liggins maintained her resolve once she got to the jail. Her family was not surprised. When her grandmother came to the building, about a mile from the campus, she asked to talk to the young woman. The officer on duty said Liggins would have to be bailed out first.

"I don't want to bail her out yet," her grandmother said. "I want to talk to her to see what she wants me to do." Indeed, Liggins told her to wait. The incarcerated women had vowed to stay together until everyone could be freed. Street was convinced that the mass arrests had averted violence. Brumfield thought he was wrong in his assessment, arguing with him when he called her in to be interviewed about the event. He kept referring to "a riot," and she retorted, "No, Mr. Street. It wasn't a riot. It was a disturbance." Never for a minute, she explained, did she think anything violent was going to happen.

The day after the judicial council announced its punishment, John Brittain, Jr., a legal services lawyer representing the black students, said the eight facing immediate suspension would appeal their punishment to Chancellor Fortune. Apparently Brittain's willingness to represent the students was unpopular in some quarters. The lawyer, a black who was a member of the Connecticut bar and permitted to practice in several federal courts, was arrested that same day on the charge of practicing law without a license. He was released on $500 bond and speculated later that "someone is after me."

Within a few days Fortune had made his decision on the appeals: The disciplinary action would stand. "I find no basis to interfere in any way with the punishment recommended by the Judicial Council," he wrote to the eight in letters. They were to be considered suspended effective immediately until the next January.

Brittain quickly filed a lawsuit in federal court, and a hearing was held April 1 and 2 before Judge Orma T. Smith. Because she had taken pictures used to identify the students, Brumfield was called to testify and faced intense examination by Brittain.

Before this entire episode, Brumfield had considered herself a typical student, walking around in what she called "my sorority girl fog." When she had worked on a piece about the campus for *Life* magazine, the most significant thing to say about the women students was that most of them got up at 6:30 A.M. for an 8:00 A.M. class because "it was important to look good." If young women at other campuses were already burning bras and wearing tattered jeans, many at Ole Miss were still hoping to be named the next week's "campus cutie."

The Fulton Chapel affair was an awakening for Brumfield—never more so than when John Brittain cross-examined her in federal court. A white woman in Mississippi was not used to being confronted by a black man in a position of authority, and Brumfield was no exception. She was unnerved and intimidated. She also knew she had to answer his questions about the pictures she took and whom she saw, even though she was very uncomfortable about having to identify people who were her classmates, especially Linnie Liggins. (After these proceedings were over, Brumfield got a taste of the taunting so many black students had faced. She was walking to a class one day when a group of black students saw her across the street and yelled, "Go to hell, Patsy Brumfield, go to hell." She was afraid, but her mother had been concerned enough to call the campus security office and request that Brumfield be escorted home every evening after she finished work at the *Mississippian*.)

As soon as the hearing on April 2 was over, Judge Smith ordered the students reinstated temporarily while he considered the full merits of their lawsuit. Four days later he continued their reinstatement pending individual disciplinary hearings before the board of trustees.

Mayfield had few illusions about how he and the others would fare before M. M. Roberts and his colleagues, and although he was still in school, he found it hard to go to class. So did Sam Givhan, though he faced no threat of suspension, just probation. Both the young men were still grappling with the realization that the university that had let them in, even encouraged them to come, had now turned on them.

Givhan felt radicalized. In three semesters, he had never skipped a class, had never even been late, and was doing well in all of his courses. Now, he wondered, "Why bother?" and for several weeks, until he decided he would continue his studies, he was just going through the motions of being a student.

Mayfield, too, was ready to call it quits, wondering why he should keep studying if the university was going to punish him and take away his credits for the semester. Wayne Johnson, a black minister who had been counseling students over the last several months, told him that was the wrong attitude. He all but ordered Mayfield back to the library. "Hawk," he told him, "no way this judge is going to take away this semester. You finish it."

Mayfield turned out to be right in his assessment of the board of trustees. After two days of hearings to accommodate each of the eight individuals, the trustees unanimously decided after the last hearing on April 24 that the students would be suspended until January 1971. They also urged the state of Mississippi to consider criminal prosecution. The eight students were notified of the board's action in writing, and the trustees made their decision public about a week later.

The students were still counting on Judge Smith to throw out their punishment. But early in the summer, Smith dashed those hopes when he upheld the suspensions. Reverend Johnson, though, had been right about one thing: The students had gotten credit for the spring semester.

Mayfield and Cole had just been named the top officers in the BSU, and both of them were angry at what had happened. Cole, no longer a timid freshman, told the *Mississippian* that Smith's decision showed "no deep thought or consideration" and that "all basic law principles were shattered." Mayfield said Smith "acted like a pig and offered injustice."

Cole, Mayfield, and the other six students knew they had no immediate future at Ole Miss. Seven of them headed to other schools—three, including Mayfield and Cole, to Tougaloo in Jackson, and Donald to Howard Law School in Washington, D.C. Liggins, a senior, was allowed to finish her course work and participate in an honors convocation, where she received an award as an outstanding French student, but she was not permitted to attend her graduation. She had been the first in her family to get a college degree, and family members from out of state had made plans to attend the ceremony and see this milestone for themselves. But the university, having singled her out with the other seven for particular punishment, refused to relent.

While all of this was going on, faculty senate members were working on their response to the black students' demands. English professor John Crews, who had supported Bradley's call for lenient treatment for the protesters, was deeply involved. Linnie Liggins had done a work-study project with him, and he found her to be both bright and mild mannered, as far from militant as one could imagine. He considered her the "kind of person we need in society," not one to be tossed out of school. His distress at the administration's harsh attitude toward the demonstrators reflected his continuing reassessment of a racial order he had accepted without question growing up in Vicksburg. He remembered the times some of the whites would deliberately push the black kids off the sidewalk when their paths crossed on the way to school. He knew inside that was wrong, yet he was not quite bold enough to step forward and say, "You can't do that." Now as a professor at a university struggling to move beyond prejudice, he had a chance to step up, and he intended to take it.

Among the things Crews was looking into was the possibility of better jobs for the black students. A number of them worked in the cafeteria but mostly doing menial tasks, like cleaning up. None was allowed to be a cashier. Crews realized what he was up against when he went to interview the cafeteria supervisor. When he talked about the possibility of blacks' getting better jobs, the supervisor told him they did not really want to work and just wanted "to sit on their butts." After the meeting, Crews wrote himself a note about the supervisor: "hostile as hell . . . I am not convinced he would readily hire Negroes as cashiers or other front-line positions."

Crews found the same kind of attitude when he talked to one of the leading businessmen in Oxford about the possibility of at least one black teller in a downtown bank. Can't be done, he was told. "The people won't tolerate it." By early summer, though, it appeared that at least in some areas, the black students' concerns were being heard. The university announced June 25 that Jeanette Jennings, a graduate of Jackson State with a master's degree from Tulane, would become the first full-time black faculty member, appointed an assistant professor of sociology. Robert Walker had actually been the first black to teach a class. In 1968 he was an instructor in the history department while working to finish his graduate degree at the school. His affiliation with Ole Miss ended when he moved away from Oxford.

Plans were also in place for a black studies program to begin in the fall, and three black students were in line to be managers of their dormitories.

Even more important was the athletic department's new interest in a talented young black basketball player from Indianola.

If Coolidge Ball would suit up for the Ole Miss Rebels in the fall, it would mean that one of the most visible barriers was crumbling, even if Donald Cole, John Donald, and Kenneth Mayfield would not be there to cheer him on.

7

>⊱⊰<

Ole Times There Not Yet Forgotten

When it came to sports, Ole Miss was no different from most other universities. They were a vital part of campus life, a focal point of social activity and a vehicle for fund raising from alumni happy about their teams' successes. At Ole Miss, sports were also cultural, one way white southerners could assert their heritage. The team nickname, Rebels, had been chosen in 1936 in a contest sponsored by the *Mississippian.* The previous nickname, Red and Blue, was deemed inadequate, and the one before it, The Flood, had been dumped for lacking that certain something. But Rebels, the paper said with some understatement, was "suggestive of a spirit native to the old south and particularly to Mississippi." Fittingly, perhaps, Ole Miss played its first football game as the Rebels against Union University of Jackson, Tennessee, and trounced them 45–0.

Along with the new name came a new mascot, Colonel Rebel, a southern gentleman in the image of a plantation master: flowing white hair, bushy mustache, wearing a long coat nipped at the waist, light pants, dark shoes, and a big broad-brimmed hat. In a few years, two other southern symbols would be added to the campus pageantry, the Confederate flag and "Dixie." Both first appeared in the fall of 1948, the year of the university's one hundredth birthday and just as southern Democrats—the

Dixiecrats—bolted the party over civil rights. It was a happy marriage of politics and school spirit, a way to celebrate white southern pride in the safe confines of a stadium.

"More and more it looks like the confederates will rise again as Rebel boosters don their blacks hats, wave the southern flag and whistle 'Dixie,'" a commentator noted in the midst of one football season, his remarks hinting at the kind of neonationalism found in the previous century's religion of the Lost Cause. The uniforms of the Ole Miss marching band were also a throwback to an earlier era: gray outfits and small-brimmed hats that evoked the dress of Confederate soldiers.

Every now and then the stadium celebrations could be dangerous. Cheerleaders had developed a pregame tradition of throwing bundles of flags up into the stands to be distributed. Each of the bundles had about fifty flags, and when the men on the squad got off a good throw, the flags arrived with considerable force. An unsuspecting person who didn't happen to be looking the right way could get smacked in the head. Band members were particularly vulnerable because they were sitting down close to the field. During one game, a trumpeter caught the flag bundle squarely in the forehead, knocking his glasses off and leaving a bloody gash. To his surprise, nobody noticed his distress. His fellow revelers were all going for the flags.

Regardless of who had composed "Dixie" (the speculation was a black man in Ohio had actually written it) or its first use (for a minstrel troupe), by the mid-twentieth century it was the anthem of the white South. The Dixiecrats had made that clear when they adopted the song for their cause, singing chorus after chorus as they marched around meeting halls carrying Confederate flags.

Ole Miss students may not have been thinking about politics when they waved their flags in the football stadium or rose in unison to wish "I was in the land of cotton," but the song and the flag by now were inextricably linked to segregation and white supremacy, not just school spirit. The angry southerners who waved their flags at James Meredith had provided one more piece of evidence.

Any black coming to the university, particularly anyone thinking about playing sports, had to realize he would be confronted with these symbols day in and day out, and not solely in the athletic domain. When Al Hirt, the great New Orleans trumpeter, came to the campus, for example, the climax of the program was his impromptu version of "Dixie,"made all the more rousing by the fact that the three-hundred-pound musician was wearing a Confederate flag vest given to him by student leaders.

Coolidge Ball knew all of this and had resolved not to let it bother him as he considered his options during his senior year in high school. He knew that he was the best basketball player on his team in Indianola, and he knew that basketball was the road out of the despairing poverty of the delta. He felt lucky that his most important decision after graduation was which college to attend. Scouts had been coming to see him play for more than a year, some thirty in all, each hoping to snag him. Among the most ardent pursuers in the winter of 1970 were the University of Kentucky, New Mexico State, and Ole Miss.

Ball was ten years old when Meredith integrated the university. He remembered the event but had put it away in his mind as history. It didn't even register when he went to Oxford to look at the school. What was uppermost in Ball's mind was the atmosphere around the sports program. He wanted to know if he would be accepted as part of a team he thought needed help. He knew he could provide it.

During the campus visit, Ball attended one of the games and was introduced at halftime, along with another potential recruit. The applause he received was warm and sustained. He was delighted when coaches and players later told him they knew about his storied high school career, appreciative when they said they hoped he would be a Rebel.

When Ball returned home and thought over his options, that warm welcome in the coliseum stuck in his mind. He was leaning toward New Mexico and had even taken preliminary steps to enroll there, but he decided Ole Miss wanted him more, and like so many other Mississippians, white and black, a sense of home was important. He didn't want to be so far away. He changed his mind, called the coaches in Oxford, and told them he was coming.

Ball certainly appreciated the cultural freight of the flag and Dixie, but he reminded himself when he got to school that "*I* didn't play Dixie. *I* didn't raise the flag." If white students wanted to do it, well, that was their business. He just wanted to get along with his teammates and his coaches and let his performance on the court speak for itself. His biggest concern was to be treated "like a human being, like any other eighteen-year-old freshman."

But Ball was different. He was instantly visible and couldn't stay in the shadows even if he wanted to. He tried to ignore the fact that he was breaking a barrier on campus, and the university treated his arrival quietly. The announcement in the *Mississippian,* though, betrayed some old habits. His parents were mentioned but not given courtesy titles. Nor was Ball mentioned in a later article about the 1970–1971 roster, even though his high school career had been more illustrious than that of the other freshmen.

Such perceived slights might not have bothered Ball, and he may have been able to shut out the distractions of "Dixie" and the flag, but they nonetheless had been factors, albeit indirect, in the timing of his arrival at Ole Miss. After all, it was 1970—sixteen years after the *Brown* decision ordering desegregation of public education, six years after the federal civil rights law that opened up public accommodations to blacks, a year or two after several other southern schools had integrated their sports teams— and there were still no black athletes at the university and barely two hundred black students.

If Ball was ready for Ole Miss, Ole Miss had to be ready to accept Ball. Eighteen months earlier, the coaching staff had not been so welcoming to Donald Cole. He was a gifted athlete, and although he had not played basketball regularly in high school in Jackson, he wanted to try out for the Ole Miss freshman team. He went to the gym at the start of the season to participate in the tryout, and he thought things were going pretty well the first few days. As he assessed the white players around him, he knew he was better than most others though perhaps not the best on the floor, so it was a surprise one day when he came for practice to see that no gear had been put out for him as was customary. Instead there was a message that the coach wanted to talk to him. He was told that he could not play anymore because he wasn't going to make the team. The reason? Only players on scholarship could do so, and there was no more scholarship money. Still in what he called his "naive" period, Cole was too surprised to argue. He figured the coach was telling the truth and didn't stop to think that the money issue was a convenient cover for keeping the Ole Miss team all white.

By the time Ball was ready to play at Ole Miss, the racial dynamics had changed not only in the political arena but in the athletic one. Faced with integrated teams all around them and under constant pressure to win, the coaches and the Fortune administration realized that Ole Miss was not going to be competitive unless it tried to get the best players around, whatever their skin color. To make things a little easier, Southern Mississippi, located in the Hattiesburg home of trustee chairman M. M. Roberts, had recruited its first black basketball player two years earlier, and there had been no hell to pay from the board or Southern's alumni. On top of that, Ball wasn't just any black player. He was among the best in the state. To come to Ole Miss he couldn't be ordinary. Just like Meredith eight years earlier, he had to be special.

Added to the pressures of breaking a racial barrier was the issue of Ball's place in the black student community. Although his classmates were glad to cheer for him in the coliseum, more than one expected that he would automatically be one of their leaders. Some were disappointed that his focus was basketball, not realizing that Ball's first family on campus was his team and not appreciating that the brotherhood of athletics was stronger than the brotherhood of skin color.

In his four years at the university, Ball would prove to be a good entrée for future black players and a high-yield investment for the Rebels. He would average twenty-two points a game and rebounds in double digits. He was selected as an All Conference player his sophomore, junior, and senior years and was honored by his teammates three times as the most valuable player. His last year he was named captain of the squad.

Basketball was important, but it could not compare to football. By the time Meredith sought to break the color line at the university, the program was one of the more reknowned in the country thanks to its highly successful coach, Johnny Vaught. He had compiled such an enviable record that his 1959 team was later declared the South Eastern Conference Team of the Decade. In twenty-three years at the helm (1947–1970) he compiled an extraordinary 185-58-12 record and fourteen consecutive postseason bowl appearances.

Vaught thought he had retired from coaching in 1970 after suffering a heart attack, but he was called back into service in 1973, when his successor was unceremoniously dumped in midseason for his poor record—poor by Mississippi standards, that is (16-9 over two and a half years).

One of Vaught's most famous players was Archie Manning, a red-haired, freckle-faced boy from the Delta who set quarterbacking records and, perhaps most important, beat arch-rival Alabama in 1970 after dropping the previous year's matchup by one point. He typified for many all that was good about Ole Miss and its football. He was not only superstar but folk hero. To help readers understand the hold of football in the state, and in that moment the importance of Manning, *Sports Illustrated* began one story, evocatively titled "Archie and the War Between the States," with this vignette: "Mississippi is the place where a doctor hangs up a picture of Archie Manning and then wonders: 'Is it wrong for a 40-year-old man to be in love with a 21-year-old boy?'" Vaught's football program was a white man's haven, a place for the young, the strong, the committed—boys like Archie—where a victory on the football field in front of thousands of adoring fans could stand for more than just a notch in the win column. It was another reassertion of southern pride and a victory on the cultural battlefield. For four months every year, football was the university's secular religion, and as one astute observer put it, "If you were not waving the Rebel flag, then you were not part of the congregation."

The stellar years of the Vaught era had offered a certain stability that was a welcome antidote every fall weekend to the pressures and cross-currents of change that were buffeting the university. If other schools, like Southern Mississippi, Mississippi State, and even the University of Alabama, wanted to integrate, that was up to them. Vaught was convinced he could keep winning with the sturdy white boys who came to Oxford to play for him, and the fall of 1962 had only deepened that conviction.

Meredith's lawsuit to get into Ole Miss was nearing the end, and sooner or later he was going to be on campus. Vaught worried that the "terrible thunderhead" building up in the state could swallow up his football team if he were not disciplined and focused. His goal was "to keep business as usual." The week before Meredith's fateful entrance, the team played an away game at Memphis and won handily. It won again in Jackson two days before Meredith actually enrolled. Vaught could feel the emotions swirling through the stadium, especially when Governor Barnett arrived to a tumultuous reception that grew in intensity when he went to a midfield microphone to reiterate his loyalty to Mississippi's heritage and traditions.

Vaught was in his office on campus when the riot broke out, and his first thought was to get to his players. He went to their dorm—like many other schools with major sports programs, the athletes were housed separately—and ordered them to stay inside. He also directed that the doors be locked so no one could get inside.

As Vaught walked through the campus the next day, he was aghast at what he saw. The beautiful Grove looked more like a trash dump. How, he wondered, could he and the team keep their minds on football? But that was his job, and he made sure his team followed suit. What made things difficult, though, was the presence of the federal troops. Four days after the riot, helicopters were landing on his practice field, and army tents had gone up at second base on the baseball diamond. The team had to move to the stadium to practice. Famous for secret sessions, Vaught now was preparing for the next week's game, which was the all-important homecoming, under the eyes of some two thousand soldiers.

To make matters worse, the team was in limbo all through the week about where the game would be played. University officials wanted to keep it in Oxford to demonstrate that everything was under control. The federal government, which had threatened to cancel the whole thing, finally said no, and the game was moved to Jackson.

Vaught never considered himself in the Knute Rockne mold of delivering motivational speeches. He relied more on planning, training, and execution instead. In the dressing room before the game, his comments were direct and brief: "It is very important that we play this game, boys, and we have to win it." The team obliged, easily beating Houston 40–7. Every touchdown was lustily cheered, and an equally loud roar went up when the score of another game was announced. The University of Michigan had defeated Army 17–0. Ole Miss didn't play either of those teams, but that didn't matter to the throng gathered in Jackson. "Ole Miss has been fighting the Army all week," one spectator yelled.

For Vaught the win over Houston and the rest of the unbeaten season was more than just a victory. "Successful football kept Ole Miss from closing its doors," he insisted, though it was a view not shared by many involved in the crisis.

James Meredith had enrolled in 1962. Cleve McDowell spent a few months as a law student in 1963 before being expelled. Cleveland Donald enrolled in 1964 followed by a trickle of other students until 1968, when dozens of blacks were in the fall entering class. But the football team had remained all white. Indeed, ten years after Meredith, a Saturday afternoon at the packed stadium was the loneliest place on campus for Ole Miss blacks. Eugene McLemore had reminded faculty members of the racial slurs he regularly encountered when he went to games. And now that Ole Miss was playing integrated teams, taunts aimed at opponents' black players were common. "Kill that nigger" or "Kill that black SOB" were among the favorites.

One of the more obscure taunts was "Give 'at ball to LeRoy," a catch phrase from a racist football joke that had been making the rounds in the state and was particularly popular at Ole Miss. "Two colored schools were playing," the joke begins. Late in the game, the coach of one of the squads knows he needs a score and tells the quarterback, "Give 'at ball to LeRoy." Instead the quarterback hands off to Willie, who is promptly stomped in the backfield. "Give 'at ball to LeRoy," the coach yells again, but the quarterback gives the ball to Sam, and he is pummeled to the ground. "Give 'at ball to LeRoy," the exasperated coach hollers. The quarterback turns around and yells back, "LeRoy say he don't want 'at ball."

The insensitive joke illustrated that if the face of the campus was changing, the mores and folkways of the past would not disappear so easily. Although blacks were no longer "unwelcome guests," as a faculty committee had put it, they were not yet full partners in university life. They were becoming a permanent part of the landscape yet in some ways still invisible to many of their white classmates. Little, if anything, in their childhoods had prepared the white students to recognize blacks as their equals, entitled to the same things they were and striving for the same kind of stable, productive future they wanted. What's more, there seemed to be in the minds of some the notion that their lives were somehow diminished by the expansion of opportunity for blacks—almost as though a once-exclusive club had become less so when the membership rules were changed. The continuing racial slurs were a way to remind themselves of the old power structure.

During one important game in 1970, Ole Miss found the tables turned with its "LeRoy" joke. Confident of beating Southern Mississippi, which had already integrated its team, fans were taunting Southern to "Give 'at ball to LeRoy," halfback Willie Heidelberg. When Southern did, Heidelberg scored two touchdowns on the way to a 30–14 drubbing of the Rebels. By the fourth quarter, Ole Miss revelers were yelling, "Don't give 'at ball to LeRoy."

Given this kind of atmosphere at Rebel games, many of the black students chose to stay away from the stadium. Others, determined not to be deprived of one part of college experience, developed their own ritual protest. They sat together in the end zone and blatantly cheered for the opposing team, ever more lustily when a black player made an outstanding play. They refused to stand for the Alma Mater or "Dixie." Occasionally someone in the group would hold up a homemade banner: "Racist Athletic Department," or "Ole Miss Racism," or "Right on Wright," a reference to the talented black running back from Houston, Elmo Wright.

By this time, the issue of integrated athletic programs in the South had become a topic of public discussion. Civil rights groups were monitoring the progress at various schools. One article in the *Race Relations Reporter* noted in March 1970 that "even the University of Mississippi" was making moves to get black football players. But the article reported that these initial recruiting efforts were not going so well. One potential player was offended when "a university recruiter referred to him as 'boy,'" the story explained. He subsequently chose another southern school.

In the fall of 1970, a columnist for the *Clarion Ledger* wondered in print whether Ole Miss would ever integrate its football team. He pointed out that Mississippi State and Southern already had done so. Indeed, to improve its recruitment efforts, the administration at Southern was making a determined effort to diminish the use of Old South symbols on campus. One important step was getting rid of "General Nat" as a mascot. "General Nat" was Nathaniel Bedford Forrest, one of the founders of the Ku Klux Klan.

But at Ole Miss, Colonel Rebel, the flag, and "Dixie" were virtually sacred. Indeed, a year earlier, when a few students sought to come up with a new "spirit" flag—imposing the initials "UM" over the Confederate flag—alumni who opposed the idea put enough pressure on university officials to shelve the proposal. As long as "the real Ole Miss anthem is 'Dixie,'" there will not be an integrated football team, the *Clarion Ledger* writer predicted. "There will be no Negro flashes in the Ole Miss backfield, or lightning-fast black flankers in the flats or tough Negro troopers in offensive or defensive lines so long as the Stars and Bars of the Confederacy remains the true standard of the school."

Much of the column was on the mark, yet the writer misjudged recruiters' ability to go out and sell Ole Miss when they really wanted to, and he didn't know of a young man from Yazoo City who, like Coolidge Ball, was confident of his skills and possessed the internal resolve to succeed in Oxford. He would treat the flag and "Dixie" as just so much cultural noise, however unpleasant. His name was Ben Williams.

Ole Miss was not the only college that sought Williams's talents. By his senior year in high school, he was well known around the state as a top defensive prospect. He was big for his age, quick, and, perhaps most important, a thoughtful young man who appreciated that good football playing was something that could be learned. It was not only instinct. Recruiters knew that Williams possessed one important trait: he was coachable.

He also seemed to be more proof that in many cases Ole Miss makes a good first impression, despite the offending comment made to a previous black recruit. Williams liked what he saw as soon as he set foot on the campus. Perhaps more important, that first visit to Oxford was but one step in a process that had started nearly two years earlier.

The assistant coach assigned to recruit in the Yazoo area was Junie Hovious, who had worked with Vaught since the day he came to Ole Miss. Although Hovious was a defensive backfield specialist, when it came to recruiting the assistants were assigned their tasks by geography, and Hovious got Williams's home town. The coach had not been sent out to find a black player for the Rebels, and he had not been told that if he did, to go no further. In his mind, he was just looking for the best available recruit, regardless of color.

During one of his many trips to the high schools in central Mississippi, Hovious watched Williams play when he was just a sophomore. He immediately liked what he saw. Hovious introduced himself to Williams and his grandmother, Molly Haymer, with whom he lived, and planted the seed about recruiting Ben for Ole Miss. He realized that Mrs. Haymer would play a part in Williams's decision about which school to attend, and he cultivated his friendship with her as much as with Ben. He made sure to visit with her every time he came to Yazoo City, often stopping by the house for coffee before going to watch Ben play.

By the time Williams was a senior, Hovious was determined to get him to Ole Miss. He not only liked the young man's football skills but also his attitude. He tried to convince himself that Williams's color was not a factor, but that defied reality. Simply put, if Williams came to Oxford, he would be the first black to play football for Ole Miss, and there was no denying he would be under extra pressure. It was important to make sure the young man understood this and could handle it. For his part, Hovious had no doubts. He was also confident that Williams would be "a good advertisement" for the program. He would certainly help the image of Ole Miss, and he would make it easier to get more players like him.

Williams graduated from high school in the spring of 1972, eighteen years after the *Brown* decision decreed an end to segregation in public schools. Yet he had spent virtually all his education in school with black students, even at St. Francis, a Catholic school in Yazoo City. When that school closed after he finished ninth grade, he spent his sophomore and part of his junior year at the all-black high school. Finally in January 1970 the Yazoo schools were integrated, two and a half years before he graduated.

At St. Francis, Williams had been taught by white nuns. He had been coached by white men, and for a year he had played with and against white boys, so going to Oxford was not going to be the same kind of eye-opening experience as it was for many of the black students who preceded him. Besides, Williams reminded himself, "when you're six foot three and weigh two hundred fifty pounds, you really don't have any problems."

The day Williams ran out on the field as the starting defensive tackle, there was something different in the roar of the crowd. The rebel flags were flying, "Dixie" was blaring, but there was a new chorus of cheers. The black students in their end zone seats finally had one of their own to root for.

If Williams felt any extra pressure as the first black football player, he kept it to himself. He ignored the flags waving in the stands and closed his ears to the music. "How can you be worried about 'Dixie' or the rebel flag," he explained, "when you've got a 6-5 three hundred pound white boy foamin' at the mouth across the line ready to kick in your teeth?" He also reminded himself of one truism in sports: "If I play a good game, those white fans are going to stand up and cheer for me."

He was right about that, and although his special cheering section in the end zone took pride in his stellar play, many of them smiled bittersweet smiles, remembering the personal slights that were a part of so many of their days on campus. Sam Givhan found it just short of schizophrenic. Watching the white crowd go wild over a particularly good play by Williams, he would ask himself, "Didn't I just experience you rejecting me?"

The arrival of Coolidge Ball and then Ben Williams was undeniably important at Ole Miss. Equally so were the slow but obvious adjustments in the academic program, none more so than the hiring in the fall of 1970 of Jeanette Jennings, a young social worker from Jackson, as the first black full-time professor. After earning a master's degree at Tulane University, she had been teaching part time at Jackson State and also working full time at the state Department of Public Welfare—one of a handful of blacks in state government service.

Jennings hadn't asked for the job in Oxford. The university came to her after a decision was made to start a social work program in the sociology department. She would fit the bill on two counts: Her background was appropriate, and there was no denying the school was anxious to hire its first black professor.

John Crews and his special race relations committee had been meeting regularly and giving interim reports to Chancellor Fortune about their assessment of black-white relations on campus. As important, they had been gathering information about what other southern schools were doing. An observation from one report was clear and direct: The university lagged behind these other schools "in the areas of black student leadership, black participation in athletics, faculty and administrative positions held by blacks. The most significant difference that we can detect in race relations at the University of Mississippi and the majority of institutions responding to our inquiry is that of policy. Several of the schools, notably the University of Arkansas, Florida State, and Virginia, appear to have a systematic policy of recruiting blacks and in aiding their participation in campus life." Ole Miss was making strides in some areas, the committee said, but it was far behind in others.

Crews was certain this kind of information was important in getting the university to move forward. If he and his committee could demonstrate that other schools in the region were making racial accommodations, then it made their suggestions "less subversive" in the eyes of conservatives like trustee chairman M. M. Roberts, who were still clinging to a bygone era. The announcement that Jennings was hired was a good sign and a significant step.

As far as Jennings was concerned, she would have to wait and see. As a student at Jackson State eight years earlier, she had never thought much about Ole Miss, though she did remember the agitation over Meredith. During the height of the tensions, there was a bomb scare at her dorm, an apparent threat of retaliation that never materialized.

It didn't dawn on Jennings until after the hiring process was well underway that she would be the first full-time black professor. She took some time to reflect on that fact, reminding herself that she had been in situations before where she was one of a very few blacks among many whites. Her current work situation was exactly that, so too her graduate study at Tulane.

As she thought about the actual teaching, Jennings again reminded herself that she had made presentations before in front of all-white audiences, and by this time she accepted as a fact of life the knowledge that because of her skin color, she had to be better prepared than anyone else. There would also be special adjustments in the classroom.

To minimize potentially awkward moments, she would make sure she got to class a few minutes early so it would be clear that she was the teacher. She prepared herself for white students who would walk in, take one look at her, and decide they did not want to be taught by a black woman regardless of what she had to offer. It would happen at least once a semester. And she readied her retort to those who would presume to call her "Jeanette," explaining politely but in no uncertain terms, "I did not give you permission to call me by my first name." She expected to be challenged by some of the white students with just a little more edge than usual, but she could handle that by making sure she was thoroughly prepared.

All in all Jennings felt well armed internally to handle the academic side of being the university's first black professor. What she had not understood was the impact she would have on the other black students and the special place she would hold in the hearts of Oxford's black community.

Until her arrival, black adults had looked at Ole Miss as a source of employment, but only for the most menial tasks. They cooked, they cleaned, or they took care of the grounds. They never taught. So these families took special care to make sure that Jennings was made to feel welcome and protected. She was their heroine. For her part, Jennings came to regard the families outside the campus as home—an emotional center to offset the more distant relationships available to her in the sociology department. To be sure, her colleagues were decent and friendly, but it was always clear that she was not an intimate part of that group.

Jennings's impact on the students was even more profound. Finally, thought Mary Thompson, "there is somebody we can relate to, somebody of our own skin color." It didn't matter that only one or two black students were in her classes. The important thing was to see a black adult in a teaching position—a black professional on the Ole Miss campus. Thompson never took one of Jennings's courses—it didn't fit with her academic interests—but almost instantly she and Jennings became friends. Race bound them together, a natural kinship. The story was repeated countless times, and during the five years Jennings spent in Oxford, there was a steady stream of students, male and female and from every academic discipline, in and out of her office.

All of this caught Jennings by surprise. She had imagined she would get to know the social work students quite well, but she never thought she would come to know virtually all of the three hundred or so black students on campus. It enabled her to become a one-person repository of the students' concerns—everything from running short of money to buy a book to problems with teachers who would not recognize someone in class, to dealing with occasional harassment in the dorms.

Jennings felt it was a help to the students just to have someplace to go, and she saw herself as kind of an adjunct to the informal counseling Wayne Johnson was doing at his campus ministry, the de facto headquarters for black students. There was no formal assistance from the university. "We took care of ourselves," Jennings said.

While Jennings had been settling into her teaching routine in the fall of 1970, Harry Owens, who had come to Ole Miss in 1964 from Florida State, was putting together the first courses in the black studies program. It was important to find the right teacher for this task, and given that the university wanted to fill the post from within, Owens was a good fit. Perhaps most important he was a southerner, not some outsider arriving in Oxford to teach a foreign view of the region's history. He was an Alabama native educated in the South and for the first twenty years of his life admittedly had "no liberal ideas whatsoever." But he had come through his own journey on matters of race.

It started when he was an undergraduate at Auburn, after his English professor insisted that Owens go to hear a campus speaker, Harry Golden, editor of the monthly *Carolina Israelite*. A New York native and Jewish, Golden had moved to Charlotte, North Carolina, to write and considered the *Israelite* "a personal journal" of items he believed were of interest to Jews and non-Jews alike. He did not shy away from racial issues, bringing a folksy iconoclasm to the subject. One of his solutions to the race problem he called the "vertical Negro plan," pointing out that whites and blacks conducted many daily affairs without difficulty, such as standing in the same grocery or bank lines. "It is only when the Negro 'sets' that the fur flies," he wrote. So Golden proposed that public schools be equipped with desks but no seats, just like in a bookkeeping office. "Since no one in the South pays the slightest attention to a VERTICAL NEGRO, this will completely solve the problem."

The proposal, one among several Golden offered, made Owens realize the absurdities inherent in segregation and triggered a rethinking of his own philosophy. From then on he went through a gradual reassessment of much that he had believed about the racial order. By the time he finished his doctorate at Florida State, he felt far removed from the conservative young man who had come out of rural Alabama. To be sure, outside events—Meredith's coming to Ole Miss, John Kennedy's call for a civil rights bill, the murder of Medgar Evers—had made him pay attention, forcing him to "try to figure out what it all means."

Owens ended up at Ole Miss by happenstance: He was looking for a job in history, and one was available in Oxford. He chuckled to himself that he was, like many other graduates, seeking work and hoping to stay in the South. "We'll go anywhere except Mississippi," they told themselves, not anxious to walk into a maelstrom of tensions and one that didn't pay that well either. Yet when Ole Miss offered Owens a position, he took it.

Within a year he was teaching a course on Negro history. The first class was a summer session for forty southern high school teachers: twenty white and twenty black. It was part of a program that also offered the group classes in political history and labor history, taught by other professors. In his class Owens lectured part of the time and brought in guest speakers, among them the preeminent black historian John Hope Franklin.

He was grateful for Franklin's calming presence during one testy period when the class had gotten polarized over race. A black teacher from Louisiana had spoken out about the long history of white bigotry, and some of the white teachers considered the comments too harsh. A group that initially had taken seats in the classroom at random was now split up by race—blacks on one side, whites on the other. When Franklin came to speak, his combination of grace and authority in dissecting the issues diffused the tensions and turned the group back into one class, not two factions. Owens marveled at Franklin's ability to discuss issues in a way that reached across the racial divide. It was a reminder of why Franklin's major work, *From Slavery to Freedom,* was so important. Writing about the emergence of the Jim Crow era, for example, Franklin captured the essence of the matter in a simple, profound statement: "It was a dear price the whites of the South paid for this color line. Since all other issues were subordinated to the issue of the Negro, it became impossible to have free and open discussion of problems affecting all people." White Mississippians knew better than most how true that statement was.

Owens taught his first Negro history class to Ole Miss juniors and seniors in the fall of 1965. By the time he was tapped to develop a black studies curriculum, he had a set of lectures prepared and a solid reading list that included *From Slavery to Freedom* as the main text, along with writings by Gunnar Myrdal and Kenneth Stampp. In addition he had just finished a year of postdoctoral work at Johns Hopkins University studying southern and black history and was in the midst of the program when he was called by Ole Miss and asked to put together a black studies curriculum.

Although the history of black Americans was an essential ingredient of Mississippi history—indeed, the history of white Mississippi is profoundly bound up with its treatment of blacks—Owens was surprised to realize how little his students knew, and that included the few blacks who took his course. But then how much could they have known? They were being taught out of the same books that the white student used, though in the black schools they were well-worn hand-me-downs. Even more important, the history imparted was the history envisioned by the founders of Ole Miss a century earlier so their sons "would not be estranged from their native land"—the careful presentation of information that had molded the "closed society" so aptly described by Jim Silver.

The initial black studies program was Owens's history course and a survey of black art taught by an outside professor. Over the next few years, the program expanded to include a sociology course, "The Black Experience," which Owens insisted be taught by a black professor, and classes in political science, literature, and anthropology. The enrollment was never large, and Owens worried that he and his colleagues were "preaching to the choir," not reaching the students who most needed to understand their own society and history, whatever its bleak and ugly moments. But it was still worth it.

A year and a half into the program Owens wrote an article for a short-lived publication of the Black Student Union, the *Spectator,* laying out the reasons. "No teacher should go into the classroom without having had a black history course," he said. "Particularly in the South, black and white business and professional people will be serving the total community; they would do well to prepare for better service by having studied black history and sociology." But the most important reason for such a course, Owens said, is that blacks' "heroic struggle against almost overwhelming odds, not only enlarges our understanding of American history, but it also offers a great lesson to all Americans. The history of millions of black people fighting, not only to survive, but more important, to overcome institutionalized racism, can provide an historical perspective of the present and a hope for the future."

Even if the course offerings were small, the black studies program was a start—something the school could build on. In fact, a recruitment letter sent to potential black students included a paragraph describing the black studies program as a point of interest. With some candor, the letter added that although there had not yet been any "dramatic accomplishments on campus," communication among black students and university personnel was improving. Noting the efforts of John Crews's special committee, the letter said that the panel's work "is an example of the university's concern for its black students."

A decade earlier James Meredith received no acknowledgment from the university of its concern for his welfare, but on the tenth anniversary of his admission, the work of the Crews committee, indeed its very existence, was directly related to what he had done. Although Ole Miss was hardly a hotbed of liberalism, there was now more open discussion of all manner of subjects and more outspoken faculty members. One of them, David Sansing, had joined the history department in the fall of 1970. He was not as brash as Jim Silver but considered himself an heir to Silver's style, pushing his students to think in new ways about old issues, encouraging them to challenge what they saw and were told. He was proud of the inscription Silver had written in his copy of *The Closed Society:* "To David Sansing, who is in my old office and carrying on."

When Sansing learned that Meredith would be in Oxford in the spring of 1972 to campaign for the U.S. Senate (an unsuccessful effort), he invited him to speak to his class. More than one hundred students and faculty crammed into a small room to hear him. After Meredith finished his informal presentation, the audience gave him a standing ovation. A slightly bemused Meredith acknowledged the applause and then answered questions for another forty minutes.

"What do you think is the difference between the students today who gave you a standing ovation and the students who rioted when you arrived ten years ago?" one of them wanted to know.

"If you had been here ten years ago, you would have acted just like these students," Meredith replied. "If those students were here today, they'd be acting like you were acting. The difference is time and an understanding of events. You're not any different from those students."

The *Mississippian* editor at this time, Otis Tims, was in fifth grade when Meredith entered the university, and he had no idea what the campus was like in 1962, particularly coming from Waynesboro, a small town in southeastern Mississippi, "where all the incidents of the civil rights movement had passed us by." But even if he had not grown up consumed by racial issues in the way those from Jackson, Oxford, or the Delta had been, Tims nonetheless was shaped by the policies that kept him in a segregated high school and exposed him to the racial appeals of Mississippi's political campaigns. He remembered one with particular clarity: when John Bell Williams won the 1967 gubernatorial election by painting his opponent, William Winter, as too liberal and too sympathetic to blacks. One Williams handbill stuck in Tims's mind—a picture of Winter addressing a group of black voters. The message to the state's white community was obvious: Look where Winter's sympathies lie.

Tims thought it was important for Mississippians to examine their history, particularly the history of his own college, so with the help of his staff, which now included the first full-time black writers, he put together a special package on the event that featured interviews with Ross Barnett, Meredith, and a reprint of the *New York Times* assessment of how the campus had changed in the past decade.

Tims wrote the opening editorial. Its firm tone put him in the camp of earlier, outspoken *Mississippian* editors, particularly Sidna Brower, who had contributed a special piece on her memories of the 1962 riot. Critics were accusing the paper of "opening old wounds, of trying to create trouble" by writing again about the turmoil of 1962, Tims wrote, but that was shortsighted: "The Meredith crisis is as much a part of the heritage of this academic community as the Lyceum. Our purpose is to look at this crisis, after the decade of change it inaugurated, so that we may be more aware of where we are today." Tims conceded that this might be "unpleasant," or as Ross Barnett had told him, "'water under the bridge.' . . . But that water will keep on flowing, will continue to affect the shoreline of ideas in Mississippi. It will continue to affect our lives. We cannot ignore it. If we in Mississippi continue to ignore our past, even the dimmest aspects of it," he concluded, "we will never be able to understand a seemingly gloomy present nor plan for a none-too-certain future."

Since the Fulton Chapel episode, the paper had become an occasional forum for discussions among black and white students. In one
guest column, for example, Lawrence Weeden, a BSU leader, said "campus racism" was the reason blacks were unable to participate in more
activities. One white student wrote back to say Weeden was right about
racism, but it was black racism that was the problem. The student cited
a demonstration some weeks earlier when a group of blacks and a few
white sympathizers burned a Confederate flag. Another wrote in to say
that beliefs cannot be forced and that racism "will always be a way of
life for some people." Weeden signed his piece, and his picture ran with
the article. But these two letters carried no names. The first was signed
"a white student," the second "A Mississippi Coed"—an indication of
the discomfort among some whites about having a public discussion
about race.

Like Weeden, Burnis Morris, one of the paper's regular black contribu-
tors, was not shy about putting his views in print with his name. He had
developed self-confidence during high school in Laurel, where he was a
top student at one of the state's best all-black high schools, Oak Park
High, and editor of the student paper. The school was one of the few in
the state that had a junior ROTC program for blacks and a Latin program. Morris was on a classics team that had qualified for a statewide
competition in Jackson, but white school authorities would not let the
students go. One official told them the organizers hadn't known the Oak
Park team was black and that they would not be welcome. Morris took
the slap as just part of the racial territory. There was no other way of life
for comparison, and nobody protested publicly. "It didn't occur to anybody that that was an option," he explained.

Morris was determined to achieve, and he never considered any other
school than Ole Miss. He knew what so many whites knew: that Oxford
was the training ground for leaders, and he intended to be successful on
the campus whatever slights or difficulties came his way. He was angry
when he was jeered and pelted with debris at a football game, but he
didn't think once about leaving Ole Miss for a friendlier college. He was
convinced it was the best school in the state, and he was determined to
have a University of Mississippi degree.

Morris originally thought he would be a chemical engineer, but he changed his mind when he did well in an elective journalism course. The teacher cited one of his first pieces as an example of good writing, and after that Morris never gave engineering another thought.

By 1972, Morris was a well-established writer at the *Mississippian*. A few days before the special Meredith package, he had published a pointed article interviewing black students about their lives at Ole Miss. Ten years after Meredith, it was obvious that race was an issue every day for those who followed him. Few whites gave it a thought. They have accepted the fact that blacks are on campus for good, one student told Morris. "It doesn't mean they want us here."

Morris offered a trenchant conclusion to the story. Certainly things had changed: there were a few black athletes now, one black professor, and a few black faces on Ole Miss recruitment brochures. "Many blacks call this 'tokenism,'" he wrote. "Whites call it 'progress.'"

Morris's article was like the half-empty, half-full glass. On the one hand the public discussion about race was now not just among whites of differing views but among whites and the growing number of blacks. On the other, the comments on the pages of the *Mississippian* suggested that the white and black students were attending two different institutions.

Perhaps they were. By this time, one could argue that there really were two schools occupying the same campus in Oxford: the University of Mississippi and Ole Miss. At the former, a student could get a good education and a degree. But "Ole Miss," in the words of anthropologist Peter Aschoff, was "where you go to learn to take your role in the halls of power in the state of Mississippi."

Black students had been admitted to the university. None went to Ole Miss. Nor did every white student. Race was the most obvious dividing line on campus, but there was another cleavage, class, and it manifested itself most clearly in the split between those young men and women who were in fraternities and sororities and those who were not. By and large the students in the Greek system, its shorthand name, dominated campus life. They generally were from well-to-do families, although that was not always the case, and they set the social standard. Patsy Brumfield, for example, did not come from a wealthy family in McComb, yet her mother went to work before Brumfield left for Ole Miss so that her daughter could afford the wardrobe that would be necessary to be a sorority girl. She knew it was Brumfield's best chance for success in the fullest sense of the word at Ole Miss.

For black students the social stratification amounted to a double whammy. Harold Reynolds, who had joined Morris as one of the regular black commentators in the *Mississippian,* wrote perceptively in one column that a black fraternity—he was commenting from the male perspective—was necessary because "the Ole Miss black student's path to social equality is blocked by intangible and unmentioned, yet very real barriers." The social life of an Ole Miss black student "is virtually nil," he went on. "Because he has no permanent social center he must shuttle back and forth from place to place in search of entertainment and recreation. . . . He has no voice in relation to the campus concerts that he is allowed to attend and because of his cultural differences he is not often satisfied with the Elton Johns and Cat Stevenses," a reference to two mainstream white artists.

By 1973 a group of young black men had organized a chapter of Omega Psi Phi on campus, designed, they said, not only to provide social and fraternal activities for black men but to provide a more organized means for involvement in campus activities. The first black sorority would follow in two years.

Not all black students thought this was a good idea. Morris countered in one of his columns that a black fraternity amounted to "a paraphernalia of ridiculous pretensions" and worried that it would lead to stratification in the small black community on campus.

The social issues Reynolds and Morris raised were bound up in financial ones. Roughly 90 percent of the 350 black students received some kind of financial aid, many of them cobbling together loans, grants, and scholarships to meet expenses. Some students were so strapped that they stopped eating in the university cafeteria and made meals in their dorms. They had no extra money for a social life off-campus or to invest in the wardrobes or other accoutrements that would have made them candidates, however unlikely, for white sororities or fraternities.

The social inequality that Reynolds spoke of meant that blacks were also cut out of virtually all traditional campus leadership positions, a reality that nagged at Patricia Taylor. She had grown up in Oxford with Mary Thompson, and like her friend she had chosen to stay at all-black Central High School her senior year even though she could have transferred to the white school under the state's freedom of choice plan. Beyond the wish to stay with her friends, Taylor thought she was getting a decent education where she was. Living in Oxford meant that her school got its second-hand books from the university-sponsored high school, and most of the time they were just a year or two old. Compared to other black schools around the state, Central was lucky. In other less affluent counties, particularly the Delta, black students were making do with much less.

Taylor had thought she wanted to go to Mississippi Valley College, one of the historically black schools in the state, but she was offered a better scholarship to attend Ole Miss. Besides, her grandfather wanted her to attend the university. He was a groundskeeper and cafeteria worker on campus, and it tickled him no end to realize that now he had a granddaughter who was a student there.

It was further incentive for a highly motivated young woman to do well. Yet she realized that even with her drive and determination, her experience at Ole Miss was an incomplete one. "There was no opportunity to develop leadership skills," she explained, "or for that matter followership skills." The sense of what was missing in Oxford was always most acute when she and her friends would go over to "Valley," as it was known, or down to Jackson State. "It was so amazing to see so many black students having a good time," she said, marveling at the palpable sense of freedom that did not exist for her at the university.

Taylor considered Ole Miss a proving ground, her degree not only making her grandfather proud but showing that she could succeed "against all odds." Twenty years later, armed with a law degree from Oxford, she was a state judge in Jackson. In her mind, the university lost out by not allowing her to display some of her leadership skills in campus activities. Perhaps the most telling legacy of her time there was the encouragement she gave to her daughters to go to historically black colleges for their undergraduate education.

It was not only black students who felt cut out of Ole Miss social life. Whites who were not part of the Greek system felt similarly excluded, although in theory they had the opportunity, simply by the fact of being white, to seek admission to one of the social clubs. Many found other outlets, such as joining the band or getting involved in student religious organizations like the Baptist Student Union. That was the preferred route of Kent Moorhead, for whom Ole Miss was a family tradition. His father was dean of the school of education, and older siblings had preceded him on campus. The riot and subsequent occupation of the city by federal troops in the fall of 1962 was the major event in young Moorhead's life. He alternated between fear and fascination as he watched soldiers set up camp not far from his home, heard helicopters buzzing over his school, and learned to negotiate roadblocks around his neighborhood. Moorhead quickly understood that race was serious business and complicated. At Oxford High School, where he was a star student, football player, and student leader, his understanding of this reality only deepened when integration finally came. His modest proposal of securing school buses to take students to out-of-town football games was turned down. The bus ride would have meant that black and white students were together, possibly becoming friends and developing relationships. His high school may have been desegregated, but the old racial and sexual taboos were still plenty powerful.

On the football team, Moorhead made friends with several of his black teammates, getting close enough to some of them to be invited into their homes. One particular visit was both eye-opening and moving. "I'll never forget the shock of seeing how little his family had," he recalled of one friend, whose father was the janitor for a local white church. "This was a man with a full time job that involved cleaning a Christian church, and he was forced to live along with his rather large family according to standards that would shame a Third World country." He was paid $2,500 in 1972, a dozen times less than what Dean Moorhead made.

Almost immediately after starting college, Moorhead joined the band, which included a few black musicians. He felt some of the camaraderie of his high school football team, but at the same time he felt a chill on the campus between white and black that seemed a throwback to the earlier days of segregation.

Undaunted by his new surroundings Moorhead was willing to take a huge step across the racial divide. He wanted to ask one of his bandmates out on a date: a black woman whom he had admired from afar. Realizing this was a potentially volatile move, he thought his parents deserved to know his plans, given how small the Oxford community was and his father's prominent position. "Ask your father," Moorhead's mother instructed when apprised of his plans. "Do what you want to do," he told his son.

So Moorhead asked the young woman out. She declined. He was never sure whether it was because she didn't want to cross the racial divide or because she just wasn't interested. Moorhead got over the disappointment, but it confirmed for him that he was living in a confused time, where the old society had broken apart but there was not a new one in place yet. The old ideals still held force.

Although Moorhead never felt he was part of Ole Miss, his life was perceptibly different from the blacks on campus. "I didn't have to worry about my right to be there," he said. "I was part of a system that blacks didn't fit into."

One of the many traditions at Ole Miss was the selection each year of honorary campus leaders, Colonel Rebel and Miss Ole Miss—essentially popularity contests that for the most part featured nominees from fraternities and sororities. In the fall of 1975, Ben Williams, by now a defensive standout for Ole Miss, decided to run for Colonel Rebel. He put together a campaign of personal visits at every dorm and every sorority house; he knew his good looks and boyish charm would go over well with many young women who found him affable, even alluring, like some forbidden fruit. He didn't waste time with any of the fraternities, sure that they would back their own candidates and that his visit would be a waste of time. Like the other candidates, he took out ads in the *Mississippian* that featured his picture and some kind of pithy saying to get readers' attention. "He's been a 1st all his life," noted one, a reminder of what Williams's presence on campus represented.

When he subsequently won the honor, Williams was the first black student to attain such prominence. Some of the other black students found it ironic, even disconcerting, that this accolade was attached to a symbol of white power and authority that had only recently been circumscribed and then only under the most extreme outside pressure. Many whites, on the other hand, saw Williams's victory as an institutional watershed, a way for students to say things were different. This was only a college campus, but it was the same kind of important moment in Otis Tims's view as when blacks and whites in Greenwood that same year attended an Urban League dinner together.

It was standard for the yearbook to have a picture of the winning couple, and the June 1976 annual was no exception, though some on the campus wondered if the annual would really show what was, in effect, an interracial couple. They were expecting separate pictures on facing pages. But the picture of Williams and Barbara Biggs, his Miss Ole Miss, featured the two of them in an outdoor setting that was friendly but not intimate. They were standing next to each other, not quite touching, and there was a fence between them. A smiling Williams was leaning on one side, Biggs casually resting on the other. It seemed an appropriate metaphor for the time: we've come a ways, but we can't go too far.

Williams's selection as Colonel Rebel was the most obvious recognition of a black presence on campus, but there were some other important milestones. Dottie Chapman, who had graduated in the spring of 1974, became the first black admissions counselor. It seemed to be a natural progression for the young woman, who had first become interested in Ole Miss when she was invited to visit by two black students from her home town of Water Valley. She liked the campus and what she sensed was the special kind of black students who would be her classmates—smart and determined like she was. She watched with pride and amazement one day during her visit as a group of black students refused to be cowed by a few white football players who had been harassing them. One of the young black men had quietly called for help, a standard procedure among the blacks. If they sensed trouble, they tried to get reinforcements, and quickly. Chapman was in a dorm helping to celebrate a birthday when word came that there was trouble at the Grill, one of the campus gathering spots. She and the others arrived just as one of the older blacks, a law student, told the football players to leave the group alone. To Chapman's surprise, the men left. But she and her friends decided to stay as a show of unity and determination. To make their point even more obvious, they sat on the Grill steps and conspicuously ate watermelon in a playful imitiation of an old stereotype.

Chapman knew she wanted to develop that kind of moxie, and what better place than Oxford. It might be easier and more comfortable to go to Jackson State, Valley, or another of the predominantly black schools around, but Ole Miss would be a challenge that would set her in good stead for the future if she survived. Coming from an all-black high school, she was surprised at first to realize that she was often the only black in her class except for one, a course called "Effective Study," which was designed to help students learn how to study for their college classes. Here most of the students were black, and it was the way most of them got to know one another. Implicit in the enrollment was the dubious legacy of "separate but equal." Many of these students, while high achieving in their high schools, had to play catch-up to succeed at the university because their schools had not had the resources and the tools to prepare them to compete academically.

As important as anything else, though, was Chapman's route to the university. She was the third black student to come to Oxford from Water Valley, and as such was the beginning of a network in the black community similar to the one that had operated so well for so many years among whites. As an Ole Miss admissions counselor, Chapman realized she would have a chance to build on her own experience. She could make a compelling case when she went to high schools around the state on behalf of the school, presenting herself as living proof that being black, going to Ole Miss, and doing well there was possible.

A year before Williams had been elected Colonel Rebel, Harold Reynolds had become the first black named to the Ole Miss Hall of Fame. A talented writer who had been interested in journalism since his high school days in Gulfport, Reynolds was well known around the campus by virtue of his regular column in the *Mississippian*, "Reynolds' Rap." While he had had the opportunity to go to other schools, Reynolds chose Ole Miss not only because he thought he could get the best education there but also because of what he felt was a duty to the state's black community: "I wanted to continue what James Meredith started."

In the winter of 1974 Reynolds had supervised a special section of the paper, "Focus," written exclusively by black students. It was an attempt, Reynolds explained, to provide readers with "black-oriented views of life in a predominantly white environment"—or as one of the writers so aptly put it, the section was an effort to gauge "black progress under the Rebel flag." In a sense the observation seemed like a contradiction in terms because to these students, the flag and "Dixie" were impediments to, if not progress, surely comfort on the campus. The black students interviewed could not treat these symbols with as much equanimity as Coolidge Ball and Ben Williams, who could associate waving the flag and singing "Dixie" with their accomplishments. Shorn of that personal connection, most blacks found the symbols degrading and deflating. The common theme through the "Focus" section, like Burnis Morris's much briefer survey two years earlier, was that Ole Miss was still unfriendly territory for blacks—their successes and Dottie Chapman's efforts notwithstanding.

As if to emphasize that point, two black students denied admission to the law school filed a suit in the the spring of 1974, claiming that the school's heavy reliance on a standard law school admissions test discriminated against them. They charged that there was "a deliberate lack of effort" to seek black students for the program, noting that a few years earlier the school had stood out for its significant black enrollment while only 14 of the current 627 students were black. It would take six years of legal maneuvering before the suit was eventually settled.

Jeanette Jennings had been interviewed for a story in Reynolds's package about black faculty members. The writer lamented the fact that by 1974 only one other full-time teacher had been hired, also in the sociology department. In less than a year she would be alone. Jennings decided to leave after she had been passed over for an appointment she thought should have been hers: running the social work program. One of the reasons she did not get the position, she was told, was that she did not have a Ph.D. She decided that she would get her doctorate so that no one could ever make that excuse again, but she was also convinced that even if she had had a Ph.D., the University of Mississippi in 1975 was not going to let a black woman run an important academic program.

There was a counterpoint to Jennings's departure, however. Lucius L. Williams, a 1951 honors graduate from Jackson State with a doctorate from Columbia, had been named assistant vice chancellor for academic affairs, the first black in the university's administration. It was one more step for blacks, albeit "under the rebel flag."

8

Tradition Under Challenge

By any measure Rose Jackson was an Ole Miss success story—from how she got to the university, to her accomplishments while on campus, to her achievements in the business world after graduation. Like so many other black Mississippi high school students in the mid-1970s, she understood that Ole Miss was an option for her, but she never thought seriously about going there even though she was on her way to becoming the first black valedictorian of her racially mixed high school in Clarksdale. She was destined for Jackson State, where both of her parents had gone, until she received an invitation from Ole Miss to attend the National Achievement and Leadership Conference. This was the brainchild of Kenneth Wooten, the school's registrar and later head of the admissions department. By now diversity was a national policy and one that Ole Miss had to embrace to keep up with other campuses and to keep its share of federal money coming in. Wooten knew the school's history and reputation would be obstacles in recruiting blacks, so he designed a program to bring them to the university "to show that blacks don't get lynched on campus."

The word *conference* was a misnomer. Wooten had not planned a weekend of dry academic debate. It was really a precollege orientation where the high school students could attend classes, meet professors, talk with other black students about their experiences, and, perhaps most important, see the place and imagine themselves reading a book under one of the beautiful big oaks in the Grove or having a snack in the cafeteria.

That is exactly what happened to Rose Jackson. Until then, her image of the university was what she had seen in newspaper pictures or on television: hordes of white faces in a football stadium awash in Confederate flags. But a few days in Oxford changed all that—precisely what Ken Wooten had had in mind. Talking to some of the black students made a particular impact on Jackson. They seemed down to earth, and none offered a sugar-coated view of the campus. Instead the message was that Ole Miss was what the rest of the world was like, and this was a place to learn to adjust. But, they cautioned, the university worked best for a student—and Jackson remembered this with specificity—who was "self-confident, had thick skin, a person who was inspired from within."

Jackson went back home to Clarksdale and told her parents she wanted to go to Ole Miss. What helped clinch the decision was the journalism department, the only accredited one in the state, and Jackson thought she wanted to be a reporter. Jackson's parents were surprised, somewhat disappointed, and concerned, but she managed to allay their worries in large part by her enthusiasm for what lay ahead.

Although she had won over her parents, Jackson was anxious about the reaction in the black community. She was clearly one of the stars and had been throughout her childhood. There was pressure on such gifted individuals to support historically black colleges, yet here she was casting her lot with Ole Miss. On the one hand, it was a measure of how much had changed that she was invited, even wooed, to attend; on the other, what would it mean for schools like Jackson State if the best students went to predominantly white schools?

Jackson had to do what she thought was best for herself, hoping her success would prove her decision to be the right one. She was not only determined to succeed. Like so many white students, she hoped to make contacts at school that would help her later in life. She wanted to be part of the effective, far-flung network of Ole Miss alumni who looked out for their own, and she saw no reason that race should interfere with that goal.

By the time Jackson was a junior, she was president of the main campus women's organization, a member of several honorary organizations, a national board member of the Society of Professional Journalists, and a winner of academic honors with a 3.72 grade-point average. She was keenly aware of her achievements as a black student and told the *Mississippian* in one interview that she wanted to show that blacks "can achieve in a white culture and not lose all sensitivities in a white community." She also believed that she was evidence of the increasingly open doors, opening minds, and changing attitudes that were defining Ole Miss.

Jackson had already been a member of the homecoming court—a first for any black on campus—and given her other accomplishments, she thought at the start of her senior year that she was just the kind of candidate who could become the first black Miss Ole Miss, an honor voted by the student body based on leadership and service. It was the companion to Colonel Rebel, which Ben Williams had won four years earlier.

Jackson had shown "that I loved the university," as she put it to friends, and her activities demonstrated her leadership abilities. Her grades spoke for themselves. But to her chagrin, she was brought up short by race. It was hard to decide which was more upsetting: seeing one of her campaign posters defaced by the word *nigger,* or having white friends tell her on visits to dormitories and sororities that although they respected and liked her, they couldn't support her. It would be difficult, they said, for a black woman to represent Ole Miss to the state and the alumni.

Jackson did not win the election, and for one of the few times in her young life, she was deeply upset. She believed she had done everything that was required to win, yet she was unable to get over the final hurdle. Ben Williams had been more easily accepted as Colonel Rebel because he was an athlete, and in white minds athletics and entertainment had been accepted areas of achievement. Basic leadership and academics, however, were still new territory.

What was so painful for Jackson was the fact that friends were reluctant to support her. It would have been one thing if her opponents had been strangers who saw only a black woman, but here were fellow students she had worked and studied with who could not get beyond skin color.

It was a reminder of her first encounter with racism, a moment she knew every black child faced sooner or later. For her it was at age eight, when she was driving back to Clarksdale with her father from an afternoon outing on a hot summer day in 1967. Young Rose was desperate for an ice cream cone and begged her father to stop and get her one. He did so at the first roadside shop he saw, which was run by a white man. He approached the window and asked for a cone.

"We don't serve niggers," the man said.

Taken aback at first, Jackson paused, took a breath, put aside his pride, and asked, "May I take it from the back then? My daughter really wants some ice cream."

"We don't serve niggers," the man repeated.

"It's a shame that you don't," Jackson replied quietly before turning back to the car.

Rose could not understand why she didn't have her ice cream. Calmly, her father told her that the world was made up of all kinds of people, good and bad, and there were some of each in both races. That was the moment, she remembered, when he gave her the most important lesson for handling the racial insults he knew she would encounter later in life. An example of what her father meant came their way in a matter of minutes when they were pulled off the road by two white highway patrolmen who had obviously been contacted by the shop owner. One walked over to the window and told Jackson, "You don't talk back to a white man."

The potential for an ugly scene evaporated when the patrolman's partner came up to the car, saw a frightened Rose in the front seat, and told the other lawman, "Leave 'em alone. There's a child in the car."

In her most disappointing moment in Oxford, Jackson remembered her father's lesson. Individuals like Will Norton, a journalism professor and one of Jackson's teachers, helped her realize that his lesson was the right one. She considered Norton both friend and mentor and joked that he was her "great white father." After graduating, she would not make a professional move without his consultation or blessing. Norton had been so upset about a sorority's putting up a rival candidate for Miss Ole Miss just for the sake of opposition that he spoke about it in class. Rose was clearly the outstanding student on campus, he said, and deserved to be given the honor. To do so would enhance the university and demolish its image as a home for white racists.

After the election, Norton resigned himself to the fact that her defeat was an accurate reflection of campus sentiment. "The students just couldn't take that symbolic step to say, 'Ole Miss is not what your stereotype of it is.'"

Jackson's disappointment over the Miss Ole Miss contest was eased a few weeks later when Chancellor Fortune called and asked her to enter *Glamour* magazine's contest for the top ten women college students in the country. He wrote one of the supporting letters on her behalf.

In early April 1979 Jackson was notified that she had been selected as one of *Glamour's* honorees. She was featured in the August issue along with nine other young women. How ironic, she thought, that those who would not let her represent the school within the state would see her now as the university's representative on the much larger national stage. The administration, not surprisingly, couldn't have been happier. What better advertisement for their efforts, what better index of change at Ole Miss than Rose Jackson smiling on the pages of *Glamour*?

On matters of race, the campus was still taking one step forward and then one step back. A positive, ennobling moment, like the achievements and honors of Rose Jackson, could be followed by a conflict that threatened to split the university apart. It served as a constant reminder of the complexities inherent in bringing blacks and whites together in a world that was unraveling the mores and customs that had been created to keep them apart. There was no preprinted formula for this enterprise, and Fortune, like J. D. Williams before him, was the senior chemist in the living laboratory of Ole Miss. He knew the ingredients he was dealing with; he did not always know the proportions and could not predict when the volatile mix might explode.

One near-certain flashpoint was anything to do with Civil War icons and ceremony. For more than a century these had been woven into the fabric of Ole Miss—from the stained glass window honoring the University Greys to the memorial to the Confederate war dead to the Confederate flag and "Dixie." They were reminders of how the past shaped the present. The football team, in particular, served whites as a powerful link to bygone years even though by 1980 some two dozen players were black. One year, for example, the Ole Miss yearbook likened the team to the revered war heroes a century earlier: "Amidst a sea of Rebel flags waving to the strains of 'Dixie,' these Confederate Soldiers fight for the Gallant

Cause. . . . The Soldiers know that the Cause is not Lost," for each victory means "the Confederate troops rise again."

To the white students who wrote these words, such evocations were innocent reflections of pride mixed with a bit of literary license. They reflected the stories they had heard growing up about a valiant fight and the South's supreme will that was ultimately denied. These same words rang hollow to black students confident of their right to be at Ole Miss but still uncomfortable with so many allusions to a past that for them meant slavery and second-class citizenship at the hands of the whites their fellow students were honoring.

It was not surprising that a conflict arose when a group of students decided in the spring of 1979 that they wanted to have a horse for Colonel Rebel to ride at football games and that the animal should be named Traveller, in honor of Robert E. Lee's mount. The Fortune administration was uneasy about the Traveller option, fearing that it would stir up new unease among black students about Civil War memorabilia. Another flap about race would surely not help the university's image, and another allusion to the era of slavery would not help its recruiting.

Mississippian columnist David Robinson was incredulous at such concerns, wondering in one column how this could hurt a school "that is nicknamed after an ante-bellum plantation owner's wife, the Ole Miss, where athletic teams are called Rebels and where the band plays 'Dixie' while 40,000 fans wave Confederate battle flags." A native of Greenville and nurtured on the bold journalism of Hodding Carter's *Delta Democrat Times*—though admittedly more conservative than the moderate-to-liberal Carter—Robinson was typical of so many other whites who loved Ole Miss because of its traditions. He had learned about them as soon as he was old enough to learn anything. He had been destined for Oxford from the moment he was born. His birth announcement in the newsletter at his father's company listed his probable graduation date from the university, and he was one of dozens of freshmen in each incoming class who had considered themselves "Ole Miss students-in-waiting."

To them the Confederate symbolism was a source of pride linked to individuals who had fought to their death for what they believed in. "There is something about that sacrifice that needs to be honored and deserves to be honored," Robinson explained, and he resented the fact that someone wanted to deny him and like-minded classmates the right to observe their traditions, especially on a campus that put so much value on tradition. In that tradition, Robinson believed, was a sense of identity, "and any time you start denying tradition you lose your anchor, your identity. You lose your purpose."

Robinson found an almost fascistic cast to the criticism of naming the horse Traveller. He riled up black students with a second column that equated concerns over the animal to book burning and suggested that the school might be renamed "Medgar Evers University."

This was not about tradition, the black students countered, but racism. The symbols were its badges. "Now just think about it and tell me what significance does the rebel flag hold for the black man," wrote one in a challenge to Robinson. "Remembrance of suffering, years of bondage and working for the white man against our will, our women as bedwenches, and our men being beaten and whipped to death. You have your rebel flags, your segregated activities, the KKK on the rise and even Robert E. Lee's horse's namesake. I suppose you feel all you need now is us in chains."

The controversy threatened to erupt into something much more serious, but Fortune put a stop to it before matters escalated when he sold a horse that had been donated to the university for Colonel Rebel.

By the fall of 1981, the university's two major sports teams, the basketball and football squads, were well integrated, but the cheerleading squad was not. It had started to rankle the black students that they were not represented in this highly visible position even though so many of the athletes the crowd cheered on at football and basketball games were fellow black students. It was another reminder that their spheres of opportunity on campus still were limited.

Ole Miss was the only school in its athletic conference that still elected cheerleaders. The process seemed to have worked well, for the squad was regularly ranked among the top groups in the country. The prevailing sentiment was that it would be difficult for a black student to be elected cheerleader, not because of skill but because the election was really a popularity contest and black students were not involved in enough activities to make them well known across the campus. Jackson's quest to be

Miss Ole Miss, however, suggested a more troubling reason: a reluctance to elect blacks to positions that went to the core of the Old South pageantry so much a part of the university's ethos.

A group of white students wanted to change that. They were members of a special advisory committee that had been set up by the chancellor five years earlier to monitor racial issues on campus. It was called the Black Student Concerns Committee, the name reflecting the special status of these matters. One of the vice chancellors was a permanent member, and the faculty and student slots rotated each year.

By the spring of 1982 the group had come up with a new program to recruit blacks interested in cheerleading and to expand the training sessions before the final selection. Much of the work was spearheaded by Steve Ray, a senior from Tupelo who was head of the campus student government and a member of the committee. Ray was one of those white Mississippians destined for the university from childhood. Both parents, his sisters, his maternal grandfather, and an assortment of uncles had gone to Ole Miss, so the road out of Tupelo after high school led directly west into Oxford. Ray was too young to remember the *Brown* decision and just a toddler when Meredith entered the university, but he was just the right age to be part of Tupelo's school integration. The process had gone more smoothly than in other areas of the state. Part of it had to do with the decision by local leaders to integrate voluntarily rather than fight the process every step of the way. And part of it, Ray knew, was that the black population of Tupelo was smaller than in other cities and counties where white resistance to integration had been much more fierce.

When Ray got to Ole Miss, he could see that he was different from classmates who had left public school for private academies that had sprung up in the aftermath of court-ordered desegregation. He had never gone to a completely segregated school; they had never related to black individuals as peers or colleagues. The only blacks they had known had served them—cooks, gardeners, or maids.

Ray recognized the seriousness of the black students' concerns about the cheerleading squad and understood that an all-white group at this moment was detrimental to the university's standing as a whole. What's more, he realized that no black was going to be elected to the squad without a concerted effort.

By March 1982, the Black Student Concerns Committee was pleased to learn that four black students were taking part in the clinics to train for the final competition. Among them was John Hawkins, a junior from Water Valley (and coincidentally a cousin of Dottie Chapman). Living barely fifteen miles from Oxford, Hawkins had always known about Ole Miss. Now he could think of it as an option for himself. He had fine credentials: good grades, star athlete, and band member—one of the few to be invited to a statewide summer camp for outstanding student musicians. He had to audition to be accepted.

By the time he graduated from high school in the spring of 1979, Hawkins had decided that there were two important things about the immediate future: to stay close to home (he was the third of nine children) and to get a good education. So when Ole Miss recruited him, he paid attention, pushing aside the slight disappointment that he had been recruited for academic reasons, not for the basketball team. It was more a matter of pride than the desire to play, for even if he had been offered a sports scholarship, he knew by now that he wanted to concentrate on academics and participate in as many campus activities as possible. An older sister had started college, but she dropped out, so Hawkins was even more determined to do well as the first in his family to get a college degree.

Like Steve Ray, Hawkins had spent most of his schooling in an integrated setting, but he understood the racial boundaries that still remained. He played sports with many white friends and sat next to them in class, but at day's end, everyone went back to his own home environment. He thought of that time as "integrated but segregated," but it helped prepare him for Ole Miss. Nearly twenty years after Meredith, the university was still not a hospitable place for blacks to attend, but as the recruiters had said, Ole Miss was the place to go for the best education and the chance to connect with future leaders.

As a member of the Black Student Concerns Committee, Hawkins was well aware of the effort to integrate the cheerleading squad. He knew there was a shortage of black men available because virtually all of them with the requisite athletic skill were already playing football or basketball for the university. He had no thoughts of trying out until he learned of the efforts of a black classmate, Clara Bibbs.

She had tried out for the squad the previous year but had not been chosen. Her friends thought she didn't have the right partner, so Hawkins agreed to help out. His mission was to maximize her chances of getting elected, not to get a spot himself. "I'm doing this because I want you to live your dream," he told her.

Hawkins and Bibbs worked diligently in the clinics and on their routines. They made it through the trial stages and into the final competition, when a slate of the top men and women was presented to the student body and voted on. In the past the top five men and women vote getters were named to the ten-member squad. But as a result of the advisory committee's work, the squad was expanded to twelve—six men and six women.

By this time Hawkins was fairly well known around campus. He had been active in the Black Student Union, had played in the band for a year, and he had gotten involved in student government. More important he had the backing of a group of white students, led by Ray and Allison Brown, head of the campus women's organization, who were working very hard to help both Hawkins and Bibbs. Brown wanted to make sure they knew how to campaign on a campus that had its own political network, and she made it a point to give them entrée into the fraternity and sorority houses whose members would turn out and vote.

Brown disagreed with the notion that a majority-white campus would not elect a black cheerleader. Rather, she believed that it was unfortunate though true that black students did not know how to play the system. If they put together a solid campaign strategy, they could win. "That was our little challenge," she explained. "We said it was not impossible."

The campus election was April 22, 1982. Brown's prophesy proved correct. To Hawkins's surprise, he was elected. To his chagrin, Clara Bibbs was not.

By virtue of breaking one more racial barrier at Ole Miss, Hawkins's election was a news event, and by day's end a number of reporters were on campus to interview him. One wanted to know whether there would be any problem having a white partner, an obvious reference to the volatile issue of racial-sexual taboos. Hawkins said no. This is "a new age and the time has passed for prejudice." An interracial cheerleading couple would pose no problems on the squad, "and only old-fashioned people wouldn't accept a black cheerleader, and I pity them."

In fact, the transition for Hawkins and his eventual partner, Laura Smith, went smoothly, although they had to find private places to practice because people were so curious about a very visible interracial partnership. Smith asked that they be left alone to hone their skills, and while she adjusted to the extra attention that was focused on them, Hawkins knew their partnership was not easy for her father. "He has to go to the country club and hear his friends say 'there's a black guy holding your daughter with his hand under her dress'—it's not something he looks forward to." And the squad captain made sure the two were rarely, if ever, photographed during their stunts when national newspapers came to write about the university.

Though Smith always described her partnership with Hawkins as an easy and amicable one, she declined to talk about that period fourteen years later except to say that people got along fine at Ole Miss when they were left alone. Another of the questions to Hawkins during that hectic postelection time was whether he would, as the first black cheerleader, honor tradition and wave the rebel flag.

"The answer is no. I will not," Hawkins replied.

From that point on, his life changed. Unlike Coolidge Ball or Ben Williams, who could privately ignore the sea of Confederate flags around them, Hawkins had no such cover for a symbol he found at odds with his heritage, for his job was to run out onto the field with an oversized banner and stir up the crowd. Standing his ground, he knew, would mean stepping on sacred tradition, and even more important, publicly demonstrating that something very fundamental had changed about Ole Miss. It was no longer the homestead of white Mississippi. Or as the *Clarion Ledger* put it, "an anachronistic tradition linking Ole Miss symbolically to the Confederacy and the system of white supremacy will have been subtly but irrevocably compromised."

Not everyone had looked at the flag with such charged history in mind. Many students and alumni considered it a manifestation of school spirit, something they had grown up with when their parents brought them up to Oxford to go to football games. It represented their first memories of Ole Miss—sweet, fun, and most of all innocent. In their minds it had to do with school spirit, not racial attacks. They were, in a word, reluctant to make the cultural accommodations blacks believed were necessary to make diversity work.

William Ray, who had just succeeded Steve Ray as head of the student government, was brought up short by Hawkins's action. He had always waved a flag at football games and hadn't given it a second thought. But the controversy changed his mind, not only because it could offend one portion of the university but, Ray realized, it was not good for Ole Miss. Regardless of the intent of students and alumni, he came to understand, use of the flag "subjects the school to intense bad feelings among a big part of the world."

The William Rays were very likely in the majority, but they were drowned out by the angry voices of those who subscribed to the *Clarion Ledger*'s view of a "compromised" history. Their reactions were an ugly throwback to the time of Meredith. The door of Hawkins's dorm room was set on fire; graffiti appeared around campus calling him a "nigger"; he received harassing telephone calls and one or two death threats; pranksters poured buckets of water in the hallway near his room so that it flooded, forcing Hawkins to move out. Eventually he went to his fraternity, Phi Beta Sigma, one of the several black Greek organizations that by now had chapters on the campus. What galled him the most, however, was the pressure one angry white tried to put on his father, a factory worker in Water Valley. The man called the senior Hawkins and told him that if his son valued the elder Hawkins's job, he would "stop this nonsense."

Before the first football game, Hawkins attempted to quell any further controversy by holding a news conference. "It has not been written anywhere that an Ole Miss cheerleader has to wave a flag," Hawkins said to reporters from state and national news outlets, the presence of the latter one more indication of how loudly racial conflict resonated at Ole Miss. "While I'm an Ole Miss cheerleader I'm still a black man. In my household I wasn't told to hate the flag," he continued, "but I did have history classes and know what my ancestors went through and what the Rebel flag represents. It is my choice that I prefer not to wave one."

Hawkins's position on the flag prompted debate about changing the banner so that it would still represent Ole Miss yet not conjure up so much controversial history, but even the mere suggestion brought dozens of angry calls and letters to the chancellor's office. A few were particularly hostile, reflecting a discomfort at the fact that Ole Miss was even integrated. Lawyer John C. McLaurin of Brandon, Mississippi, chided Fortune that "a negro boy is now running the university. By now he has probably moved you out of the Chancellor's home and is now occupying it himself. If he doesn't like the times and places for the games to be played, he will change that, too." When Hawkins was elected cheerleader, McLaurin went on, "he knew that the Confederate flag was displayed. Why, then is he allowed to dictate the change? . . . Maybe we should just give the university to the blacks and start anew in another direction." After signing his name, McLaurin added this postcript: "Does the new king know who his daddy is?"

Football coach Steve Sloan had contributed to the debate when he told the *Clarion Ledger* before the season opened that he favored modifying the flag in some way so that it was unique to Ole Miss. He acknowledged that the symbol, along with the ritual playing of "Dixie," created distractions for his team and was an often an impediment to recruiting good football players. But when they did come, he insisted they were "extremely happy here." The problem remained the school's image. "It's somewhat our fault," he admitted, "because we stay vulnerable."

A cartoon in a newspaper the next day underscored this point: Colonel Rebel leaning nonchalantly on a walking stick, but with one leg chained to a ball. On the front of the ball was the distinctive stars and bars of the Confederate flag.

A few days after Sloan's remarks, the *Mississippian* devoted most of the editorial page to the subject. Editor Paul Crutcher admitted that he had been worried before the first game that there might be trouble in the stadium, but then he realized his concerns were groundless. He made an important point about the views of the vast majority of white students: This was not 1962, but 1982, and "attitudes had changed." "I knew that there had been no campus uproars over Hawkins' decision from the students who elected him in April—no bonfires had been built, no demonstrations had been staged, and no shots had been fired." Students were more concerned about whether Ole Miss won than "about who waved what flag."

Next to Crutcher's editorial was a personal plea from history professor David Sansing to change the flag. "The use of the rebel flag as a spirit symbol has created a dilemma for many people who love Ole Miss. It has for me," Sansing wrote. "I have never waved a rebel flag at a football game because I have not been able to separate and sort out all the other things the flag, through no fault of its own, symbolizes. I have often wished that our flag, the Ole Miss flag, which I love and cherish according to my own definition, could be modified in some way to free it, to pare it, to disassociate it from those sentiments and philosophies and images that it sometimes conjures in my mind."

He understood and appreciated that waving the flag had no racial connotations to most of the students in the stands, recalling one young woman who told him she had been waving the same flag her father had given her when she was just five years old—and she planned to continue doing so. White Ole Miss students with "few exceptions, think of the flag in its present shape and configuration only as a spirit symbol of the University of Mississippi," Sansing wrote. "But it is not."

Despite the intense discussion—or perhaps because of the strong and sharp response from alumni—the flag remained unchanged. But the controversy was not over, just in abeyance.

For his part, Hawkins was doing his best to be both normal student and good cheerleader, trying not to let the pressure affect him. He had alerted Fortune about the harassment he was encountering, and although the chancellor never did anything publicly to put a stop to such activities, Hawkins knew that university security personnel were quietly watching out for him to make sure he was not harmed.

Privately, Fortune was plenty worried about the flag issue. He was trying to walk a careful line between maintaining his authority on campus and riling up angry alumni who would treat any change in the flag as a personal affront. Most disturbing were calls from people he considered long-time friends who told him, "Porter, if you do anything to the flag, I'll never speak to you again." He confided to Sansing that if he was getting this kind of pressure, "what must John be going through?"

Hawkins did not face these difficult weeks alone. His fraternity brothers and friends in the Black Student Union also took care to protect him, moving him to what they called a "safe house" the morning of game days and then escorting him to the football stadium to join the rest of the squad.

The intensity of the reaction to his personal decision had been a surprise to Hawkins, and it troubled him that he was being portrayed by some whites as a troublemaker and a maverick. He was distressed enough about such comments that he wrote a guest column for the *Mississippian* to explain his views. "I am in no way a racist or a radical person. . . . But I am a person who believes in what is right," he wrote. His choice of Ole Miss was deliberate, he said, a choice he hoped would be "a university I would be proud to call my alma mater and a place that I would be happy to call my home."

His refusal to wave the rebel flag, he said, was not a revolt against the school but an effort to highlight the unfairness of the university's subsidizing a symbol—by paying for and helping distribute the flags—that were not used by black students and offended them. Black students wanted to care about the university and feel that it was a place they could belong. Being surrounded by the symbols of a white supremacist society worked against that.

Adding fuel to the flag controversy was a decision by the Ku Klux Klan to stage a demonstration in Oxford the last week in October to show its support for the Confederate flag and hold a recruitment drive. On the day of the demonstration twenty-nine Klan members staged a short march in the center of town, most of them dressed in full regalia: white robes, hoods (a few wore masks), and carrying large Confederate flags. About 450 people gathered at the square to watch the spectacle. There they heard Grand Dragon Gordon Galle tell them whites must unite, blacks should be sent back to Africa, and school integration should be stopped.

Will Norton was there and took the moment to observe the reactions of some of his students. He could tell by the expressions on their faces that this was the first time they had made the connection between the Klan and the rebel flag. The shock of understanding was palpable. Some would no longer wave the flag in the spirited atmosphere of the Ole Miss stadium. Others would find a way to distance themselves from the darker purposes on display that afternoon and return to their own personal traditions.

The event was peaceful and well covered by the media. Photographers nearly outnumbered the marchers and had an easy time shooting the event. Klan members were more than willing to be photographed. The young man working for the *Mississipian* and the yearbook had no idea that the pictures he took that balmy October Saturday would reverberate on campus six months later.

Hawkins, meanwhile, made it through the football and basketball season without incident, never wavering from his initial position on the flag. But at the end of March 1983, after the last basketball game, he decided he had had enough. He announced that he would not try out for another year, explaining simply, "I just don't want to."

The twentieth anniversary of Meredith's admission to Ole Miss had come in the midst of the fall controversy over the flag. It was a moment university officials wished they could have ignored. "Why celebrate a riot in which two people were killed?" wondered Charles Noyes, one of Fortune's top assistants and the man who wrote virtually all of his important speeches and other communications.

But months before the September 30 anniversary, Fortune and his aides understood that even if they wanted to let the moment pass unnoticed, others were going to pay attention. The anniversary had become a common benchmark for measuring how far the university had come on race, and twenty years seemed a particularly good vantage point. The chancellor's office had already gotten media requests for information as far back as the winter of 1981. Administrators decided the better course of action was to put together their own program with an agenda of progress, not struggle.

The university's success in attracting black students was obvious—by 1980 there were 688 on a campus of 8,900—more than double the enrollment of 316 black students six years earlier. And black students were now participating in a wide range of campus activities. The faculty picture, however, was more dismal. There had been only one black professor until 1974, when there were three. But by 1981 there were only 7 on a faculty of 424—the lowest ratio of the major southern universities.

The reasons were no surprise to Bela Chain, the university's affirmative action officer and the individual most responsible for making sure the university complied with federal mandates to desegregate. They boiled down to the history of racial prejudice in the state and university—so many people viewed Ole Miss "as one step shy of the Klan," Chain lamented—and competition from other institutions. The pool of black professionals, admittedly growing, was still relatively small, and there were intense efforts by schools around the region to bring more blacks onto their campuses. The university had only so much money and on many occasions could not compete in salary or put together an attractive enough package, such as research opportunities or the promise of program development, to woo a candidate.

On top of that was the location. Oxford was a small town with its certain charms, but there was not a large black professional population where faculty members could find comfortable camaraderie outside of their academic lives, and Memphis, the nearest big city, was roughly two hours away by car.

It was a source of disappointment to the faculty recruiters that they had such a hard time even finding interested individuals. By the mid-1970s, the school was advertising openings in traditionally black publications and at predominantly black institutions and in professional journals, but the results were dismal. When there was some interest, it was hard to close the deal. Chain remembered the case of one woman who was recruited but nearly stopped the process without even coming to Oxford. Her son had begged her not to go south, worried that she would not be well treated. She was impressed with the university when she finally saw it but elected to take an offer elsewhere.

Chain knew the university was behind its projections. Indeed in one report to the board of trustees, the administration had predicted that by 1979 there would be thirty-seven minority faculty members, but in fact there were only eighteen.

The lawsuit filed in 1974 by disgruntled black students had finally been settled in the spring of 1980 after languishing in federal court nearly six years. The terms were revelatory. The university agreed to keep up its recruiting efforts for students and faculty, and it agreed that it would no longer use a minimum cutoff score on the law school aptitude test or weight a grade-point average from one university higher than another—a subtle way of saying that an A from Jackson State or Alcorn should be considered the same as an A from Ole Miss or Mississippi State. The law school also promised to make sure tutors were available for black students needing assistance to help ensure their completion of the three-year program.

The agreement contained one other paragraph alluding to the difficulties of finding minority faculty willing to come to Oxford. It stated the university's promise to "vigorously continue" efforts to have black visiting professors every summer "so long as needed to attract black applicants for professorial positions."

Fortune understood that an assessment of the twenty years since Meredith would have some down sides, but he believed that the progress on race far outweighed the setbacks. He also knew that the decision to commemorate the event would not be universally well received around the state.

Within days of the announcement of the twentieth-anniversary program, angry letters streamed into his office, revealing a bitterness many had thought passed long ago. One of the more vivid protests came from Jackson lawyer Richard Barrett: "Ludicrous as it may sound, I sincerely believe that celebrating the birthday of Benedict Arnold or, perhaps, the burning of Atlanta would rank higher than 'celebrating' such an event that slaps the face of every Mississippian who still holds constitutional government and educational excellence as a heritage worthy to pass on and to fight for."

Enough angry letters came into the chancellor's office that Noyes created a stock response for Fortune's reply. "First of all," began one of the key paragraphs, "we are not paying tribute to him [Meredith] in any way. Our intention is strictly to stress the progress that has occurred in our state and at Ole Miss during the past 20 years." Because of the many media requests well in advance of the event, Fortune went on, "it became evident to us at an early date that these reporters would be placing a great deal of emphasis on James Meredith and on the events of 20 years ago and that the University might be pictured in an unfavorable light by these reports. In an effort to take the emphasis away from James Meredith and the events of 20 years ago, we felt we should plan a positive program that would stress the enormous progress that has been made during the

20-year period and would show the rest of the world not only our progress but also the accomplishments of some of the blacks who have graduated from the University of Mississippi."

The line-up of individuals by itself, Fortune concluded, would be evidence of change, among them William Winter, "our progressive governor," a description well accepted across the South, and Dr. Robert W. Harrison, a black dentist from Yazoo City, who was president of the board of trustees.

In these letters Fortune also criticized some of the stories that had already been written about the university, stories "probing into the past and printing negative statements that . . . have rekindled fires of prejudice and intolerance that have been dormant for years." Fortune's concerns were understandable, but his observation about the dormancy of prejudice and intolerance was a dubious one, particularly in light of the harassment and intimidation John Hawkins had endured for his stand on the rebel flag. Both were evidence that the fires of prejudice and intolerance still smoldered.

The twentieth anniversary was cause for rumination not just by outside parties but within the university as well, particularly in the *Mississippian* and in a special issue of the Ole Miss magazine put out under the auspices of a journalism class taught by Willie Morris, the well-known native son who was writer-in-residence. Morris had written his own two-page essay to commemorate the event for *Time* magazine, reflecting on the university's transition and the changes in his "beautiful and tragic and bewitched state."

But it was the white students' writings that were particularly instructive as they grappled with history while trying to assess progress and their own feelings about the world they were living in. *Mississippian* editor Crutcher was one of those self-described Ole Miss students-in-waiting. His grandfather was former chancellor J. D. Williams, and Crutcher grew up thinking of the campus as his own playground. Countless weekend afternoons were spent running through the Grove and playing with his grandfather at the chancellor's residence. Going to Ole Miss was as natural for Crutcher as getting up in the morning. He assessed the twenty years between Meredith's admission and the present from an insider's view, given his many visits with his grandfather, and an admitted perspective of privilege—he had gone to a well-established private school, Marshall County Academy, in nearby Holly Springs.

In an editorial in the September 30 *Mississippian,* Crutcher was both proud and impatient—proud of what he believed had been progress over two decades amply demonstrated by statistics that showed a growing black enrollment at the school, the success of Ole Miss black graduates in a variety of fields, and increasing involvement of blacks in all phases of life in Mississippi. He conceded that things were not perfect, but they were improving. He was impatient with critics who refused to concede that things had gotten better. Look at the most recent controversy on campus, he wrote; it is over the flag. Listening to his grandfather remind him of racial attitudes twenty years earlier and "the physical violence they sometimes spawned and the ugliness they represented, I begin to believe one thing—we must have come a long way in race relations in Mississippi if the biggest problem we have to address these days is who waves what flag at a football game."

Allison Brown, editor of the special Ole Miss magazine, offered a different take in a long editorial anchoring the publication. She wrote of the students' journey back into history to learn the story for themselves even in the face of critics who wondered—as they had at the ten-year anniversary—"Why are you dredging this up?"

Recalling her own integrated schooling from fifth grade on in Pascagoula's public schools, she concluded on a note of optimism: "We are of a generation that knows first hand that blacks and whites can actually work together, grow up together and share common experiences. We all know deep down that it is just plain wrong to look at people purely on the basis of their skin color. The hardest thing is admitting it. Even at Ole Miss, where tradition hangs on until the very last thread, much progress has been made."

The theme of the twentieth-anniversary commemoration, coordinated by Vice Chancellor Lucius Williams, was "Inspiration to Achieve." The centerpiece of the event was a black alumni reunion that stretched over three days and included the first awards given to black graduates of distinction. Among them were Reuben Anderson, the first black law school graduate; Cleveland Donald, the second black student to graduate; basketball player Coolidge Ball; and Rose Jackson.

Fortune opened the ceremonies with a careful presentation—words painstakingly crafted by Noyes to set the right tone: "It is an insult to the language to say that we are 'celebrating' what happened 20 years ago. We are commemorating the opening of this university to black students, and pausing to look at ourselves and to be looked at."

James Meredith was not the keynote speaker—that honor belonged to Margaret Alexander, a prize-winning black novelist who was professor emeritus at Jackson State—but he was the emotional center of the commemoration. Administrators held their breath before Meredith's speech. What would this occasionally prickly and mercurial man say at a moment of maximum exposure? They had to envy fellow administrators a few hundred miles away in Georgia, whose first black students, Hamilton Holmes and Charlayne Hunter, were much more conventional, much less threatening to whites than Meredith. Holmes was a distinguished physician, Hunter a nationally known journalist. But it was also true that Georgia was not Mississippi, and it had to have been someone cut from a different cloth to withstand what Meredith had endured—and he had done it alone. Rose Jackson would remind classmates of this when they complained among one another that Meredith had not been more of a leader or mentor to them.

The first part of Meredith's speech to a packed Fulton Chapel was a call for the "reunification of all back people" and a plea to support black African countries. Then he turned to Ole Miss. Though much remained to be done, Meredith said, the university "was still the best place in the state for blacks to get the best possible education. The black leaders of Mississippi will come from the University of Mississippi in the future and I strongly recommend to every black high school student in Mississippi that they put the University of Mississippi at the top of their list of prospective colleges that they want to attend."

Meredith then said that the Confederate flag, Colonel Rebel, and "Dixie" "must be removed as school symbols and songs. There is absolutely no difference between these symbols and the segregation signs of twenty years ago such as White Only Waiting Room, Colored Drinking

Water . . . and so forth." If the university did not take action, Meredith said, he would recommend that the NAACP file a lawsuit to force these changes.

These comments were near the end of Meredith's remarks, and about this time, a large group of white students got up from their seats and walked out. Once outside, they started to sing "Dixie" and go through the well-known "hotty toddy" football cheer that ends "Who the hell are we? . . . Ole Miss by damn."

As the audience filed out of the chapel, a number of black students were visibly upset by the white students' departure and their subsequent actions. David Sansing knew the situation could get out of control and worried that visiting reporters might exploit the tense moment and make matters worse. With help from two colleagues, he told the crowd that everyone should go over to the Ole Miss Student Union, just a few hundred yards away, and sit down and talk with each other—not at each other, he said, but to each other. For the next two hours they did just that, taking turns saying what was on their minds about race, the past, the present, and the campus.

Sansing knew that only the ones who were willing to listen and learn had responded to his suggestion, but for the moment he was optimistic that there had at least been some dialogue. "I have never been as proud of Ole Miss students as I was then," he remembered. That moment of good feeling was going to give way to another racially tense episode before the academic year was over, but those in the Ole Miss community had learned that it was important to embrace the positive moments of racial interchange—if for no other reason than having a cushion for whatever new hostility was on the horizon.

The dialogue that had started in the Union continued on the pages of the *Mississippian*. Despite some angry exchanges, there was an overall tone that was more conciliatory than confrontational, typified by one of Crutcher's columns. "We can either go on trading punches to show each other who is right and who is wrong," he wrote, "or we can begin to find some common ground upon which we may stand, and from there proceed to the realization of progress—in our schools, in our jobs and in our lives. . . . We cannot afford to be apathetic or gutless, for it is only through us that real progress will be made."

When the twentieth-anniversary celebration was completed, Lucius Williams prepared a report for Fortune outlining what had been accomplished. In addition to the Inspiration to Achieve program, there had been a symposium on media coverage of Ole Miss, a folklife festival in downtown Oxford, and a three-day symposium at the law school, "Law and Social Change," that featured Reuben Anderson and Meredith's lawyer, Constance Baker Motley.

"It was a major accomplishment just to be able to review such a controversial event," Williams wrote. Furthermore attendance at all events— roughly 11,200 (almost 9,000 at the folklife festival)—illustrated the interest in the observance. Some twenty states were represented. Overall, Williams continued, "a more positive image of Ole Miss and the State of Mississippi has emerged nationally," apparent, he said, from comments by the national media following coverage of the event.

But the observance served another less appealing purpose. University and state officials "were keenly re-awakened," Williams said, "to some of the problems that remain to be solved." Avid segregationists reemerged to challenge the notion of rights for black citizens, and, he noted, the university received more than seven hundred negative letters and telephone calls relating to the anniversary commemoration. They presaged another difficult episode that was just around the corner.

One of the traditions in the last month of the academic year was the release of the yearbook, the *Ole Miss*. The editor for the 1982–1983 book was John Hall, a native of Meridian who considered editing the yearbook the achievement of an important goal. Since the day he had arrived in Oxford, Hall had wanted to be the editor by the time he was a senior, and he had planned his activities and his academic life in the previous three years to make that dream come true.

Hall came from a family that believed in the public schools and supported integration. When it finally came to Meridian—Hall was in fourth grade—he and his family gave no thought to his leaving for a private academy. Because enough other families felt the way the Halls did, integration in this east Mississippi city was accomplished with relative calm.

Hall knew he was headed to Ole Miss—his father, a brother, a sister, and many friends had attended—but he deferred his entrance for a year, deciding instead to travel with Up with People, the musical group that promotes cultural understanding and, coincidentally, the group performing in Fulton Chapel in 1970 when black students staged their protest. The year offered Hall a chance to visit Europe and to be part of an integrated group of young people; he felt the experience broadened his horizons literally, because of the group's itinerary, and figuratively, given the makeup of the organization.

By the time he was elected yearbook editor, Hall considered himself as qualified as anyone else to put together a publication that would reflect the important and sometimes difficult events of the previous year. He was especially pleased, indeed thrilled, that Willie Morris had agreed to write an essay to open the annual about Ole Miss and the university's passage through the academic year. It would introduce the editor's section, a dozen or so pages whose content was completely within Hall's discretion.

Ole Miss, Morris wrote, "is a subtle blend of everything the Deep South was and is"—the rebel flags, young white sorority girls "who at age twenty-one will marry in their Delta weddings." All this, he said, "is the best and worst of an older South which has survived into a new age. Many of the white students live the most sheltered of lives. Their proximity with the young blacks of Ole Miss seems both mystifying and exhilarating. . . . It is a different age," Morris concluded, "yet much remains the same."

In the editor's section, Hall had chosen to include coverage of Hawkins's election as cheerleader, the twentieth-anniversary commemoration, important sports events, and the Klan march in Oxford. Six pictures of the Klan were included in the section, one of them nearly a full page and another, filling a half-page, showing a young black child staring uneasily at the hooded man a few feet away. Excerpts from Morris's essay framed the pictures; for this one, it was his observation that "a sense of history, of the pride and despair of Mississippi, is here as it always has been."

Although Morris had written an essay that was inside the annual, Hall had written his own comments that were on the dust jacket of the book. The observations, while perceptive, came unmistakably from a white perspective. "This has been a year of challenged traditions at Ole Miss," Hall wrote. "Students and alumni have been forced to forfeit a part of their culture in the name of harmony, progress, and compromise. Some people ask why we have a change while others ask why it has taken so long. The fact is whether we like it or not, Ole Miss has changed in 1983." He ended on a note of optimism: "Black and white—we live together here—a crucial difference that separates us from other places. All racial problems have not been worked out, but when they are, I believe the South will be the place where it happens."

Hall was anxious for the annuals to arrive and was pleasantly surprised when they were shipped to the campus early in April 1983, several days ahead of schedule. He had not given much thought to his own section after putting it to bed, and it was only after a student, one of the more conservative whites, had picked up his copy, saw the several Klan pictures, and came up to tell Hall, "Way to go," that a sinking feeling came over him. He suddenly realized that his effort—to show how the rebel flag takes on a different meaning when held by a Klansman—might not be understood in that vein. Here was someone who suggested he was applauding the Klan, and Hall was heartsick at the thought.

Right then he expected there would be controversy. Within a day the Black Student Union lodged a formal protest. The Klan march, which had been in Oxford and not on the campus, was not a university activity, they said, and had no business in the annual. To put it there for whatever reason gave the group free publicity and tarnished the image of the school. It would be unpleasant to say the least, several said, to take their yearbook back home and have their families open it up, only to see pictures of robed men and women holding Confederate flags. It conjured up a terrible history. Lydia Spragin, head of the Black Student Union, said Hall had the right to mention the Klan march but not in so much detail. "You have an eight-by-ten [picture] you can take out and frame," she exclaimed, referring to the full-page picture of several men in full Klan regalia.

Adding to the tense atmosphere was a petition drive underway since the beginning of April to require the university to recognize the rebel flag formally as a school symbol. A proposal submitted to the student governing body was reminiscent in its language of Chancellor Hume's emotional defense of the university a half-century earlier, pleading that his sacred shrine stay in Oxford. The latter-day resolution asked that the flag, Colonel Rebel, and "Dixie" "remain our endeared traditions until the stones crumble from the buildings and Ole Miss is a mere whisper in history. We submit that a University which betrays its traditions is a University not worth the respect of its students, prospective students or former students."

John Hall, however unsuccessfully, had tried to use the annual to show that tradition is subject to interpretation, but he didn't fully appreciate that interpretation is almost always shaped by context. Because so much of the criticism was directed at him, Hall wanted to address black students directly. He did so at a tense two-hour meeting the evening of April 11. "My intent with these photos was to show white people how black students at Ole Miss perceive the Rebel flag," he said to a chorus of boos and catcalls that interrupted his comments. "The symbol jumps to the other side of the spectrum when placed with a hood. I certainly didn't mean to offend black students. . . . When I look at the photo of the klansman with the Rebel flag, it turns my stomach in knots."

Only later, upon painful reflection, did Hall realize that he had been presumptuous in assuming that he could somehow make other whites understand what he believed to be a black perspective. He was devastated that the entire annual, the prose of Willie Morris included, had been reduced in so many people's minds to six pictures.

The black students may have admired Hall's willingness to speak to them directly, but they were not satisfied with his explanation and apology. As distressing to Hall, none of them would speak to him privately about the issue—not even black students he had considered his friends through their classes and work on other campus activities together. He had sought to promote understanding. Instead, he had polarized. Equally distressing was the lack of support from white friends and the administration. Fortune's aides had little to say except to complain about the problems the entire matter was causing the university.

For someone who had been a campus leader, a member of the Hall of Fame, and an Ole Miss star, Hall had never felt so isolated. The conflict literally made him sick, robbing him of sleep as he waited for morning to come each day so he could buy the newspaper and see what new criticism was being leveled at him and the annual. He was determined to stick it out on his own, however, and while he immediately shipped a book to his parents so they could see firsthand what prompted the brouhaha, he told them to stay put in Meridian. He knew that if he could survive the ordeal, it would be good training for whatever came later in life.

Only Will Norton, the journalism professor, told Hall he had done the right thing in featuring the Klan march. Though it wasn't much solace at the time, Norton told the shaken young man that years from now, he would be proved right in trying to illustrate the events that had shaped the year. As a former practicing journalist, Norton himself was surprised at the reaction to the annual. In the darkest days of Mississippi's history, he had thought that the closed circle of power that controlled politics, law enforcement, and the press had contributed to violence against blacks. It was rarely discussed, hardly ever condemned. Norton believed it was a step forward to shine a light on extremists, not realizing, as Hall had not understood, that the black community could see any publicity about the Klan as a glorification.

John Hawkins, who was about to succeed Spragin as head of the Black Student Union, suggested that black students could ask for a refund of their student fees that had helped pay for the annual; other BSU members suggested burning the annuals.

When David Sansing heard about the possible book burning, he was aghast. He rushed to find Hawkins and implored him not to go forward. "You don't want an image of black people burning books," he told him. "That kind of thing is what dictators and demogogues have done throughout history."

In fact, BSU members did not go through with any book burning. It was just one of many ideas tossed around in the tense moments. Adding to the chaos was angry white reaction. On Friday, April 15, carloads of white students waving Confederate flags drove through the campus shouting, "Save the flag." Some scrawled racial slurs on elevator walls and bulletin boards in dorms that housed a number of the black students.

By Monday, April 18, with rumors of book burning still rampant, more than a thousand white students gathered in front of the Lyceum for their own protest. Shouting racial epithets and "Hell no the flag won't go," the group marched through campus looking for Spragin and Hawkins. They finally made their way to his fraternity house yelling, "We want John. We want John," though Hawkins was not at the house.

By the time he made his way there, he could not believe what he was seeing or hearing. All he could think was, "This is a damn lynch mob." He and his fraternity brothers remained calm until the Oxford police dispersed the crowd. But the scene was uncomfortably reminiscent of the ugly reception that had greeted Meredith two decades earlier. It was a sobering reminder of how race was still a flashpoint, of how much room there was for misunderstanding even among individuals of good will who only months earlier, on the anniversary of Meredith's arrival, had been talking publicly about the need to find common ground. The mystic chords of memory, in Abraham Lincoln's apt phrase, rang constantly at Ole Miss, and this was one of the most dissonant moments in years.

The next day, April 19, some two hundred black students staged a brief and peaceful counterdemonstration in front of the Lyceum. The group recited the Lord's Prayer and sang "We Shall Overcome" and "We Shall Not Be Moved," two songs associated with the civil rights movements twenty years earlier, and then they dispersed.

Although Chancellor Fortune was a target of demonstrators on both sides of the issue, he was at an educators' meeting in Texas and had to rely on reports of the incidents through his aides. They counseled him to get back to Oxford as soon as possible. He returned to the campus the evening of the nineteenth.

Fortune had been well aware of the escalating controversy over the flag, and he had asked a group of colleagues to give him ideas about what to do. He realized now that he had to act promptly. Sansing and Willie Morris were among the small group of professors who had been drafting proposals for Fortune, and the two spent much of the evening of April 19 riding around Oxford putting additional touches on a statement they had already sent to the chancellor's office. Morris was looking for a personal touch to enliven the drier recitation of history and policy.

By midmorning April 20, the chancellor was ready to make a public presentation. He decided to issue the statement in a closed setting to news reporters and take no questions. "This flag has never been adopted by the University as an official symbol of this institution," Fortune said. Its identification with Ole Miss started in the 1950s and resulted from national television coverage of football games. "However, the shaping of public perceptions is a complicated process. The coverage of racial violence by the national news media, and especially television, planted in the American mind the image of this flag at scenes of racial conflict. Many see the flag as a vestige of an earlier and troubled era. . . . It seems self-evident to me that the integrity of this or any other great university, cannot rest upon the outcome of a public debate over the nuances of the symbols associated with that university," he went on. "A university cannot be accountable for the imputations of a continuing public controversy. It is time that the University of Mississippi disassociate itself from the debate over what various symbols might mean to various groups and individuals."

Only those symbols registered by the university would be given official sanction, he explained. The rebel flag was not an official symbol of the school and would not be used by official representatives of the university. Fortune added that he had no authority to ban the use and display of the rebel flag by individuals because that would be infringement of free expression. But even with this disclaimer, the chancellor's decision confirmed for many whites what John Hall had expressed so clearly on the jacket of the controversial yearbook: "Students and alumni have been forced to forfeit a part of their culture in the name of harmony, progress and compromise."

Fortune ended his statement with a personal appeal for calm and understanding from present and former students—largely Morris's addition from the previous night. He spoke of his love for Mississippi and the university, and then he observed that "the young whites and blacks at Ole Miss spring from a shared heritage, and I plead with them both to respond to the better side of our nature, as Mississippians always have." The use of *heritage* had been inapt. Black and white Mississippians had a shared history, but they had a deeply divided heritage. The very controversy Fortune was trying to quell was proof of that. In a subtle request to alumni, who numbered among the most ardent flag wavers, the chancellor added, "I plead, too, with our older Mississippians to aid us in our quest for a better Mississippi."

When Fortune was finished, he left quickly for a college board meeting in Jackson. A group of testy white students milling around outside calmed down when Sansing read a copy of Fortune's statement and stayed to answer questions.

The practical effect of Fortune's decision meant that cheerleaders would no longer carry flags onto the field, the university would no longer buy the small flags that cheerleaders had tossed into the stands at football games, and the book store's stock of flags would be sold out and not restocked. Nothing was said about "Dixie" or Colonel Rebel, issues left for a later day.

The response among whites on the campus and throughout the state seemed to have one central theme: the policy probably would not make much difference in practice, despite its symbolic intent. Students and alumni would continue to wave their flags; the fact that Ole Miss would not provide them wouldn't matter much. But former *Mississippian* editor Ed Williams, by now associate editor of the *Charlotte Observer*, wrote a guest column in the *Clarion Ledger* pointing out that Fortune's action was not unimportant and not without effect. Symbols stand for something, Williams wrote, and must be treated carefully. Recalling a campus awash in Confederate memorabilia every football weekend, he observed that "for a black student, it takes an unusual appreciation of irony to feel at home there. . . . The descendants of slaves now sit alongside the descendants of slave owners in the classroom at Ole Miss," he went on, and the symbols "of earlier days no longer suffice. . . . It is right to honor that which is honorable from history," he concluded. "But our responsibility is to the future. We must not sacrifice it in a misguided devotion to the past."

To Black Student Union leader Spragin, Fortune's gesture was only a start. Three days earlier, the group had issued a list of thirteen demands, and to call attention to their concerns, BSU members staged a silent demonstration when Governor Winter spoke at the dedication of a new athletic facility. The demands were remarkably similar to the list of grievances put forward more than a decade earlier by the students who had marched into Fulton Chapel seeking more black faculty, more financial aid, and more support services for the black student population.

This new protest with its list of demands for action struck many white students as ill timed and ill advised. They couldn't understand the persistent anger, particularly because in their view so much had changed just in their own lifetimes. They went to class with blacks, ate with them at restaurants, shopped with them at the same stores, relaxed with them at the same parks. William Ray, just finishing his year as head of the student government, was disheartened, feeling that this latest blast from the BSU reflected a burgeoning separatism on the campus between the races.

Some of the white students used the *Mississippian* letters page to express their consternation and dismay. One of the more pointed comments came from freshman R. E. Reed, who said he was "both amused and disgusted with the recent actions of blacks on this campus. I just couldn't believe how they could so readily tear down all the progress that they had already made." He warned of a backlash to persistent complaints about alleged mistreatment. "Will these types of people ever realize that others have only so much Christian spirit and are tired of giving them everything that they want?. . . . I especially resent the fact that they say I owe them something because of their history. I never have owned a slave (of ANY color), nor have I ever committed any atrocity against any black. If they really want these things, they must prove it, and stop acting like greedy, violent little children and more like mature adults."

Whatever administrators may have thought privately, they took the BSU demands seriously. Thirteen years earlier, after the Fulton Chapel demonstration, Fortune had had a few informal meetings with black students and periodically reported to the faculty on how he and his aides were addressing the students' concerns. This time he appointed a special committee to respond to the demands. On May 6, the chancellor released a fourteen-page single-spaced reply to the black students. There was little publicity about the matter. Summer school had not yet started, few students were on campus, and the *Mississippian* had suspended publication for the month.

The chancellor essentially rejected most of the demands and provided lengthy explanations. Most telling was the measured and detailed reply about the paucity of black faculty members. He explained the university's extensive effort to advertise openings in a variety of journals and post them at schools, particularly predominantly black schools. And he said that approximately $70,000 was available for attracting and retaining black faculty, either to increase the pay of an existing position or to help fund additional education that would make a potential candidate meet the school's qualifications or to get visiting professors on campus in the hope that exposure to Ole Miss would result in their wish for a permanent position. "In spite of our good procedures for seeking out Black faculty members and our reasonable explanations and rationalizations for our failures," Fortune wrote, "the fact is that the University has not succeeded in attracting and retaining more Black faculty. This is a cause of official concern and regret, and the University will be making a renewed effort to improve this situation."

On the subject of symbols, Fortune said there would be no effort to curtail the use of "Dixie" because of freedom of speech concerns. As for Colonel Rebel, that was a registered symbol of Ole Miss and would remain so. "The university does not consider it 'racist' and will not discontinue its use," he said.

The chancellor used particularly strong language to reject a demand for a separate budget for black cultural affairs, invoking the *Brown* decision to give his answer resonance. While the university recognized the "diverse interests" of different ethnic, political, and racial groups on the campus, Fortune said, the school "is philosophically opposed to any practice which promotes racial division. The concept of 'separate but equal,' found discriminatory on its face by the Supreme Court nearly thirty years ago, is not espoused by the University." He noted that the administration had rejected previous requests for a separate black student union, black dormitory, and "separate racially designated classes within departmental curriculums." The goal instead is to "promote the good of the *entire* University. We believe that the goal of quality educational service and scholarship is entirely consonant with the goal of equal opportunity and affirmative action."

Once he had answered the BSU, Fortune believed that a difficult episode had come to a close. In more ways than one it had. By then he had decided to step down. He was tired after fourteen years at the helm, and his family was concerned about his health. He had already suffered one heart attack on the job; they feared another. Fortune announced his retirement late in May.

There was an eerie coincidence to his decision. His predecessor, J. D. Williams, had been suffering through a long illness, and on May 29 he passed away. His death, combined with Fortune's announcement, served as a kind of denouement to the initial "P.M." period of Ole Miss—post Meredith. It would be left to a new chancellor, one not encumbered by these controversies as a former student, teacher, or administrator, to guide the university on the next phase of its journey. But like his predecessors, he too would hear the mystic chords of memory chime through the campus.

9

The Power of Perception, the Reality of Place

"This is the University of Mississippi for all Mississippians—white, black, brown, red…. If you as alumni are not ready for this to be, get out of the way."

Gerald Turner had not officially been installed as the new chancellor when he leveled this challenge at the Ole Miss graduates who had gathered on a hot August day in 1984 to get their first look at him. It was his way of alerting the university community that a new day was at hand on matters of race. It was impossible to imagine Porter Fortune making such a statement or J. D. Williams. Thirty years earlier Williams had in fact taken pains to assure Mississippi officials that he had never taught at an integrated school. Turner, on the other hand, made sure to point out in his interview with the board of trustees that he had taught at predominantly black Prairie View A&M in Texas and was proud of it.

The board had obviously taken a chance on this confident young man to head the school. He had come from the University of Oklahoma, where he had been made a vice president by age thirty-three and was now only thirty-eight, admittedly young to head a state university. And although he was from Texas, Turner did not consider himself a southerner but a Texan—born and educated there—with a bachelor's degree from Abilene

Christian College and a master's and doctorate (in psychology) from the university in Austin. He had made clear to the board that if he was named chancellor, he would commit himself to getting more minorities on the campus. He believed the members when they said they shared that goal.

Turner had never been to Ole Miss before interviewing for the chancellor's job, but he certainly knew its history. Walking around the campus for the first time, he was struck by its beauty and by how much change had already taken place. Turner knew the thirtieth anniversary of Meredith's admission would be approaching, and all around him he could see the "cosmetics of progress" in the apt phrase of C. Eric Lincoln, the elder statesman of southern religion studies. Black students mixed easily with whites, sitting together in classes, studying at the library, and walking leisurely through the Grove.

He knew that Dixie Week still existed, but he also knew that there were no more slave auctions or reenactments of Confederate enlistment. B. B. King and the Neville Brothers were headlining entertainment along with a healthy mix of black jazz musicians and an annual shrimp and beer fest at a nearby lake. But Turner also realized that these surface changes masked deep cultural differences between whites and blacks that were fueled by widely variant views of history. Ole Miss had always been an option for whites, but there were no blacks on campus, even those born *after* Meredith arrived, who did not understand that their parents could not have come to study, but only to cook food, clean rooms, or take care of the grounds. To make the campus "psychologically accessible" to these students, as Turner liked to put it, was a daunting goal but one he was determined to pursue.

The number of overt racial incidents on campus had been decreasing, but their recurrence suggested the sobering truth that a plateau had been reached. The boundaries of racial accommodation were becoming more clearly defined, and they were not where so many had hoped they might be thirty years earlier, in the most buoyant moments of the civil rights movement. By the late 1980s and certainly in the 1990s, there would be no talk of a "color-blind" campus in Oxford or even a "race-neutral" one. Indeed, that would have been impossible given the obvious efforts to attract black students, faculty, and staff. The talk was of diversity, and the reality was racial coexistence, if occasionally strained.

There was a price for this march toward diversity, a backlash among many whites that prompted a defensive reaction among blacks. Whites who resented encroachments on their traditions to accommodate black students were becoming more vocal in their concerns. One group even started its own newspaper, the *Ole Miss Review,* which was modeled after the conservative Dartmouth publication, to get the point across. After all, an anchor of the Old South was what many of these students were looking for in Ole Miss, and to curb displays of the Confederate flag or silence "Dixie" was to diminish the college experience they had expected. Some openly resented the array of financial help earmarked for blacks.

At the same time an increasingly cohesive black student community sought to create its own campus culture, largely through fraternities and sororities, rather than seek admission into the established white groups. Furthermore there was subtle and sometimes overt pressure on black students who sought to cross the divide to stay within the fold. It was a throwback to the early years of integration, when junior and senior high schools had two of everything: two class presidents, two homecoming queens, black and white cocaptains of the sports teams. Back then this was intended to ease the transition from forced segregation; now it was more a matter of choice among the black students, albeit one borne of past resistance and rebuff. The result, however, was the same: separation.

At many universities around the country, fraternities and sororities had diminished in importance, particularly in the turmoil of the late sixties and early seventies, when challenges to authority and conventional structure were the norm. Not at Ole Miss. The Greek system had remained the center of student life, providing virtually all of the campus leaders—and that meant that nearly all of them were white. The lack of integration bothered Turner, and as soon as he took office he ordered the fraternities and sororities to send him their bylaws. If any had whites-only clauses, they would have to be stricken.

Getting rid of inappropriate language was easy. It would take more than words to change behavior. Even if a charter said that a fraternity was open to white and black alike, there was little likelihood of this occurring if, as happened in one house, upperclassmen made disparaging remarks about black women when they teased the incoming pledges or when the fraternity men taunted and leered at young black women as they walked near Fraternity Row to their classes. Nor was the goal of integrated fraternities helped when members of one house celebrated Halloween by dressing up as Ku Klux Klan members and parading around the yard with a Confederate flag. Many in the house were upset that the *Mississippian* reported the incident, contending that it was a private party. Black students found it an example of gross insensitivity that only hurt the image of the university.

There were further complaints from black students about being refused admission to what were supposed to be open parties after football games. Occasionally fistfights would break out, with charges and countercharges of who hurled what epithet at whom. It galled the football players that they could be cheered on the field for a touchdown or a tackle but not be welcomed at some of the postgame celebrations.

Adding to the problem was the reluctance of black students to go through white rush. By now there were seven black sororities and fraternities, and even if black students would be treated courteously by the white fraternity houses, those who ventured to Fraternity or Sorority Row were often derided as "Uncle Toms," or as sell-outs. More than one had confided this to Turner when he called them in to talk about ways to integrate the Greek system.

Fraternity life held no interest for Damon Moore, a softspoken young black man from nearby Coldwater who had come to Oxford with the same focused determination that so many black students before him had exhibited. A sixth-generation Mississippian with a deep pride in his family's roots, Moore grew up drenched in his family's history. Ancestors going back six generations, to 1830, were buried in small, out-of-the-way cemeteries in the rolling farmland just outside Oxford. He often visited their graves to remind himself of his link to the land around him.

Born two years after Meredith enrolled at Ole Miss, Moore had understood from the time he could understand anything that the citadel of learning just fifteen miles away had been closed to his great-grandparents, grandparents, and parents. His mother and father were teachers, each educated at Mississippi Industrial College in Holly Springs, and they wanted something better for their son.

By the time Damon was ready for first grade in the fall of 1969, fifteen years after the *Brown* decision, the Coldwater schools had just integrated. Jean Moore did not worry at all how her son would fare with white children. She told him he would be the best, and he was. He graduated from high school first in his class and prepared for four years of study in Oxford.

"He had to go to Ole Miss because we couldn't," Jean Moore explained, "to show them that blacks could compete." Damon considered his enrollment there "my birthright."

Moore was typical of so many other black students who arrived on campus with a special coat of armor to ward off anticipated racism. Many had been schooled by a parent or grandparent, as Moore had, to believe in themselves as they entered a majority white world and to ignore the racial slurs that might come their way. It was hard to imagine such conversations with such regularity in the homes of incoming white students who, after all, were moving onto a campus that had been created for them and where they were expected to thrive, even if so much had changed since Meredith.

Once at Ole Miss, Moore lived up to his parents' expectations. He was certain he wanted to be a doctor and used his innate talents and willingness to work hard to make up for the deprivations of an education in a modestly equipped high school. There had been no physics course in Coldwater, and the science lab was much more rudimentary than anything available at most private white academies.

Moore ignored everything on campus but his studies, going home to his family in Coldwater all but two weekends of his entire college career. If there were occasional low moments, he reminded himself that "I have a mission. It is to do well."

At the end of his freshman year, Moore had shared the outrage of fellow black students at the 1983 *Ole Miss,* appalled at the number of Ku Klux Klan pictures that had appeared. It made such an impression on him that more than ten years later he could quote verbatim from Willie Morris's essay in the front of the book and editor John Hall's shorter piece at the back. When Hall wrote of the sacredness of a southern ground "rich with history," Moore believed he, too, was part of that history. He had the same special feeling for place as Hall and any other white Mississippian did, particularly because he could trace the Moores back more than a century. And it was with some irritation that he remembered Morris's observation that whites' "proximity with young blacks seems both mystifying and exhilarating."

"My mother didn't send me to Ole Miss to be mystifying," Moore said, irritation in his voice. "She sent me to get an education."

Moore graduated summa cum laude, won a prestigious award for his work in English—he had sandwiched as many humanities courses as possible between his science requirements—and a passel of other honors. He headed to Johns Hopkins Medical School in the fall of 1986, and a year later, as he was starting his second year at Hopkins, he was awarded a Rhodes scholarship.

In his four years at Ole Miss, Moore had never been to a football game, but the university wanted to honor him at halftime once his scholarship had been announced. At first he balked, but then he decided that his parents deserved to see this moment, and he acceded to the administration's wishes. He came out to midfield at halftime accompanied by Chancellor Turner, and when he was introduced, the crowd rose to its feet for an ovation that lasted several minutes. Moore was lost in the moment, hoping his parents were bathed in the same goodwill he was feeling. He was wrenched out of his reverie as the applause, which had started to die down, suddenly picked up again. The Ole Miss Rebels were running onto the field to begin the second half, and as they raced toward their sideline, the band accompanied them with a boisterous version of "Dixie." Standing at midfield, Moore felt the past fuse with the present, and in this moment of personal glory, he said to himself, "Damon, remember where you are."

Moore had blocked out the Confederate flags waving in tribute to him—signs that Porter Fortune's announcement five years earlier that the flag was not a university symbol had hardly ended the matter. What it prompted instead among some students and alumni was a resurgence of the siege mentality of the early sixties tinged with more vocal expressions of racism, and that had had a demonstrable effect on black student enrollment. In the fall of 1982, twenty years after Meredith's admission, there were 715 black students on the campus. A year later, in the wake of the flag conflict, the number had dropped to 656, and in the fall of 1984, it had dropped further to 536. In the minds of many blacks, it was as though the Ole Miss community, Fortune's effort notwithstanding, had put up a new whites-only sign at the campus gate.

To understand the emotions generated by the flag and some of the reasons it remained so controversial, one had only to pick up the *Mississippian*. Barely a week went by without some letter or column on the subject. One by Victor Kermit Hervey, a black student, was among the more perceptive. It was not a harangue but an attempt to explain in straightforward, nonhysterical prose why so many blacks felt such discomfort with the flag. Even if very few who waved it or hung it from a dormitory window did so as a gesture of racism, there was, Hervey wrote, "an inner message intended to be conveyed—that is, we love our past, we do not regret we were forced to accept social changes." The flag, he went on, celebrates a past of prosperity, and because his great-grandfather had been a slave, that was not a past he could identify with—his way of drawing the distinction between a shared and deeply entwined history and a decidedly different heritage. For whites it was power, for blacks oppression, and the flag represented that dichotomy.

"This is the most prevalent argument for setting aside 'tradition,'" Hervey explained. "As long as this university is perceived as still trying to grasp to those ideals, Ole Miss will always be under the scrutiny of the national media: 'Ole Miss: 102 years, 3 months and 17 days after James Meredith—tonight on TBS.' It refuses to be washed away."

Hervey's barbed wit struck a chord with Turner. He agreed that attachments to the Confederacy remained a barrier to the diversity he wanted to achieve. He knew how important alumni can be in recruitment, in the best of circumstances serving as informal ambassadors for the university. He was bluntly told by one black graduate that connecting with the black alumni was going to be a problem. Many felt so "abused and mistreated" during their time in Oxford, the graduate continued, that they chose not to have any relationship with the school once they received their degree.

That was an understatement. The list of black alumni who stayed away from the campus after they graduated was long. Verna Bailey had come to Ole Miss by choice in 1965, fiercely determined to make it through. In hindsight she realized what it had cost her: the social life with newfound friends most young adults expect in a college setting, an experience she could never recapture. She had no desire to revisit the scene of so much pain.

Linnie Liggins, who was from Oxford and still had family there twenty-five years after she graduated, remained bitter over the fact that she had been denied the right to attend her graduation. Even more important, the university's branding her a troublemaker had ruined her hopes of getting a scholarship for graduate school and the chance to teach school in the Oxford area, as she had hoped to do. She ultimately moved to the Midwest, and when she came back home to visit relatives, she didn't go near the university.

So if these first black alumni believed their struggle had been worth it for the piece of parchment that said "University of Mississippi," it had at the same time left so many of them with complicated and negative memories of the school. Otis Sanford, a 1978 graduate in journalism who went on to become deputy managing editor of the Memphis *Commercial Appeal,* captured the feeling with a cryptic summation of the Ole Miss experience: "It did more for me than to me."

When Chancellor Turner checked with alumni officials, they told him that only Rose Jackson and maybe one or two others responded to invitations for one activity or another, let alone appeals for money. University officials believed they had taken decisive steps to improve relations with black students and alumni: Black History Month was now a formal program, Martin Luther King's birthday was honored and his daughter had spoken on campus, the first black law professor had been given tenure, and new scholarships and tuition waivers for minority students were now available. But Turner decided that something more was needed. He wanted a new program targeted specifically at the black community—if nothing else, as a gesture of recognition. Alumni officials were skeptical. In general Turner agreed with their argument that a uniform approach to university activities was preferable, "but this is a special case," he told them, and one that needed special attention. His basic idea was simple: "Some kind of event to honor the very people we kept out of here, to let these people come back and to put the university's arms around them."

David Sansing, the history professor, heartily endorsed Turner's concept. So did Michael Edmonds, a black student who had graduated in 1984 and had moved easily in the white world of Ole Miss. He had made it a point to involve himself in student government and more pointedly often ate with white friends in their fraternity houses. Black classmates criticized him for "acting white" because of the friendships he formed and the way he sometimes dressed—in khaki pants and sport shirts, the informal uniform of the fraternity crowd. Edmonds tossed off the barbs, determined to give himself as complete a college experience as possible, a goal that had been impossible for James Meredith and Verna Bailey twenty years earlier. He went to football games and refused to be bothered by the plethora of flags around him. In fact, he even had one of his own. After graduation he stayed on to head up the student programming department.

Sansing and Edmonds came up with the idea of an awards program—"Awards of Distinction," they called it. The Black Student Union was already honoring black alumni, but these awards would be from the university. In Sansing's mind it was a way to acknowledge the discrimination of the past and to honor those who endured and survived it. Some of the awards would be given to alumni, others would be recognized for their achievements regardless of where they went to school, and one of the awards each year would be given posthumously.

Turner liked the concept and agreed to find the money to make it work. He decided that the ceremony would be combined with a dinner, and each honoree would be allowed to invite a number of friends and family to the event. The idea of a dinner seemed particularly significant to Sansing. In the days of segregation, it had been unthinkable as well as illegal for whites and blacks to sit down to a meal together. To do so now made a statement, and to have the banquet in a building at the University of Mississippi made that statement indelibly. For the same reason that James Meredith had chosen to integrate Ole Miss rather than Southern or Mississippi State, Sansing knew that it made a special statement for the university to present these awards. In his mind this was more than the cosmetics of progress. It was progress—a public way for the university to reconcile with its past—and in a way, Ole Miss would be a proxy for the entire state.

When the university announced the first Awards of Distinction early in 1987, Turner was surprised at the angry mail and telephone calls he received. "That's when the colonels came out of the woodwork," he said, one of the "colonels" pointing out with irritation that "you are honoring the very people who integrated Mississippi." But Turner stood firm, even in the face of some obvious anxiety from board of trustees members. He told them and reminded himself that it was "the right thing to do."

The first group of honorees included author Richard Wright, who was the posthumous recipient—and the university provided the money for his daughter, Julia, to fly in from Paris to receive the award; Reuben Anderson, the first black law school graduate and in 1987 a member of the state supreme court; *Washington Post* columnist William Raspberry; Beverly Hogan, a senior state government official; and two civil rights activists, NAACP leader Aaron Henry, whose speech on campus fifteen years earlier had been so controversial, and the Rev. R. L. T. Smith. Later posthumous honorees would include of two of the state's most celebrated civil rights activists, Medgar Evers and Fannie Lou Hamer.

Some of the speakers began in anger. They raised their voices, and they cried as they recounted the bitter moments in their lives at the hands of whites. And then they said, "Thank you," willing to return the university's embrace. For Raspberry it was a marvel just to be there: "Here I am in a place that was beyond my imaginings when I graduated from high school," he said. "Today I was invited here to be honored."

Turner, Sansing, and Edmonds knew they had done a good thing when Reverend Smith told the audience, "You have made my life complete."

Verna Bailey understood that emotion when she returned to Ole Miss in 1996 to accept an award on behalf of her late father. For him, she said, the university's honor was "coming full circle." She had agreed to come back from her home in Oregon, where she was a middle school principal, to a place that held such painful memories because she knew he would have wanted her to. She also realized it had helped her make some peace with an important, if difficult, part of her life.

By the fall of 1987 Turner could see that his gestures toward the black community were paying off. For the first time in two years, black student enrollment was up—563 out of a student body of 9,200. But at the same time there was backlash from white students who were irritated and even angry at some of Turner's policies and the obvious attempt to attract black students. Frank Hurdle was one of the chancellor's most voluble critics.

As a child in Holly Springs, Hurdle was another Ole Miss student-in-waiting. He joked that his father told him he could go anywhere he wanted to college "as long as it was Ole Miss." He felt a part of its traditions while still in grade school, when he got his first Confederate flag, a souvenir from his parents after a day at the football stadium in Oxford. "Anyone who says waving that flag is promoting slavery, well, it's insane," he would say during controversies over the flag. His comfortable upbringing combined with his education with like-minded whites at Marshall Academy gave him confidence in his views and the right to express them. He was not afraid of conflict or criticism, willing to take what he freely dished out. When Turner had spoken out against perceived racism in the Greek system, Hurdle countered in the *Mississippian* that the chancellor was unfair and had no common sense.

He was the founder of the *Ole Miss Review,* and though it would fail after six issues, it nonetheless encouraged others to come forward unapologetically to state their views. In the summer of 1985, a few months after the *Review* had died, *Mississippian* columnist Robert McLeod stepped into the fray. "If you are a white male, look out," he wrote. "There are countless organizations, scholarships and grants for everybody, but white males." He criticized the number of scholarships now available for minorities—a $100,000 grant from the Gannett Foundation for minority journalists had just been announced—and said he was "tired of working. I'd like some of that scholarship money, but I have something wrong with me. I'm white." He debunked the argument that because whites had discriminated against minorities for so long, "it's time they got a taste of their own medicine. Well, I haven't been around that long, and don't want to pay for my predecessors' mistakes. I wasn't the one who paid women less than men. I wasn't the one who turned people down for jobs because they were black. I don't owe anyone anything. I just want to be treated the same as everyone else."

Once the *Review* folded, Hurdle was given his own column in the *Mississippian,* and he did not shy away from racial issues. One of his more provocative pieces criticized students and faculty at Rust College in his home town of Holly Springs for coming to the defense of an accused rapist. The perpetrator was black, the victim white. He was eventually convicted by a jury that included five black members, but in Hurdle's words, Rust students and teachers "had decided that the case was one of racial injustice instead of rape. Unfortunately," he concluded, "the civil rights movement seems to have devolved to the point that any black or black position, regardless of how wrong, must be supported. Forget right or wrong, forget morality, just get honky no matter what you have to do to accomplish your goal. . . . If blacks allow the civil rights movement to become a pro-rape movement they will soon find it screeching to a halt."

Gregory Sykes, the president of the Black Student Union, fired back an angry letter, lambasting Hurdle for this and other "quasi-racist columns." Hurdle wanted to be editor of the *Mississippian,* and Sykes promised him that because of his "blatant insensitivity," the five hundred plus black students would mobilize to vote against him. The concern, Sykes went on, is that Hurdle "is committed to the furtherance of race relations problems at the University of Mississippi. On a larger scale, we don't have race relations problems. We have 'Frank Hurdle hates American black people' problems. For too long have a few people like Hurdle made things bad for the entire university. Ole Miss has had enough."

Hurdle did not win the editor election in the spring of 1986, but he ran again the next year and won. He couldn't wait for football season to begin. "Wave a flag, drink a pint and yell a cheer" were his instructions. "The Rebel flag is still the official flag of Ole Miss as far as students are concerned, and it always will be," he wrote in his homecoming column. "Just because a bunch of pointy-headed intellectuals say different is no reason to modify our behavior. . . . If you are against the flag, go to hell," he went on. "Because my preacher told me that heaven was full of the things we love, which means it is full of Rebel flags."

Each editorial predictably encouraged a spate of letters pro and con, and if nothing else, Hurdle ensured that the issue was kept alive. Over in the Lyceum, Turner found the subject to be an irritating wound. "If we could just get rid of the flag," he would periodically muse to himself.

Fraternity Row was the seat of student power at Ole Miss. Running along the western edge of the campus, it was a literal training ground for senators, governors, and members of the legislature who learned some of their first political lessons vying for votes to lead their own houses and to win campus-wide elections. Its location put it roughly a quarter-mile from two important landmarks: the Lyceum and the football stadium. It was soaked in tradition and history. The main cross street was Confederate Drive.

If Turner was unable to get individual white fraternities to integrate, he could at least integrate the row by getting a black group there. The symbolism would be on par with the university's honoring outstanding black citizens. Members of Phi Beta Sigma, which had a house on the edge of campus, and their sponsors began working with Turner aides to buy a vacant house on the street. Two of the men deeply involved in the negotiations were the associate dean of students, Thomas "Sparky" Reardon, and Thomas Wallace, the principal of a nearby elementary school and an adviser to the fraternity. Though Reardon was seven years older than Wallace, the two men were different sides of the same coin— both Ole Miss graduates, but one white and the other black. Each had come through his own journey on race. Reardon, who is white, shed the attitudes and prejudices he had learned in his childhood in Clarksdale, the heart of the Delta; Wallace, who is black, learned how to succeed in a majority white world that would on more than one occasion be hostile to him.

In Reardon's mind it was a measure of how far Ole Miss had come that a black fraternity would be on the row. He had been a student in the winter of 1970 when the fledgling Black Student Union had staged its protest in Fulton Chapel during an Up with People Concert. He remembered the event not so much because of the protest but because of what had happened before it.

The original plan was for the performers, some from Africa, to stay at the sorority and fraternity houses. When the groups realized that some of the cast members were black, the various houses held emergency meetings to vote on whether they would allow these individuals to stay there. Reardon's own fraternity, Phi Delta Theta, which included mostly young men from the Delta, voted against the proposal. So did a number of other houses, and the idea was shelved. Reardon recalled that moment with neither pride nor remorse but as a statement of fact. Like others on

Fraternity Row, he explained, "my way of life had taught me that blacks were called one thing and played a certain role."

Wallace had come to Ole Miss as a transfer student from Northwest Mississippi Community College. He had done very well there and had gotten a scholarship to the university. He was committed to being an elementary school teacher, and he stood out for two reasons: He was a man and black. In his elementary art class, he was the only male and the only black among fifty white women. Most of them, he felt, tried to make him feel welcome; he ignored the hostility of the others. He had come to get an education, and like those determined black students who had come before him and would follow him, he refused to be deterred. He was committed to two years of hard work and reminded himself, as Damon Moore would tell himself a decade later, "I came here with a purpose."

By early August 1988, the deal for the Phi Beta Sigma house was virtually complete. The necessary legal papers were in order, and Wallace planned to be on hand when they were signed the morning of the fourth. Around 3:00 A.M., he was awakened by a ringing telephone. It was Sparky Reardon. "Tom," he said quietly, "the house has burned." Both men were devastated. Reardon already had been to the scene. The university police had called to tell him there was a fire on the row. He had misheard the location and thought it was the nearby Sigma Pi house. But as he rounded the corner in his car and saw the flames and the commotion, his heart sank. The police suspected arson.

Chancellor Turner was upset and angry. He knew right away how badly this would reflect on the university, and he would have to speak out strongly about what happened. It was next to impossible to go back to sleep, and he stayed up a good while talking with his wife, Gail. "There can be something positive from this," he told her. "Good whites will demand that we move on."

Phi Beta Sigma members were in shock. They had met with no ill will as their move to Fraternity Row became public and had no idea who might have burned the house. They vowed to press on, one of the members telling reporters, "We've been working hard for it, and we've seen a lot of positive things at the University of Mississippi. We're going to continue to be positive."

The probability of arson carried a disturbing resonance: An anguished David Sansing thought to himself how much arson had played a role in southern strife. Slaves burned barns, crops, and fences to revolt; Klan members burned crosses, churches, and homes to intimidate.

The next day Turner kept his scheduled meeting with a group of alumni in Memphis. "They will not defeat us," Turner told the group, which rose in unison to applaud him. In the audience was Rose Jackson, like everyone else deeply pained by the incident but gratified to hear the university chancellor speak out so forcefully. For black graduates like Jackson, who cherished their Ole Miss degrees and tried to encourage others to attend the school, such moments were particularly difficult. They had gotten used to defending their decision to go to Oxford—some of them had been booed in church when they announced they were going to the university—and when incidents with racial overtones occurred, the naysayers were quick to jump. That same day Turner announced a $200,000 fund drive and reported that an alumnus had already guaranteed a $100,000 loan.

Student leaders also wanted to help. Stuart Brunson, president of the Intrafraternity Council, was not on campus when the fire broke out. As soon as he heard the news, all he could think was, "Here we go again," another blot on Ole Miss that would wipe away how much progress had been made. He headed right back to campus to see what he could do.

Brunson had always had a special sensitivity about race even though he had grown up in a segregated small town in Tennessee, just over the Mississippi border. He went to an all-white private school and could see around him that old habits died hard. Unlike many of his chums, he made mental notes of these things: that in the late 1970s, blacks still sat in the balcony of the local movie theater and stayed out of certain restaurants. Local folks knew that when they saw blacks in some of the eateries, they most assuredly were from out of town.

Brunson's family owned a farm where much of the help, particularly in the busy summers, were local black residents. An outstanding student and high school leader who had won several honors, Brunson was used to getting compliments around town. One he remembered most vividly and with pride came from Pearl Jackson, a black woman who often helped chop cotton at the Brunson farm. After one of Brunson's awards was mentioned in the local paper, she told him she knew he would be a success. Pleased, he thanked her but wanted to know why. "Because you used to always come back and help me finish my row," she explained.

For Brunson the atmosphere at Ole Miss was much like that in his home town—not exactly polarized but definitely separate. Nonetheless, he realized just from his own fraternity, Sigma Nu, how important it was to have a black presence on Fraternity Row. Trent Lott, by then a U.S. senator and by 1996 Senate majority leader, was a fraternity brother and so was his son. And there were several members of Congress and the state legislature who were also Sigma Nus. Brunson agreed with Turner that such future leaders, himself included, needed to deal with blacks more closely more often and as peers.

By the time Brunson got to Oxford after the fire, he knew that he wanted to head up a fund-raising drive through the fraternities. The goal was $20,000. He went to see Reardon to explain his idea, which Reardon liked, and he secured Turner's approval. Brunson immediately called each of the fraternity presidents and asked them to hold special meetings to talk about raising money. He didn't encounter any immediate resistance, but there was some opposition, even within Sigma Nu.

One member wrote Brunson a letter criticizing his efforts because they "did not reflect the ideals of our fraternity." The fund-raising effort was "in no way bringing pride to our group," the letter went on. In fact, Brunson was "not being an honorable fraternity member."

He didn't bother to answer it. He considered the writer to be a racist and not reflective of the membership of the fraternity. But he knew there were others with that same attitude: discomfort at the notion of anything that approached social integration. They had resigned themselves to blacks' attending Ole Miss, but they wanted to keep their associations with them to a minimum. It was all right to cheer them on at football games, rebel flag in hand, but quite another to party with them on Fraternity Row.

Their views were in the minority, however. Turner seemed to be right that an ugly incident would prompt an outpouring of goodwill. The money was quickly raised for a new Phi Beta Sigma house, and by October the members were able to move into their new house. The first black sorority, Alpha Phi Alpha, moved onto Sorority Row in March 1991.

While authorities concluded that the fire was the result of arson, no one was ever arrested and charged with the crime.

Sansing feared that the general public outside Mississippi would remember only the burning, not the aftermath. But this time he was wrong. NBC dispatched a reporter and camera for a piece on the efforts to help the Phi Beta Sigmas, and the *New York Times* made space for a long story on the move with a picture showing white and black young men carrying furniture into the new house.

"Nothing short of such a cooperative effort among fraternities, students and citizens throughout Mississippi can do as much to show the world we're not about to surrender to incendiary idiots," the *Clarion Ledger* had written in an editorial.

The image of Ole Miss to the outside world had been of perennial concern to members of the university family since the baleful night of September 30, 1962. They understood that image was related to the recruitment of students, faculty, and money.

Turner believed that one of his jobs was to showcase the progress of the school, much as Porter Fortune had tried to do with the twentieth anniversary of the Meredith imbroglio. But there was a difference. Fortune and his top aides would have been happy to ignore the event but were pressed into it because of so much national interest. Turner, on the other hand, wanted to invite individuals connected to the civil rights movement to come back to Oxford, to walk around the campus and see how much had changed. The Center for the Study of Southern Culture, which had been established in 1977 to further an understanding of the South in its broadest context, was the perfect vehicle. Its very existence had given intellectual muscle to the study of the music, art, and customs of the region that often were ignored, and, to be sure, its history. Through the Center the university had sponsored a program in 1987, "Covering the South," that featured reporters from major publications who had written extensively about the civil rights movement. The spring of 1989 was an appropriate moment for another gathering, the twenty-fifth anniversary of the 1964 Civil Rights Act. So the Center put together a symposium, "The Civil Rights Movement and the Law," and invited lawyers and judges who had participated in some of the landmark events to come back to the state for three days of discussions. When plans for the event were made public, the state chapter of the ultraconservative Nationalist Movement announced it would protest the symposium. Richard Barrett, the group's general counsel in Jackson, blasted the program as "part of pro-minority sentiment" that had to be ended.

John Ates, a junior from Pascagoula, had just been elected president of the student body. As soon as he learned of Barrett's plan to protest the symposium, he published an open letter in the *Mississippian* urging students, faculty, and staff to demonstrate against Barrett and the Nationalist Movement. Then he got to work with other campus groups to organize a silent vigil to counter Barrett's message. He was determined that prominent judges and lawyers not come into Oxford, see the conservative protesters, and find no one standing in opposition. "We wanted them to know that Ole Miss does not support the hate he espouses," Ates explained.

His effort proved highly successful. When Barrett showed up, he had only one other supporter. Meanwhile Ates and his group, some two hundred yards away, numbered at least 150. Among the many homemade signs was one that read "Ole Miss Is for Civil Rights," and another, a takeoff on the famed "Hotty Toddy" cheer, said, "Peace, love, hair and Civil Rights by Damned."

Charles Morgan, Jr., a noted civil rights lawyer from Birmingham, was one of the speakers at the symposium. He surmised for the audience what Reverend King might have said had he been at Ole Miss for those three days: "Lord, we ain't where we ought to be, but thank God, we ain't where we were." It was a prophetic observation given the grim, racially charged event that unfolded in the early fall, barely five months after the civil rights experts had left the campus.

One of the continuing problems Turner and Reardon had to deal with was fraternity hazing. Technically such activities, which were aimed at pledges, were illegal; there had been incidents at Ole Miss and other schools where pledges had been injured, some badly enough to require medical treatment. But it had been hard to eradicate the practice altogether. Rarely did the hazing have a racial component; it was more humiliation at the hands of one's fraternity elders as a rite of initiation. But

Reardon knew that race was still a tool a white individual or a group could use to carve out an identity. It had a certain shock value, and it was bound to get attention. And in these times of attempted racial reconciliation it was also an act of defiance.

No one on the campus in the fall of 1989, however, was prepared for a prank pulled by fifteen or so pledges in the Beta Theta Pi house, one of the well-established groups on Fraternity Row whose alumni included past and present state officials. It would serve, as the letters to Brunson had, as a reminder of the continuing racial animosity among many whites even as they moved in a world where blacks expected to be treated as their equals.

Sometime after dinner on Monday evening, September 18, a group of pledges singled out one of the active members for what had become a traditional "kidnapping"—technically a violation of the antihazing rules but nevertheless an ongoing practice. In past years it meant taking one of the young men some place outside Oxford, leaving him for ten or fifteen minutes to wander around, and then picking him up.

This time, the kidnapping was much more elaborate. The target was an upperclassman who had been hard on a number of the pledges— harder, they thought, than was appropriate. They wanted to retaliate, so they surrounded him, hustled him into a car, and headed out of town with two other cars behind them. By the time the night had ended, the prank had escalated into one of the ugliest incidents in memory. The group had made its way to predominantly black Rust College in Holly Springs, where the ringleaders decided it was the right spot to drop off the target of the prank. "If I stay, he stays," he said, pointing to one of the pledges.

Within minutes, the two young men were stripped of their clothes, and two incendiary slogans were scrawled on their bare chests: "KKK" and "I hate niggers." They were dumped from the car as it sped off with the others, left to wander in the nude frantically trying to smudge the epithets off their skin. When Rust security guards came upon them, they hustled the young men into their small office. By this time some fifty students had congregated, growing angry when they understood the insulting nature of the prank.

Reardon was the first to see the two Betas when they were brought back to the university—still wrapped in towels—by the Ole Miss police department. "No big deal," the upperclassman told Reardon, when he walked into the small room at the university police office.

"No big deal," Reardon screamed at him, rising in his chair and about to lunge forward when a police officer nudged him back. "Do you realize what you have done?" he screamed again, well aware how the grotesque episode would once again tarnish the university.

The pledge who had been left was much more upset, crying as he told Reardon, "I've never been so scared in my life."

Brad Gunner, the Beta Theta Pi treasurer and Brunson's successor as head of the Intrafraternity Council, didn't know what had happened until close to 11:00 P.M. He had been watching a professional football game on television with some friends, and as he walked back to the Beta house, he saw people milling around. One of his fraternity brothers told him what was going on, and he was dumbfounded, heartsick, and angry all at once. He understood immediately the enormity of what had happened and how badly it reflected on the house. Clearly things were out of control.

Chancellor Turner was out of town and would not return until Tuesday. As soon as he heard the news, he expressed his outrage, called Ishmell Edwards, the president of Rust, to apologize, and told Gunner he would have to go over to Rust and apologize in person.

The reaction on the campus was also one of outrage. The faculty senate immediately passed a resolution calling for the suspension of the students involved, and the *Mississippian* condemned the event as a disgrace that "warrants severe punishment."

When a contrite Gunner went over to Rust to apologize, Edwards told the young man, "We're fortunate we're not going to a funeral." Gunner understood what he meant: that such an ugly incident could have easily escalated into something much worse, with the rage of the Rust students having nowhere to go except at the victims—not the young men who had perpetrated the prank. It struck many in an embarrassed Ole Miss community as ludicrous when Ed Meek, the school's public relations director, told the *Clarion Ledger* that the pledge members "had no idea that there were racial connotations in it."

Turner was determined that the fraternity be punished swiftly and firmly. A special committee of administrators, faculty, and students was established to take testimony. On September 24 the committee recommended that the fraternity be banished from campus for three years. Three days later Gunner resigned as Intrafraternity Council president. He apologized to the group for having his fraternity put the entire Greek system in jeopardy and apologized to the university. He was upset that the Betas now looked like a group of racists and that Ole Miss would be tagged again as a home for bigots. He understood why this would happen, he said, but found it unfair.

On September 27, Turner upheld the special committee's recommendation that the fraternity be banned from campus. There was criticism of that action from those who believed that the entire group should not be made to suffer for the actions of a few, but Turner was unpersuaded. He believed that the incident had grown out of an environment in the entire house and that a strong statement of disapproval had to be made.

Mississippian columnist Jay Oglesby believed the problem was not confined to one house but was systemwide. The thinking in too many houses, he wrote, goes like this: "'I may not be better than anybody else and minorities may have every legal right that I do. But I never will let a nigger be my brother.' This racism, devoid of a shred of logic, is the worst form of the disease and to say that it does not exist in our system is simply naive." Part of the problem, Oglesby said, is that so many students were coming from segregated academies that paid no attention to racism. One had explained to a *Washington Post* reporter that his private school kept a picture of Confederate president Jefferson Davis in the headmaster's office and that the kind of jokes told by teachers in class went like this: "What are crocodiles good for?" "They're real good at keeping niggers from fishing in your pond." "I know I've got prejudice," the young man conceded. "That's where I come from."

Oglesby's remedy was a stronger stand by fraternity leaders. Pledges, he said, have to be told, "'Look, no matter what you thought before you got here, it's just not cool to run around spouting racial slurs. . . . Everyone here earned the same right to study and have fun here at Ole Miss in the same way.' Until racism is eliminated at this level, until one frat guy will tell another after he hears a thoughtless comment that the attitude is offensive and unnecessary, this will remain a racist system."

Some of the fraternity presidents agreed that Oglesby had a point. One of them lamented to a professor that his biggest problem was with pledges who felt "they had to come on like the worst kinds of racists and drunks because this is what Ole Miss was all about."

The chancellor never wavered from his expulsion order and took as a sign of acceptance the fact that Beta alumni, including Governor Ray Mabus and Jamie Whitten, the powerful U.S. representative, did not call to complain.

Student disciplinary hearings were completed by the first week in October, and on October 8, Turner announced that one student had been expelled, four were suspended, and nine were put on probation. Dwight Ball, a political science instructor, had headed the committee that recommended this punishment. He received a standing ovation from students when he walked into class the day after the disciplinary actions were announced.

Mary Thompson had been on one of the disciplinary panels. Nineteen years earlier she had been one of those arrested at the Fulton Chapel demonstration. She had avoided further punishment, stayed on to graduate, married classmate Sam Givhan, gone to graduate school, and was now in a senior position in the financial aid office. The job was an outgrowth of work she had been happy to have while finishing up her degrees and while her husband finished his doctorate. The Beta incident had been a disturbing moment, coming just two months after she had served on a task force set up to look into minority participation in campus activities. The study had been requested by the Black Faculty and Staff Organization, and Turner had obliged by appointing a twenty-two-member group to do the work. The task force had had plenty to say about the Greek system, but members had not envisioned so ugly an incident.

On the one hand, no one could say the university had not been trying to address racial issues—and the committee cited such efforts—but on the other the members had realized, and the Beta incident underscored this point, that racial harmony was an illusive if not impossible goal. In its thirty-page report, the task force had taken special aim at fraternities and sororities for the role they played in "institutionalized racial separation": "The large number of students who are members of Greek social organizations on campus and the almost total lack of multiracial chapters suggest that the Greek social organizations are discriminatory and do not promote participation by minority students."

The last phrase was significant: Individuals join particular organizations because they believe they have common interests with other members, that they are alike in more ways than not. Fraternities and sororities at Ole Miss, the report seemed to be saying, made judgments about who might fit in on the basis of skin color. Black students did not even have the opportunity to meet whites in the fraternity or sorority setting to discover that they had much in common with fellow music students or fellow science or business majors.

The segregated Greek system, the task force added, made it difficult to attract minority faculty because of what it suggested about the atmosphere at Ole Miss—the "psychological accessibility" Turner had spoken of five years earlier. Indeed, when one professor from Oberlin College who had visited in the spring of the year was asked if he would consider an appointment at the university, he said he could not. The exclusion of blacks in white fraternities and sororities, he said, "amounts to an insidious practice the justification of which is that blacks are not worthy of participating in a certain highly valued form of social, spiritual, and intellectual flourishing." He would have to be schizophrenic, he continued, to support spiritually and intellectually, the very white students who could not see their way clear to integrating their sororities and fraternities.

His strong response was but one side of the coin. The other was the creation of black fraternities and sororities and the consequent pressure on minority students to join these houses. The bottom line was social separation that, in the professor's words, was "inimical to the ideal that all who are part of an institution should have equal access to all of its avenues of learning."

The Beta incident had served as an ugly bookend to the Phi Beta Sigma arson a year earlier. If there was a silver lining to this cloud, it was the reaction to both events. In fact Turner believed that Rust College muted its response to the Beta prank because of the swift and strong punishment meted out by the university. The hope as the 1990 academic year began was that the spirit of John Ates in organizing a counterprotest to the Nationalist Movement would prevail, and there were signs that it might.

Fifteen years earlier, in 1975, football star Ben Williams had become the first Colonel Rebel. There had not yet been a black Miss Ole Miss, though Rose Jackson had come close. In 1990 Kimsey O'Neal, a pharmacy major from Carthage and a top basketball player, decided, with Jackson's encouragement, to run for the honor. O'Neal had been a heavily recruited high school player, getting offers from schools around the country. But she knew she did not want to go far from home, and she also realized that basketball was a means for her to secure her future. She was vacillating between education and something in the medical field, and Ole Miss had good programs in both. She wasn't worried about the atmosphere in Oxford because she had been trained by her parents from the time she was a toddler to believe in herself and to toss off as a sign of ignorance the racial slurs that would come her way. "If you have brains, they can't take that away from you," her father would always remind her.

O'Neal adjusted easily to Ole Miss, in part because of the ready-made family of the athletic team. She joined an all-black sorority—Rose Jackson was their adviser—and it was Jackson at the start of O'Neal's senior year who told her she had to make a bid for Miss Ole Miss. She had good grades—she was an academic All-American—was involved in pharmacy school activities, and like Williams before her, was an athletic star.

She braced herself for the harassing calls that came after she announced she was running, but she didn't let them bother her. What was more distressing were the comments of one of her coaches, who tried to dissuade her from the effort. "You'll never make it," he told her, because the school would not elect a black woman. "You're wasting your time," he said, pointing out that a previous black player who had even made the U.S. Olympic team had not been selected.

O'Neal ignored him, too, but she was hurt that the very person she thought should be her ally, her coach, had spoken so negatively. His discomfiting words faded from her mind when she saw the support she was getting from white students. What touched her the most was the effort by classmates she didn't know who voluntarily picked up her campaign signs in their spare time when her campaign crew had to leave for class. "A barrier was crossed when that happened," she realized.

When O'Neal won the contest, Rose Jackson was the second happiest person, finding in O'Neal's victory the completion of a process she had started ten years earlier.

That same year, the campus elected another black Colonel Rebel, football player Chuckie Mullins, who had been paralyzed after making a tackle during the October 28, 1989, game against Vanderbilt. When the severity of his injuries became clear, the entire university came together to raise money to help him meet his medical expenses and continue in school. Less charitable observers noted that while it was surely important that Mullins was receiving help, the generous gesture fit the pattern of white paternalistic behavior. Even at the height of segregation, there were countless stories of whites helping individual blacks. Such actions did not offend the racial status quo because the power relationships were clear: whites from their positions of privilege bestowing their beneficence on a particular black person in need.

There were two other noteworthy racial firsts. One was the election of Katrina Howard, a senior from Clarksdale, as the first editor of the *Ole Miss*. She ran unopposed. And in the spring of 1990, Lee Eric Smith, a journalism major from Holly Springs, became the first black editor of the *Mississippian*. His appointment had generated some controversy not because of race or his credentials—he had three years of writing for the *Mississippian* and a nearby local paper—but because this was the first time the editor had been appointed by a specially selected board rather than elected campuswide. Up to that point Ole Miss was one of the few major schools in the country that still elected individuals to such positions rather than having them selected by specially qualified panels.

Smith was a good candidate to break this barrier—confident and experienced. He was another of Ken Wooten's success stories, a recruit to Ole Miss based in large part on a positive experience at the leadership conference for black high school students that Wooten had put in place in the early 1970s. That conference had helped organizations looking to give out scholarships identify promising individuals.

Smith had received two: one based on his singing ability—his rich, deep voice was an asset to any choral group—and one for journalism, which required him to publish two stories a week for the *Mississippian* or some other paper. By the time he applied to be editor, he had an impressive number of clippings on a variety of subjects. He knew there were probably some students unhappy about a black's running the paper but was unfazed by that prospect. "I think I can earn the respect of most students across campus whether they like me or not," he said.

Over in the Lyceum, Turner was making his own moves toward the goals he had so often spoken about. In February he announced the appointment of Tom Wallace as assistant vice chancellor for student affairs. The chancellor had had his eye on Wallace, who had finished a master's degree in education at the university, and he had been looking for a way to bring him on campus. That same month, the university honored Patricia Taylor, now a state judge in Jackson (and known by her married name, Wise), with one of its awards of distinction. It represented the kind of reconciliation Turner had been hoping for, given that Taylor had been one of those arrested and nearly expelled during the Fulton Chapel incident and so unhappy about her own experience at Ole Miss that she sent her daughters to historically black colleges for their educations.

The 1990 Awards of Distinction ceremony had been one of several events during the university's celebration of Black History Month. A number of special lectures had also taken place, including one by David Sansing. "Integrating Ole Miss was one of the two or three most important events of the civil rights movement," he told his audience. "It was a test of the states' will to resist the federal government. And the issue was settled that night, Sept. 30–Oct. 1, 1962. White southerners have always said, 'We've got to take things slowly,'" he went on. "If we'd taken their advice and gone slow, many of you wouldn't be here. You'd be segregated and off somewhere else."

September 30, 1992, was an evening like any other in Oxford, a cool breeze coming with sundown. If there had been any haze in the air, it would have been smog trapped in high humidity, not tear gas shot off from U.S. marshals' canisters. Most of the students walking through the Grove on this pleasant evening had not even been born when Meredith arrived on campus thirty years earlier and precipitated the riot seen around the world. Some of them barely knew the story.

Turner had not put together any formal program for this anniversary, but a few months earlier he had done something even more important, something that was unthinkable when Meredith enrolled in school: he appointed the first black basketball coach, Rob Evans. Evans had been an assistant coach at Oklahoma State, and although he had twenty-five years of coaching experience, he was not thought to be the top candidate. There was a moment of controversy over the fact that Turner might have been rewarding a buddy rather than picking the most qualified person because the two had played basketball together when they were students together at Lubbock Christian College. But the chancellor said they had not been in touch for twenty years until they reconnected in 1986. He called Evans's appointment "evolutionary, not revolutionary." For his part, Evans tried to play down the breaking of another racial barrier. "I'm the new coach and just happen to be black," he said.

Had there been an official marking of the thirtieth anniversary of Meredith's admission, the man himself almost certainly would have been part of the program. And no one could be sure what he would have said. By now he was both a mystery and disappointment to many. His politics seemed to have moved steadily right. He worked for nearly a year for archconservative Senator Jesse Helms of North Carolina—the only senator who offered him a job after solicitations to all one hundred. And then he endorsed David Duke, the one-time neo-Nazi and Ku Klux Klan leader, for governor of Louisiana and president. Meredith said he and Duke were using each other to get power for their respective constituents.

In a penetrating 1992 profile in *Esquire* John Ed Bradley let Meredith talk at length about his political views—he's no democrat, he said, but "an autocrat and aristocrat"—and his own belief in himself as a "savior" for his people. "Sadly, the diatribe seemed the ravings of a megalomaniac devouring whatever shred of reputation he had left," Bradley wrote. "And the vicious irony was that the more Meredith confessed his ambition to be the savior, the more people turned away—not in political disagreement but in pity and confusion."

Although the university didn't do anything to commemorate the Meredith anniversary, the *Mississippian* put out a special issue retelling the story and featuring reminiscences from a number of the participants, including Meredith and his Justice Department escort, John Doar, and a few university officials still on hand who remembered the ordeal. The only official campus marker of the 1962 event was a small plaque in Baxter Hall, the paper noted, and it had been installed only the year before. It gave a brief history of the building and concluded: "Baxter Hall was the home of some distinguished Mississippians—one of them being James Meredith, the first black student to enroll at The University of Mississippi in 1962." The simplicity of the plaque belied the importance of what had taken place in 1962. No matter that Meredith had disappointed and confused friends, peers, and allies. No one could take away what he had done or close the door that he had opened.

One of the suggestions from the 1989 task force had been to improve the orientation process for new students. The committee noted pointedly that many, particularly those from black families, were the first in their families to go to college and did not know what to expect at a university. What can result without a proper program, the task force said, is "self-imposed isolation of minority students from all that is good and essential" about the university.

Other schools, notably the University of South Carolina, had instituted a program that usually ran a semester on "the freshman experience." Turner supported the idea. After the Beta incident, he believed it was critical to get something like that in the curriculum to help the university deal with social and ethical problems on campus. The idea was to take a "scholarly approach to the problems of intolerance," according to Michael Harrington, a philosophy professor recruited by Turner to develop the course. Many faculty reacted negatively to the idea, objecting to a course being created outside normal procedures. Students thought this might turn into brainwashing sessions, and some complained that the classes would be little more than "how not to embarrass Ole Miss."

Though Turner wanted University 101, as the course became known, up and running as soon as possible, the first sessions did not meet until the fall of 1992. The sections were too large by everyone's agreement—roughly four hundred students—but Turner could find only so much funding for the course. Students complained that it was a waste of time, but Harrington believed it was nonetheless a step in the right direction even if many improvements were needed. He was sure of that when one of the instructors reported that during a discussion in her section about race, symbols, and intolerance, one student, the incredulity apparent in her voice, said, "But this is the place it's all right to be racist."

As one of a few dozen black students in 1970, Donald Cole had felt the sting of racism on the campus. He had been expelled, unfairly he believed, for his participation in the Black Student Union's demonstration at Fulton Chapel that year. But he had been watching Ole Miss from afar ever since his forced departure. He had unfinished business on the campus and had never given up the thought of coming back. He had finished his undergraduate work at Tougaloo, earned two master's degrees in math—one at the University of Michigan, the other at the State University of New York in Buffalo—and then had returned to the university for his doctorate in math. But that still wasn't enough. Cole wanted to teach, to be a part of the campus in a more significant way. He bided his time, leaving for a job in private industry and then taking a teaching position in Florida. He was friendly with Tom Wallace, the assistant vice chancellor, and kept in regular touch with him, particularly in moments of difficulty, like the Phi Beta Sigma burning and the Beta incident.

He had been impressed with Turner's energy and ideas and thought this was a man he could and would like to work under if the opportunity presented itself. He particularly liked one thing Turner had said: that if Ole Miss could put "more degrees in the hands of our black students, they will go out and be our advocates."

Tom Wallace had told the chancellor to keep Cole in mind when the right opening came about. Turner agreed. In the meantime, Cole was doing well at Florida A&M, where by 1992 he had been elected chair of the mathematics department.

Early in 1993, a vacancy occurred in the administration of the graduate school, and Turner asked Cole to come back as an assistant dean and math professor. The offer was too tempting to turn down—a chance for him to finish the business he had started twenty-four years earlier as a freshman from Jackson.

If an award of distinction to Patricia Taylor Wise was a gesture of recognition, inviting Donald Cole onto the faculty represented an act of reconciliation, even redemption.

George Street, one of the men most responsible for Cole's expulsion two decades earlier, was still on the campus, though long since retired. Now in his seventies, he had slowed down considerably from the after-effects of a heart attack. When Cole would see him passing by, there was no urge to get angry, to have the last word, but only the offer to help him up a flight of stairs.

It was evidence of how much Ole Miss differed from its neighboring southern schools that in the 1990s the Confederate flag and "Dixie" were still so much a part of the ethos of the university. Years earlier other regional colleges had been more successful in putting some distance between themselves and these relics, before habit had settled into ritual. Most notable was the University of Georgia.

Roger Dancz was the University of Georgia's band leader in 1974. That year he ordered the band to stop playing "Dixie," recognizing the conflict the song was creating among the growing black student body. It was a hugely unpopular decision. Bumper stickers appeared on campus— "Dump Dancz—Play Dixie"—and during one game, an irate fan hired a private plane to fly overhead with the same message.

Dancz stood firm. He told anyone who asked: "This isn't the same school as it was twenty-nine years ago and not many southern schools play 'Dixie' anymore." In fact, he said, eight out of ten southern schools no longer played the song.

Porter Fortune chose not to take such a controversial position at a time when he might have weathered the outcry, and conflict over the flag dogged him his entire tenure. Black students' unease about "Dixie" festered in the background until the winter of 1993, when black members of the pep band—Pride of the South, it was called—decided they had had enough.

As the band prepared to strike up "Dixie" in the middle of a basketball game against Alabama, four black members of the band put their instruments down and stood in silent protest, their arms folded across their chests. Tim Jones, the leader of the protest, had decided that he needed to make a statement about the continuing racism at the university. He had just attended a program on black history discussing some of Reverend King's activities in the early 1960s, and felt moved to do something. The song bothered him with its evocations of a past that had meant slavery for his people and a present that found "Dixie" coming out of the mouths of Ku Klux Klan marchers. He had not been mollified by the fact that for a few years the band had incorporated a stirring rendition of "Dixie" and the "Battle Hymn of the Republic" into its repertoire—a medley originally done by Elvis Presley.

Jones's action prompted angry reaction from some students. There were the predictable harassing telephone calls, and someone dumped a bucket of urine-soaked trash in front of Jones's dormitory room. But the Black Student Union backed him and his fellow band members, threatening a boycott of campus services unless the song was removed from the repertoire. White band members were perplexed by the conflict, wondering what had happened between the football season, when the band regularly played the song to cheer on the team, and the basketball games.

As usual, the *Mississippian* letters page served as the campus forum for the debate. Under the headline "Play 'Dixie,' Damnit," one writer excoriated the protesters for creating the problem and demanding that their view prevail.

Tracie Lee Weeden said she came to Ole Miss because of its history and tradition, and those were not going to die without a fight. "We have got to draw the line somewhere or there will be nothing left to remind us what a spirited and traditional school is like. If you take away 'Dixie,' then what's left?" she asked. "Johnny Reb? Then what have we got to call ourselves? As for African American Mr. Jones, who said the song offends him and his people, I tell you that I am very offended as a white Southern-American that you would come to the University of Mississippi and try to take something away from it that creates so much pride and spirit to our sports programs." As a former band member, she told Jones to do what she did—"play your part like it's written—*Play Dixie Damnit.*"

"Let the band play Dixie," a version of Weeden's command, became a popular bumper sticker on the late-model cars parked on Fraternity and Sorority Row.

Several members of the university's printing service sent the chancellor a blistering memo critical of the protesters and revealing a resentment at the changes being forced on Ole Miss in the quest for diversity. The protesters had accepted band scholarships to the school knowing full well that "Dixie" was played at sports events. There had been no problem during the football season, they noted. That one should surface now, the memo said, suggested that these black students came here "to cause trouble of a racial nature." "If ignorant minorities can't read well enough to learn history correctly, they have no place at Ole Miss," the memo went on. "Perhaps our motto should be 'Get your heart in Ole Miss or Get Out.'"

Coach Evans refused to be drawn into the controversy, saying that band music was "an administrative problem. My problem is to find some basketball players and coach the team."

Jack Bass, an award-winning reporter, author of several books on civil rights, and now on the journalism school faculty, offered a new idea for resolving the conflict: If the band played "Dixie" it should also play "We Shall Overcome," the anthem of the civil rights movement. "Together," Bass wrote in a column for the *Clarion Ledger*, "they represent an image for an Ole Miss facing the future." Turner's response was to take away the pep band from all basketball games and use canned music instead, not a popular decision, but one he refused to rescind.

What was continually fascinating about Ole Miss, however, was how past and present were so often merged in the same moment. On the front page of the March 4, 1993, *Mississippian* was a story about the "Dixie" controversy with a picture of two white women holding a large sign that read, "Play Dixie." The "X" in Dixie was covered with stars, mimicking the rebel flag. Just above it was a story announcing that Jesse Holland, a black student and current managing editor of the paper, had just been selected as the new editor.

The law had always been central to race relations in the South. Segregation was not just a habit; it was written into state constitutions and statutes and woven into local ordinances. The rituals of Jim Crow became hard and fast rules. In Mississippi, lawyers enforced the caste system, skillfully using white supremacist ideology to blunt a federal

Constitution that spoke of equal justice and was premised on the notion of equal rights. So it was an extraordinary moment when Louis Westerfield, who had been the first black tenured professor at Ole Miss, was chosen on March 9, 1994, to head the university's law school. Westerfield had left Ole Miss to become dean of North Carolina Central University's law school and then moved on to head Loyola Law School in New Orleans before being offered the Ole Miss position. He had been the choice of the law faculty, which had forwarded its recommendation to Chancellor Turner.

"I am well aware of the historical significance of the University of Mississippi selecting its first African-American dean," Westerfield said upon his appointment. "I appreciate those who are willing to give me this opportunity and the many others black and white, who have labored through the years to allow us to progress to this point."

He was under no illusions that his task would be easy. He came into the job girding himself for battle against those he knew were uncomfortable with his appointment. Recalling his childhood in a sharecropping family in eastern Mississippi, and then his teenage years in the hard projects of New Orleans, Westerfield understood that the struggle was over. "I didn't come here expecting to be treated equally," he remarked not long after his appointment. Westerfield shrugged off the fact that his honors in his first year as dean came only from the black community. The disappointments and frustrations in the job were worth it because he understood that the most important aspect of his position was that when he attended meetings of the local bar associations—most of them all white—and the dean of the Ole Miss law school was introduced, it was he who stood up. Even before he said a word, his presence spoke volumes.

10

Tragedy and Triumph, Shame and Honor

The chancellor's residence at Ole Miss had been the scene of many important functions over the years. Prior to March 29, 1996, it had never been the place for a reunion of black alumni, but on this sunny afternoon two hundred black doctors, lawyers, teachers, and assorted other professionals, name tags affixed to their pockets, drinks and hors d'oeuvres in hand, milled about the house, renewing acquaintances and reminiscing about their time in school.

It was the kind of scene the most optimistic integrationists had dreamed of twenty years earlier, when black students began arriving on the campus in tens and twenties, not twos and threes. The afternoon reception, the kickoff event of a three-day gathering, illustrated something Michael Harrington, the philosophy professor, and Robert Hawes of the history department had written in a proposal for the Center for the Study of Southern Culture. The university, like the entire state, the two men said, had something special to offer: "a tragic history and the experience of attempting to transcend that tragic past into a triumphant present, to transform ourselves from a symbol of racism to a symbol of racial respect."

"Racial respect" was a striking term, careful, even modest—a phrase that implied limits and boundaries and one that aimed for something less grand than "color-blind society" and more pragmatic than "race neutral." "Racial respect" is not an attempt to blur or erase differences but to acknowledge and accept them so that a working whole can come out of separate parts. On its best days, that described the University of Mississippi that Robert Khayat was chosen to lead after Gerald Turner announced early in 1995 that he was leaving to become president of Southern Methodist University. And it had been Khayat who opened the chancellor's residence to the black alumni as a gesture of welcome to make these former students feel part of the Ole Miss community.

The board of trustees had been unanimous in selecting Khayat, and in a way the decision was like honoring one of the family. He had had a long association with the university, going back to his days as an undergraduate from 1958 to 1961. He had excelled academically and was a fine athlete, a star on the Johnny Vaught football team that had brought so much glory to the school. He had been an academic All-American and a college All Star, and he had played for a few years with the Washington Redskins. He graduated from the Ole Miss law school in 1966, third in a class of forty-six. He had taught in the law school, served as a vice chancellor, interim athletic director, and head of the committee planning the university's one hundred fiftieth anniversary celebration, the position he held when Turner left.

So Khayat's opening comment at his inauguration twelve days after the alumni reunion was understandable, even if susceptible to varying interpretations. "I come not as a stranger," he told the several thousand gathered in the coliseum. "I am one of you."

Sitting in the faculty section in full academic dress, Donald Cole winced for a minute at Khayat's choice of words: "I am one of you." Who was "you"? In times past it would have been code for the white gentry. That is certainly who Ross Barnett had in mind when he declared his love for Mississippi's "people" and her "heritage" in the midst of the Meredith crisis. Or was Khayat's "you" a term for Mississippians, whoever they might be—young, old, black, white, men, women, and particularly those who had come of age, as the chancellor had, in the turmoil of the racial revolution? As Khayat went on, Cole felt more comfortable when he heard him say just that: "We are one—we must be one—regardless of our role, race or gender, economic status, religious affiliation, or political persuasion. We are one people."

Then he remembered Khayat's gesture to the black alumni group and his first comments in the black alumni newsletter about his goals for the school: "to offer an accessible, nurturing campus that mirrors Mississippi's diversity." And Cole reminded himself of his work on the committee looking for Turner's replacement. A strong ally of the former chancellor, he had often remarked how Turner understood that to get ten pounds of movement at the bottom, he had to exert one hundred pounds of pressure from the top. And he had shown in his eleven years in Oxford that he was willing to do that. Cole wasn't sure Khayat subscribed to that concept of leadership, and it had concerned him, but he had been impressed by the coalition of supporters Khayat put together: political conservatives and moderates, blacks and whites, academics and businesspeople—in short, individuals who usually did not speak to one another. That had to say something about Khayat's ability to make things happen, Cole decided, and he hoped that would be good for the university.

By the time Khayat finished his short address, Cole believed that the new chancellor's "you" included him.

Because he was a native Mississippian and an Ole Miss graduate, Khayat appreciated more than most the power of the past to shape the present and the pitfalls of a selective retelling of history. He had acknowledged as much in his inaugural remarks, referring to the "tragedy and triumph, shame and honor, darkness and enlightenment" that all were a part of Ole Miss. He understood that it was a recipe for conflict to glorify the Confederate cause and the era of white supremacy while ignoring slavery and the racial caste system.

Two federal lawsuits hanging over the university in the summer of 1996 had made that point with great clarity, one the mirror of the other. The first was a challenge to the legacy of Jim Crow in higher education, the other a challenge to some of the remedies created to undo a century of discrimination.

On January 28, 1975, Jake Ayers had filed a lawsuit in federal court on behalf of his son and twenty-one other black high school students alleging that Mississippi still maintained a segregated system of higher education. He asked that the federal courts require the state to do more than simply adopt race-neutral policies at the eight public colleges—five predominantly white schools, three historically black ones. The black schools were still decidedly inferior and still where the lion's share of young black Mississippians were getting their education.

For more than a decade, the parties dickered with potential voluntary settlements, but all efforts came to naught. In December 1987, U.S. District Judge Neal Biggers dismissed the lawsuit. In February 1990, a three-judge panel on the U.S. Court of Appeals for the Fifth Circuit overturned Biggers's decision, but when the full Fifth Circuit considered the case, they reinstated his dismissal.

Ayers's lawyers appealed to the Supreme Court, and on June 26, 1992, more than seventeen years after the case had been filed, the High Court ruled that Mississippi had not done enough to dismantle a segregated system. The justices sent the case back to Biggers to come up with a solution. Nearly three years later, after more intense negotiations and a lengthy trial, Biggers ordered the state to put into effect a single admission standard at all universities and to upgrade programs at two of the historically black colleges.

The plaintiffs, who had been hoping for a broader and more aggressive set of remedies to shore up the black schools, appealed his decision, and by the end of 1996, the lawsuit was working its way back through the federal appeals system.

There had been suggestions over the years that some programs at the university should be transferred or merged with similar programs at one or the other of the historically black schools to make them stronger. But such a move was highly unlikely, particularly when so many power brokers in the state had such strong emotional ties to Ole Miss.

The second lawsuit, *Texas v. Hopwood,* was much more recent and more threatening to some of the university's operations. It was a challenge to the admissions process at the University of Texas law school, where a special program had been put in place to increase the number of black and Mexican American students. Several white students, led by Cheryl Hopwood, had challenged the program as unfairly discriminating against them, and in the spring of 1996, the Fifth Circuit, which covers Texas,

Louisiana, and Mississippi, invalidated it, saying the law school could not use race as a factor in its admissions process. On July 1, 1996, the Supreme Court declined to review the decision, casting doubt on all affirmative action admissions programs in the three states.

Khayat professed not to worry about the decision's effect on Ole Miss, although the school had its own programs in place to increase minority enrollment. His mantra since he had taken over the job had been that the university would represent the people of Mississippi, and he said to anyone who asked and to anyone who listened to him speak at countless lunches and dinners that the school would aggressively recruit Mississippians, and if it did that, then by the very nature of the state's population the university would be diverse.

The chancellor's optimism was a product of what he saw every day when he looked out the window of his Lyceum office—black and white students heading into the library to study. But it was an optimism that required scrutiny. Ole Miss was one place where appearances could be, if not deceiving, incomplete because of the chasm in perception between whites and blacks, a chasm fueled by that dichotomy between a shared history and a divided heritage. "Where you stand depends on where you're sittin'," was the way Thurgood Marshall had put it. The conflict over the Klan pictures in the 1983 *Ole Miss* was a specific case in point. The continuing eruptions over the rebel flag and "Dixie" illustrated it more generally.

David Sansing and Gerald Turner were fond of saying that if integration could work at the University of Mississippi, then it could work anywhere. Had it worked? The answer depends on how the term was defined.

Many things had happened at Ole Miss since September 30, 1962. James Meredith's courageous effort had been first and foremost about creating opportunity for those who had been so long denied. It was clear that this goal had been achieved. The black alumni reunion was living proof, a sampling of the several thousand black students who had come to Oxford, stayed the course, and left with the piece of parchment that made them graduates of the University of Mississippi. As so many other whites had done before them, they moved from their Oxford experience into successful careers.

But if integration meant some kind of social melding and sense of community beyond the classroom, then Ole Miss had fallen short of the mark. It was evident by the early 1990s, with blacks making up roughly 10 percent of the student body—and a much smaller percentage of the faculty—that there were, once classes were over, essentially two different campuses—one for the white students, one for the blacks. By its very existence the black alumni reunion, successful as it was, reflected this reality, particularly the highlight of the weekend: a cheerfully boisterous competition among the black sororities and fraternities to see which one was the best "stepper." This is the term for the rhythmic dance routines each group creates for what had become an annual contest. It was an event with a cultural as well as an artistic dimension, one a white observer could appreciate only from a figurative distance.

Moments like this were instructive and not uncommon, a fact noted in a special issue of the *Mississippian* devoted exclusively to race. It was published to coincide with Black History Month in February 1996. "It is our dream," the editorial staff wrote, "that there will no longer be black events or white events on our campus, but community events." They were, the students went on, "supposed to be the generation who grew up in an integrated society, unfettered by prejudices of the past, ready to truly make America a 'melting pot.' Unfortunately, things didn't work out quite as planned."

That observation was an apt one for Ole Miss, more so than the young editors might have realized. So much of the thirty years since Meredith's arrival had exemplified the push-pull dynamic of racial change—pushing forward with the optimism of those calls for a "color-blind society" and the promise to be "race neutral," pulled backward by the punishing power of history and the tenacious legacy of oppression to forge diverse cultural identities not easily bridged. More than once David Sansing had thought to himself, "We just didn't realize it would be this hard."

In 1966 the Ole Miss law school under the leadership of Josh Morse had been in the forefront of change on the campus and in the state. The dean and his cadre of Yale-trained teachers were excited about training black lawyers in Mississippi and training a new generation of white lawyers to look at their world and the law with new perspectives. But they were brought to a halt by entrenched forces who in essence told them they had gone too far too fast. Things "didn't work out quite as planned" for Morse and colleagues.

Thirty years later the law school once again epitomized such conflict. By the spring of 1996 Louis Westerfield, who had been the dean for barely two years, felt under attack by influential members of the Mississippi bar. They had not directly criticized him, but they had criticized the process by which he had been selected. It had galled many of these lawyers that their good friend Robert Khayat, who had wanted the deanship, had been passed over for the job early in 1994.

Khayat, who was then teaching at Ole Miss, Westerfield, and a handful of other men had been interviewed by the faculty for the position. In his sessions with colleagues, Khayat expressed the desire to turn inward, to focus the law school on its Mississippi constituents. It was a precursor to observations he would later make as chancellor.

Westerfield, on the other hand, had a more expansive view of legal education. He wanted to build the school's national reputation, to recruit students and faculty from outside the state. A majority of faculty agreed with that vision and recommended him along with two other candidates to Chancellor Turner. Khayat was not among them. The rejection was a bitter disappointment to him and his many supporters in the Mississippi bar, although that disappointment was eased a year later when Khayat emerged as the consensus choice for chancellor to replace the departing Turner.

Once Khayat took office, he and Westerfield maintained civil public relations, but there were private strains between them. Westerfield frankly admitted that the chancellor "doesn't go out of his way to give me any assistance, and I don't go out of mine to ask."

In the summer of 1996, the dean was deeply troubled when he learned that members of the bar were asking the American Bar Association (ABA), which oversees law schools across the country, to change the rules for dean selection. The aim was to reduce the power of law faculties in recommending candidates. Westerfield took it personally, confiding to his friend Donald Cole that he felt singled out and did not know why—except for one obvious fact: He was black, and it was reasonable to assume a discomfort over his selection among these establishment whites, particularly because it meant that Khayat had been passed over. Apparently it was not enough that Khayat was now running the entire university.

John Bradley, who had argued so vigorously on behalf of the black students punished in 1970, was by now a thirty-year veteran of the law school and one of Westerfield's strongest allies. He fired off a blunt letter to the ABA in opposition to the state bar initiative. "It is no secret that in 1994 when an Afro-American was appointed as dean of the University of Mississippi law school a large number of active and vocal Mississippi bar members were highly displeased," Bradley wrote. "Many expressed hostility toward the law school for having voted approval of a minority candidate and disapproval of a candidate who was actively supported by many Mississippi bar members. . . . Who could think there is no significant connection between the 1994 appointment and the proposed amendment" to the dean selection procedures? Bradley went on. "Thus one critically important role of the need for faculty approval is to negate instances when political forces would deny opportunity to minority candidates."

Jack Dunbar, the Oxford lawyer who was spearheading the proposed changes, vehemently denied Bradley's claim. He was highly offended by the suggestion that race was a factor. He said it was about law school governance and power. "The faculty should not be running law schools." The ABA essentially rebuffed Dunbar's proposal to put new constraints on faculties around the country. One senior ABA official called it a "mean-spirited struggle" and expressed concern that "Louis had been required to go through the whole sorry business."

On August 24, 1996, Louis Westerfield died of an apparent massive heart attack. He and his wife had been in New Orleans attending a conference of Mississippi and Louisiana judges when he was stricken. His death stunned the Ole Miss campus. For Cole, there was particular resonance. He had lost a friend and a valuable colleague whose presence had helped the university's recruitment and image. Westerfield's appointment had been such a significant moment, one of those benchmarks that signaled the distance that had been traveled since 1962. In the previous year and a half, two senior black administrators had left the university for schools they believed would better use their talents. Westerfield's death meant that a third prominent black was gone from Ole Miss, and Cole wondered in the early days of autumn if any of them would be replaced and how long it might take. On some days he was disheartened, but he reminded himself in these sobering moments that if the University of Mississippi was not a perfect world and if its conflicts defined the boundaries for racial accord, it also stood for what was achievable: that opportunities to learn, grow, and prosper can be extended across the racial divide and in the process racial stereotypes and prejudice can give way to the racial respect so necessary to make a heterogeneous society function peacefully, if not always in harmony.

Cole's optimism was leavening against the ugly incidents of bigotry that seemed to erupt every few years. The evidence to support that optimism were the young black Mississippians who chose to follow in Meredith's footsteps and brave a new and unwelcoming world in Oxford, changing their own lives and then changing others. Cole himself had been one of them. Kenneth Weeden, a 1973 graduate from Tunica, was another.

Weeden had gotten the rude racial awakening common to his black classmates when he arrived at his dormitory to start school in mid-June 1970. He introduced himself to his white roommate, who had already unpacked his clothes, shelved his books, and set up his stereo, and then went for a walk around the campus. When he came back a few hours later, the other young man had moved out.

Weeden absorbed the rejection and buckled down to three years of hard work so that he could graduate early. He joked that he raced out of Oxford with "skidmarks on the sidewalk," so anxious was he to leave the campus. He went on to graduate school at the University of North Carolina and a lucrative career as an urban planner. He did not come back to Ole Miss until March 29, 1996, for the reunion. He hadn't been bitter about his undergraduate days, but something was missing. "I just felt this emptiness. . . . I needed to tie up loose emotional memories," he explained, so much so that he came to Oxford instead of attending an anniversary celebration in Chapel Hill for his graduate department.

Weeden was uneasy as he drove onto the campus and registered at the alumni house. Within an hour he was smiling. The enthusiasm of the younger graduates was contagious. At first he wondered where it was coming from. Then he realized that the Ole Miss he attended and the one that they did were really two different places.

Early in his tenure as chancellor, Khayat had demonstrated an appreciation for the encouraging word and the symbolic gesture. One of the first was the approval of a new memorial for the campus. This one was going to be different from the others, for it would be dedicated not to the Civil War but to civil rights. The idea had come from a group of graduate students, most of them white, who felt that Ole Miss needed to recognize its recent history in some visible way and the larger struggle for equal opportunity in education in Mississippi. The night of September 30, 1962, had ensured that there was no better place for this than Oxford.

Khayat agreed, and he chose for the site a small plot of land between the Lyceum and the main library, which was named for J. D. Williams, the chancellor during the Meredith controversy. It is a fitting location, halfway between the university's seat of power and the house of study—a reminder of where Ole Miss has been and where it is striving to go.

Photo Credits

Notes

Chapter 1: The Mystic Chords of Memory

PAGE

5 "fairyland": Federal Writers Project of the Works Project Administration, *Mississippi: A Guide to the Magnolia State*, p. 255; Sansing, *Making Haste Slowly*, p. 36.

5 "Send your sons": Sansing, *Making Haste Slowly*, p. 35.

6 "challenged": Sansing, *Making Haste Slowly*, pp. 45–53.

7 anti-Barnard forces: Cabaniss, *The University of Mississippi*, pp. 35–37, 46–49; Board of Trustees minutes, March 1, 1860; Chute, *Damn Yankee!*, p. 171; Sansing, *Making Haste Slowly*, pp. 45, 53.

8 "two abolition books": Phi Sigma Society, 1849–1867, February 22, 1861, University of Mississippi Archives.

9 "viable existence" Cabaniss, *The University of Mississippi*, p. 52.

10 "self-sacrifice": Johnson, "The University War Hospital."

12 "sons of parents": University of Mississippi, *Historical Catalogue, 1849–1909*, pp. 9–10.

12 "Lost cause": See Wilson, *Baptized in Blood;* Foster, *Ghosts of the Confederacy;* Wilson, "The Religion of the Lost Cause," pp. 220–238.

13 "her wasted fields": Witherspoon, "The Appeal of the South to Its Educated Men."

14 "white people want": Bailey, *Race Orthodoxy in the South—and Other Aspects of the Negro Question*, p. 278.

15 "sharpen his cunning": Wish, "Negro Education and the Progressive Movement."

15 "teaching Negroes": McMillen, *Dark Journey*, pp. 90, 99.

16 "an explosion": Mayes, *A History of Education in Mississippi*, pp. 162–164.

16 "without hesitation": Waddel, *Memorials of an Academic Life*, pp. 465–467.

17 Alcorn: McMillen, *Dark Journey*, pp. 91, 103, 105; Sansing, *Making Haste Slowly*, pp. 63–64; Baker, *Following the Color Line*, p. 248.

19 Sallie Eola Reneau: Berry, "A History of Higher Education for Women in Mississippi," p. 58.

19 appealing coeds: 1926, 1936 *Ole Miss* annual.

20 "never missed a train": 1926 *Ole Miss* annual.

Chapter 2: A Tattered Shrine in Oxford

PAGE

22 "not a great": Sansing, *Making Haste Slowly,* pp. 90, 98; Cabaniss, *The University of Mississippi,* p. 145.

24 "however much:" Sansing, *Making Haste Slowly,* p. 99; Graham, "Bilbo and the University of Mississippi, 1928–32," pp. 9–11.

24 wearing shorts: Graham, "Bilbo and the University," p. 37.

25 "a pentitent child": Jones, "Tenets and Attitudes of an Old Time Teacher (Alfred Hume)," pp. 33–34.

25 "a Christian institution": Jones, "Tenets and Attitudes," pp. 31, 40, 44–45.

27 "uproot": Graham, "Bilbo and the University," p. 9; *Jackson Daily News,* February 29, 1929, p. 1.

28 "alert or aware": Graham, "Bilbo and the University," pp. 2–3.

28 "spirit of conformity": *Mississippian,* April 6, 1928, p. 4.

28 "old periodicals": Graham, "Bilbo and the University," pp. 37–38.

29 new chancellor: *Jackson Daily News,* August 7, 1930, p. 14; Graham, "Bilbo and the University," p. 31; Sansing, *Making Haste Slowly,* pp. 104–107.

30 "time-worn horse": *Jackson Daily News,* June 15, 1930, p. 8.

31 "iron hand": *Mississippian,* May 18, 1929, p. 2.

31 "great good": Graham, "Bilbo and the University," pp. 78–85; Sansing, *Making Haste Slowly,* p. 108.

31 declined to censure: Graham, "Bilbo and the University," pp. 98–100.

32 "he was right": Cabaniss, *The University of Mississippi,* pp. 143, 148.

Chapter 3: Climate Control

PAGE

35 University of Texas: *Sweatt v. Texas,* 339 U.S. 629 (1950); *McLaurin v. Oklahoma State Regents,* 330 U.S. 963 (1950).

36 "qualified Negro applicants": *Mississippian,* October 27, 1950, p. 4.

37 "shocking": *Jackson Clarion Ledger,* November 8, 1950, p. 12.

37 "take it and jam it": *Mississippian,* November 3, 1950, p. 4.

37 repercussions: Albin Krebs interview, February 3, 1995.

38 90 percent: *Mississippi: Guide to the Magnolia State,* p. 261; McMillen, *Dark Journey,* p. 223.

38 "instruments for": McMillen, *Dark Journey,* p. 197.

39 Eastland: *Washington Post,* May 18, 1954, p. 1; *Clarion Ledger,* May 18, 1954, p. 6.

39 "legal subterfuge": *Clarion Ledger,* June 30, 1954.

41 "slave auction": *Mississippian,* November 5, 1954, p. 1.

42 J. D. Williams: Read, "The Williams Chancellorship at the University of Mississippi," pp. 146–168.

43 "grave intrusion": *Mississippian,* March 18, 1955, p. 4; James Autry interview, January 5, 1995; Silver, *Running Scared,* p. 35.

44 Religious Emphasis Week: Campbell, *Brother to a Dragonfly,* pp. 113, 115.

45 "If Rev. Kershaw is hushed": *Mississippian,* November 11, 1955, p. 4.

45 church pulpit: Read, "The Williams Chancellorship," pp. 166–167.

46 "If I am asked": *Mississippian,* February 3, 1956, p. 4.

46 19 percent: *Clarion Ledger,* February 5, 1956, p. 8.

46 "the man can't come": Campbell, *Brother to a Dragonfly,* p. 120; Campbell interview, January 12, 1995.

46 "freedoms of thought": Morton King Papers, University of Mississippi Archives; *New York Times,* February 11, 1956, p. 1; *Clarion Ledger,* February 10–11, p. 1.

47 two chairs: Campbell, *Brother to a Dragonfly,* pp. 120–121; *Mississippian,* February 17, 1956, p. 1.

47 "turned the bees loose": Campbell interview, January 12, 1995.

48 "personal conviction": *Mississippian,* February 10, 1956, p. 1.

48 "garish flash": *Mississippian,* February 10, 1956.

48 sustained challenge: Sansing, *Making Haste Slowly,* pp. 146–147; Silver, *Running Scared,* p. 67; Clegg, "Someone Jumped the Gun," p. 61.

49 targeted as subversives: Notes from interviews conducted by Dr. H. V. Howerton, head of the Political Science Department at the University of Mississippi, June 17, 1947, from Southern Politics Collection—Mississippi, Jean and Alexander Heard Library, Vanderbilt University.

50 "Every book": July 31, 1959, article from unidentified newspaper, William Murphy Papers, University of Mississippi Archives.

50 "A belief in God": Murphy Papers; Silver, *Running Scared,* pp. 66–67; Sansing, *Making Haste Slowly,* p. 146.

51 "does not endorse": Board of Trustees statement August 27, 1959, Murphy Papers.

52 "a baseless cause": *Mississippi Law Journal* (December 1957): 110–112; excerpts from Edwin White statement, Murphy Papers.

52 pressured student editors: William Murphy interview, January 6, 1995.

53 "at the top": Mary Libby Bickerstaff Payne to Murphy, July 10, 1959, Murphy Papers.

53 "learning, ability": Statement of University of Mississippi law school faculty, June 26, 1961, Murphy Papers.

54 "Sampson": Murphy interview, January 6, 1995.

55 prohibited use of state funds: Senate Concurrent Resolution O. 155, Regular Session 1960, Murphy Papers; *Jackson Daily News,* April 21, 1960, p. 1.

55 "It is a lie": *Delta Democrat Times,* May 3, 1960, in Murphy Papers.

55 noted ruefully: Murphy to Beverly S. Burbage, May 3, 1960, Murphy Papers.

56 "ditch to die in": Murphy interview, January 6, 1995; J. D. Williams to Murphy, March 13, December 1, 1961, Murphy Papers.

56 "tiger in the gate": Cleghorn, "Tiger at Ole Miss."

Chapter 4: Meredith

PAGE

57 "one of those sons": James Meredith interviews, February 17, March 29, 1995; see also Meredith, *Three Years in Mississippi.*

59 "I anticipate": Meredith, *Three Years,* pp. 55–56.

60 "prime minister": McMillen, *The Citizens' Council,* pp. 322–327.

60 alumni statements: Barrett, *Integration at Ole Miss,* p. 36.

61 Charles Dubra: Barrett, *Integration,* p. 25.

61 Medgar Evers: Sansing, *Making Haste,* pp. 142–143; Barrett, *Integration,* pp. 25–26.

62 "we had it fixed": J. P. Coleman interview with David Sansing, Verner Holmes Papers, University of Mississippi Archives; Barrett, *Integration,* p. 33; Sansing, *Making Haste,* pp. 145–146.

62 Clyde Kennard: Sansing, *Making Haste,* pp. 148–154; Silver, *The Closed Society,* pp. 93–95; *Reporter,* November 8, 1962, pp. 30–34.

63 "The traditional practice": Meredith, *Three Years,* p. 79.

63 cutoff date: Meredith, *Three Years,* p. 58; Barrett, *Integration,* pp. 40–42.

64 "the best interests": *Jackson State Times,* February 7–8, 1961, p. 1; Barrett, *Integration,* p. 41.

64 "Other Negro citizens": Meredith, *Three Years,* pp. 60–61.

65 "not a usual applicant": Meredith, *Three Years,* pp. 69–77.

68 "because he was a Negro": Barrett, *Integration,* pp. 43–58; Lord, *The Past That Would Not Die,* pp. 104–108.

70 Motley immediately objected: *Clarion Ledger,* January 25–28, 1962, p. 1; Sansing, *Making Haste,* p. 164; Lord, *The Past That Would Not Die,* pp. 108–111.

71 "The proof shows": Meredith, *Three Years,* pp. 133–134.

71 "to be in full accord": "The University of Mississippi and the Meredith Case," the university's official report of the episode, p. 4.

71 "rise of massive resistance": Bass, *Unlikely Heroes,* pp. 177–178.

72 "full review": Sansing, *Making Haste,* p. 167; Meredith, *Three Years,* p. 143.

72 a dissenting opinion: Meredith, *Three Years,* p. 163.

73 "gentleman academician": Barrett, *Integration,* pp. 8, 82.

74 "the end of the road": Meredith, *Three Years,* pp. 165–166.

74 "We will not surrender": *Clarion Ledger,* September 14, 1962, p. 1; Lord, *The Past,* pp. 139–141.

75 "Governor Reaches Point": Barrett, *Integration,* p. 95.

75 three-hour closed-door session: *Clarion Ledger,* September 15, 1962, p. 1.

75 "solemnly and prayerfully": Barrett, *Integration,* p. 97.

76 first to show a division: Verner Holmes interviews, February 27, March 28, 1995.

76 "taught to believe": Board of Trustees minutes, September 17, 1962, in Verner Holmes Papers.

76 pressure on Riddell: Tally Riddell interview, March 1, 1995.

77 "jaundiced eye": *Clarion Ledger,* September 16, 1962, p. 1.

77 "fearless and courageous": Barrett, *Integration,* p. 100.

77 state judiciary: *Jackson Daily News,* September 19, 1962, p. 1.

77 "Students at the university": Barrett, *Integration,* p. 102.

77 cross was burned: *Clarion Ledger,* September 20, 1962, p. 1; Barrett, *Integration,* p. 104.

78 "our big mistake": Holmes interview, March 28, 1995.

78 his new power: Sansing, *Making Haste,* pp. 173–175; Barrett, *Integration,* pp. 105–106; Sansing interview, April 3, 1995.

79 impassive Meredith: Meredith, *Three Years,* pp. 193, 196–197; see also *New York Times,* September 20–25, 1962, and *Clarion Ledger,* September 20–25, 1962, for extensive coverage.

80 "Go home Nigger": *New York Times,* September 26, 1962, pp. 1, 22.

80 the young editors: Sidna Brower interview, February 13, 1995.

81 front-page editorial: *Mississippian,* September 21, 1962, p. 1.

82 attorney general: Reeves, *President Kennedy,* p. 356.

82 "to be a useful citizen": *New York Times,* September 28, 1962, p. 22.

83 "I will be there": *New York Times,* September 28, 1962, p. 23.

83 "I love Mississippi": *New York Times,* September 30, 1962, p. 66; Barrett, *Integration,* p. 121.

84 At 12:01 A.M.: Reeves, *President Kennedy,* pp. 359–361.

84 plans changed: Clegg, "Someone Jumped the Gun," pp. 188–190.

84 "I want to": *Look Magazine,* December 31, 1962, pp. 19–36.

85 "Surrounded": Barrett, *Integration,* p. 146; see also *New York Times,* October 1, 1962, p. 1, and *Clarion Ledger,* October 1, 1962, p. 1.

85 amid the melee: Brower interview, February 13, 1995; Trent Lott interview, May 15, 1995; Scheips, *The Role of the Army in the Oxford, Mississippi Incident,* p. 99.

86 "Students started out": *Mississippian,* October 1, 1962, p. 1.

87 Looking for Robert Kennedy: Transcript of conversation between Ross Barnett and Burke Marshall, October 1, 1962, 4:15 P.M.

Chapter 5: Picking Up and Moving On

PAGE

88 "sane approach": *Wall Street Journal,* October 3, 1962, p. 1; transcript of W. H. Billy Mounger comments, University of Mississippi Archives.

89 "resent the Negro": *Rebel Underground* 1, November 1, October 1962, University of Mississippi Archives.

89 "MAILED IN": Envelope with "MAILED IN OCCUPIED MISSISSIPPI," Russell Barrett Papers, University of Mississippi Archives.

89 federal officials intervened: *Jackson Daily News,* October 4, 1962, p. 1.

90 "booed and hissed": Transcript of conversation between Robert Kennedy and J. D. Williams, October 5, 1962, James Silver Papers, University of Mississippi Archives.

90 "day of repentance": *Commercial Appeal,* October 8, 1962, p. 1.

91 "unfair and reprehensible": Barrett, *Integration,* pp. 179–182; *Mississippian,* October 9, 1962.

91 "purged from the ranks": *New York Times,* October 10, 1962, p. 1; Meredith, *Three Years,* p. 216.

92 "Get out of there": Lucy Turnbull interview, March 27, 1995.

92 "Tar Baby": *Rebel Underground* 1 (October 1962); Barrett, *Integration,* pp. 190–197.

93 "It is disgusting": *Mississippian,* October 31, 1962, pp. 1, 2; "Revolt of the Professors," *New Republic,* February 2, 1963, pp. 5–6.

93 "If there are any": *Mississippian,* November 2, 1962, p. 1.

94 "Sympathy doesn't mean much": Barrett, *Integration,* pp. 198–203.

96 hate calls . . . Kappa Kappa Gamma: Brower interviews, February 13, April 22, 1995.

96 one of the prime movers: George Monroe interview, May 5, 1995; *Mississippian,* November 27, 28, 29, December 6, 1962; *New York Times,* November 30, 1962, p. 18.

98 "Dead coon": *Jackson Daily News,* December 20, 1962.

98 "Goodbye James": *New York Times,* January 8, 1963, p. 1; *Clarion Ledger,* January 8, 1963, p. 1; *Mississippian,* January 8, 1964, p. 4.

99 anti-Meredith sentiment: *Delta Democrat Times,* January 11, 1963, p. 1; *Jackson Daily News,* January 11, 1963, p. 1.

99 $2.7 million: *Commercial Appeal,* November 15, 1962; *Clarion Ledger,* December 12, 1962; Scheips, *The Role of the Army,* p. 251.

100 news conference: *New York Times,* January 31, 1963, p. 1; Meredith interview, March 29, 1995.

100 "If a white student": *Look,* April 9, 1963, p. 70.

101 left school: Barrett, *Integration,* p. 218.

102 "Discrimination?" *Mississippian,* March 20, 1963, p. 1; Ed Williams interview, April 25, 1995; John Corlew interview, May 2, 1995.

102 "no organized ostracism": *Mississippian,* April 4, 1963, p. 4; April 9, 1963, p. 9.

103 protested the exhibition: Barrett, *Integration,* p. 218; *Mississippian,* April 9, 1963, pp. 1, 5.

104 "it would be unwise": *Clarion Ledger,* June 6, 1963, p. 1; *New York Times,* June 6, 1963, p. 1; *Mississippian,* June 7, 1963, p. 1.

105 blamed the murder: Meredith, *Three Years,* pp. 304–305; *New York Times,* June 16, 1963, p. 1.

105 "we could hardly believe": *Oxford Eagle,* August 22, 1963, p. 4.

106 marched with his classmates: Meredith, *Three Years,* p. 326; Barrett, *Integration,* p. 222.

106 "serious loss": *McComb Enterprise Journal,* August 16, 1963, p. 1; *Mississippian,* September 19, 1963, p. 2A; Meredith, *Three Years,* p. 280.

107 forced by the university: *New York Times,* August 25, 1963, p. 78; Silver, *Running Scared,* p. 78; *Reporter,* October 24, 1963, p. 42.

108 credit was cut off: Cleve McDowell interview, May 10, 1995.

108 officials suspended him; *Mississippian,* September 24, 1963, pp. 1–4, September 25, 1963, p. 1; *Delta Democrat Times,* September 24–25, 1963, p. 1; Barrett, *Integration,* p. 224.

109 "cold-blooded reality": McDowell interview, May 10, 1995.

110 "totalitarian society": *New York Times,* November 8, 1963, pp. 1, 19; *American Association of University Professors Bulletin* (August 1965): 351; Silver, *The Closed Society,* p. xvii.

111 "degrading activities": Sansing, *Making Haste,* pp. 200–201; *Commercial Appeal,* March 28, 1964, p. 4; *Clarion Ledger,* April 1, 1964, p. 24.

112 Two student honor societies: Silver, *Running Scared,* pp. 186–187.

113 "I have come": *Clarion Ledger,* June 11, 1964, p. 1; *Commercial Appeal,* June 12, 1964, p. 9; Barrett, *Integration,* pp. 228–236.

113 "While I am governor": *New York Times,* January 23, 1965, p. 1.

113 installed a button: *Mademoiselle* (August 1966): 333.

114 three-page, single-spaced report: Julien Tatum to J. D. Williams, July 31, 1964, J. D. Williams Papers, University of Mississippi Archives.

114 "surely disgusting": Ben Owen to J. D. Williams, August 6, 1994, Williams Papers.

114 White cafeteria workers: Silver, *Closed Society,* p. 319; Sansing, *Making Haste,* p. 198.

115 "a concerted effort": *AAUP Bulletin* (August 1965): 346–347.

115 Admiral Benbow: Interview with William L. Taylor, June 12, 1996.

116 "leisurely integration": *Ebony* (May 1966): p. 30.

116 "romantic details": *Mississippian,* February 25, 1964, pp. 1, 4.

117 "picking up": Williams interview, April 25, 1995.

117 Southern Literary Festival: *Mississippian,* April 23, 1965, p. 1; Hamblin, "The 1965 Southern Literary Festival," pp. 83–114.

117 "endangering the future": *Mississippian,* April 23, 1965, p. 4.

118 "You people": Williams interview, April 25, 1995.

119 "a provincial outlook": *Nation,* June 23, 1969, p. 791; Silver, *The Closed Society,* p. 321; Joshua Morse interview, May 22, 1995.

119 "a new mood": *Time,* September 23, 1966, p. 76; *Ebony* (May 1966): 32.

119 write a sonnet: Michael Horowitz interview, May 17, 1995.

120 completely ignored: Reuben Anderson interview, May 24, 1995.

121 invited Aaron Henry: Walter Dellinger interview, July 3, 1995.

121 pull his chair: David Clark interview, November 18, 1995; Dellinger interview, July 3, 1995.

122 "golden era" . . . "patronizing": Gene Fair interview, April 19, 1995; Lott interview, May 15, 1995.

122 "the welcome mat": Transcript of Barrett speech, Barrett Papers.

123 "laid a hand": *New York Times,* March 19, 1966, p. 1.

123 "I come here": Transcript of Robert Kennedy speech, University of Mississippi Archives.

123 "It ill becomes": *Mississippian,* March 27, 1966, pp. 4–5.

124 past history: *New York Times,* May 6, 1965, p. 1.

124 Verna Bailey: *Mississippi Press,* May 17, 1979; *Black Alumni News,* Number 1, p. 1; Verna Bailey interview, August 13, 1996.

126 taken off the payroll: *Mississippian,* October 3, 1969, p. 1.

126 lost control: Morse interview, May 22, 1995.

Chapter 6: An Awakening

PAGE

128 "The law says": Bob Boyd interview, June 27, 1995.

129 "You should go": David Molpus interview, August 21, 1995.

131 speaker screening policy: Bridgforth, "Bomb the Ban," pp. 66–68

132 "the official determiner": George Street interview, August 23, 1995.

133 McLemore spoke first: *Mississippian,* April 5, 1995, p. 1; Eugene McLemore interview, August 23, 1995.

134 close the university: Street interview, September 5, 1995; *Mississippian,* April 17, 1968, p. 1.

134 "an atmosphere of bigotry": Memo on "Bigotry, Bias and Racial Prejudice," April 8, 1968, from "Several Black Students" to Chancellor Porter Fortune, Fortune Papers, University of Mississippi Archives.

136 "I didn't see it coming": Street interview, August 23, 1995.

137 a downside: Molpus interview, August 21, 1995; Constance Slaughter Harvey interview, September 2, 1995; *Mississippian,* February 14, 1969, p. 1.

138 breach of the peace: *Mississippian,* March 17, 1969, p. 1; Bridgforth, "Bomb the Ban," pp. 98–103; Street interview, September 5, 1995.

138 stifle political speech: *Mississippian,* March 19, 21, 1969, p. 1.

139 "I am a racist": M. M. Roberts to Board of Trustees members, Roberts's speech to state Association of University Professors, John Crews Papers, University of Mississippi Archives.

141 step out of the racial routine: Sam Givhan interviews, August 16, 22, October 16, 1995.

142 worked in the cafeteria: Mary Thompson Givhan interview, July 19, November 17, 1995.

142 four-hour taxi ride: Donald Cole interview, July 18, 1995.

142 no other black: Kenneth Mayfield interview, September 6, 1995.

144 "small minded individuals": *Rebel Magazine* section of *Mississippian,* February 13, 1970, p. 1.

145 February 24: Cole interview, July 18, 1995; Givhan interview, July 19, 1995; McLemore interview, August 23, 1995; Mayfield interview, September 6, 1995;

Mississippian, February 25, 1975, p. 1; James, "A Demand for Racial Equality," pp. 97–120.

147 doubling as a photographer: Patsy Brumfield interview, August 24, 1995.

148 full riot gear: Thompson Givhan interview, July 19, 1995.

148 "stepped out of line": Givhan interview, August 16, 1995; Thompson Givhan interviews, July 19, September 19, 1995; Cole interview, July 18, 1995.

149 Parchman: Molpus interview, August 21, 1995; Nausead Stewart interview, August 29, 1995; Street interview, August 22, 1995.

149 convened a gathering: *Mississippian,* February 27, 1970.

150 "dramatize our demands": *Clarion Ledger,* February 26, 1970, p. 1.

150 a special session: Minutes of the February 27, 1970, faculty senate meeting, University of Mississippi Archives; Givhan interview, August 16, 1995; John Robbin Bradley interview, August 17, 1995.

152 In a slap: *Clarion Ledger,* March 3, 1970, p. 1; *Mississippian,* March 7, 1970, p. 1.

153 "If you can find": Barrett memo to Fortune, March 18, 1970, Barrett Papers.

153 "grossly inconsistent": *Mississippian,* March 11, 1970, p. 4.

153 "simply fun": *Mississippian,* March 20, 1970, p. 6.

155 composed a poem: Mayfield interview, September 6, 1995; private papers of Kenneth Mayfield.

155 "my star witness": Street interview, August 22, 1995; Mayfield interview, September 6, 1995; Linnie Liggins Willis interview, July 1, 1996.

156 her grandmother came: Liggins Willis interview, July 1, 1996.

156 "It wasn't a riot": Brumfield interview, August 24, 1995.

156 John Brittain, Jr.: *Mississippian,* March 18, 1970.

156 "sorority girl fog": Brumfield interview, August 24, 1995.

157 few illusions: Givhan interview, August 16, 1995; Mayfield interview, September 6, 1995.

158 unanimously decided: Board of Trustees minutes, March, April 1970; *Mississippian,* May 4, 1970.

158 finish her course work: Liggins Willis interview, July 1, 1996.

159 "You can't do that": John Crews interview, August 16, 1995.

159 "won't tolerate it": Crews interview, August 16, 1995; memos from Crews Papers.

Chapter 7: Ole Times There Not Yet Forgotten

PAGE

162 "More and more": *Oxford Eagle,* October 15, 1953, p. 1.

162 smacked in the head: Kent Moorhead interviews, November 29, 1995, January 4, 1996.

162 Al Hirt: *Mississippian,* February 26, 1963, p. 3.

163 introduced at halftime: Coolidge Ball interview, July 24, 1995.

164 courtesy titles: *Mississippian,* November 13, 1970, p. 4.

164 wanted to try out: Cole interview, October 17, 1995.

166 "not waving the flag": Lowell Grisham comment in Kent Moorhead film footage about the Confederate flag.

166 "terrible thunderhead": Vaught, *Rebel Coach,* pp. 114–115.

168 "Give 'at ball": *Atlanta Constitution,* September 3, 1986, pp. 1, 9D; September 7, 1986, pp. 1, 12–13A.

169 sat together: Thompson Givhan interview, July 19, 1995; Patricia Taylor Wise interview, November 17, 1995; Dottie Quaye Chapman Reed interview, November 28, 1995; James Hull interviews, October 26, 31, 1995, February 3, 1996; Lawrence Weeden interview, October 24, 1995.

169 "even the University of Mississippi: *Race Relations Reporter* (March 1970): p. 7.

169 shelve the proposal: Lowell Grisham interview, December 11, 1995.

170 "no Negro flashes": *Clarion Ledger,* November 15, 1970, p. 2F.

170 watched Williams play: Junie Hovious interview, December 7, 1995.

172 "If I play a good game": Ben Williams interview, November 17, 1995.

172 lagged behind: "Race Relations at Southern Universities," Crews Papers, Crews interview, November 17, 1995.

173 prepared herself: Jeanette Jennings interview, November 21, 1995.

174 "our own skin color": Thompson Givhan interview, November 17, 1995.

175 "no liberal ideas": Harry Owens interview, October 17, 1995.

175 "vertical Negro plan": Golden, *Only in America,* p. 121.

178 recruitment letter: John Crews to Betty West, March 8, 1971, Crews Papers.

178 Sansing learned: David Sansing interview, December 16, 1995; *Oxford Eagle,* April 18, 1972, p. 1.

179 "passed us by": Otis Tims interview, October 27, 1995.

179 "opening old wounds": *Mississippian,* October 6, 1972, p. 6.

180 "campus racism": *Mississippian,* June 3, 1970, p. 3, July 3, 1970, p. 2, July 15, 1970, p. 2.

180 top student: Burnis Morris interview, January 2, 1996.

181 "Many blacks": *Mississippian,* September 29, 1972, p. 1.

182 no extra money: *Mississippian,* June 25, 1973, p. 5.

183 "no opportunity": Patricia Taylor Wise interview, November 17, 1995.

185 "Ask your father": Moorhead interview, January 4, 1996.

185 personal visits: Williams interview, November 17, 1995.

186 a fence: 1976 *Ole Miss,* p. 237.

186 watched with pride: Chapman Reed interview, November 28, 1995.

188 decided to leave: Jennings interview, November 21, 1995.

Chapter 8: Tradition Under Challenge

PAGE

189 "don't get lynched": Kenneth Wooten interview, February 2, 1996.

190 "self-confident": Rose Jackson Flenorl interview, February 29, 1996.

192 "We don't serve niggers": Jackson Flenorl interviews, February 29, March 30, 1996.

192 rival candidate: Will Norton interview, March 20, 1996.

194 "nicknamed": *Mississippian,* October 29, 1979, p. 2.

194 destined for Oxford: David Robinson interview, May 6, 1996.

195 riled up black students: *Mississippian,* October 31, 1979, p. 2, November 6, 1979, p. 2; see also Thornton, "Symbolism at Ole Miss and the Crisis of Southern Identity," pp. 26–32.

196 cheerleading squad: Steve Ray interview, February 23, 1996; statement on cheerleaders from Chancellor's Advisory Committee on Black Student Concerns, January 18, 1982, private papers of Steve Ray.

197 "integrated but segregated": John Hawkins interview, February 13, 1996.

198 play the system: Allison Brown Buchanan interview, March 19, 1996.

198 "a new age": *Mississippian,* April 23, 1981, p. 1.

199 "holding your daughter": Hawkins interview, February 13, 1996; *Washington Post,* September 27, 1982, p. 1; *Mississippian,* September 2, 1982, p. 1.

199 "an anachronistic tradition": *Clarion Ledger,* September 1, 1982, p. 1.

200 "always waved a flag": William Ray interview, February 14, 1996.

200 "stop this nonsense": Hawkins interview, February, 13, 1996.

200 "still a black man": *New York Times,* September 4, 1982, p. 1.

201 "a negro boy": John C. McLaurin to Porter Fortune, September 3, 1982, Fortune Papers.

202 "created a dilemma": *Mississippian,* September 10, 1982, p. 2.

202 plenty worried: Sansing interview, April 17, 1996.

203 not a revolt: Hawkins interview, May 20, 1996.

203 twenty-nine Klan members: *Mississippian:* October 19, 22, 25, 1982, p. 1.

203 made the connection: Norton interview, March 20, 1996.

204 "Why celebrate": Charles Noyes interview, March 11, 1996.

204 lowest ratio: *Clarion Ledger,* September 26, 1982, p. 12E.

205 results were dismal: Bela Chain interview, February 2, 1996; Black Concerns Committee, minutes of March 4, 1981, p. 2, minutes of March 9, 1982, p. 2, private papers of Steve Ray; chancellor's response to Black Student Union, special Monday report, May 1983, p. 2.

205 terms were revelatory: Settlement of *Lyndia Robinson v. Parham Williams et al.,* case number WC74-66-K.

206 "Ludicrous": Richard Barrett to Porter Fortune, September 2, 1982, Fortune Papers.

206 "First of all": Porter Fortune to Chester H. Curtis, September 27, 1982, Fortune Papers.

209 "It is an insult": *Oxford Eagle,* October 1, 1982, p. 1.

209 "the best place": Meredith speech, Fortune Papers, *Mississippian,* October 1, 1982, p. 1.

210 "trading punches": *Mississippian,* October 6, 1982, p. 2.

211 "a more positive image": "The University of Mississippi 20th Anniversary of Admission of Black Students, 1982–83," Fortune Papers, University of Mississippi Archives.

212 elected yearbook editor: John Hall interview, March 12, 1996.

213 "All racial problems": 1983 *Ole Miss* dust jacket; see rest of annual for pictures and Willie Morris essay.

213 lodged a formal protest: *Mississippian,* April 12, 13, 14, 15, 1983, p. 1; see also *Commercial Appeal,* April 15, 1983; Lydia Spragin interview, February 27, 1996.

214 felt so isolated: Hall interview, March 12, 1996; Norton interview, March 20, 1996.

215 "You don't": Sansing interview, February 3, 1996; Hawkins interviews, February 13, May 20, 1996.

215 "Save the flag": *Clarion Ledger,* April 16, 1983, p. 1B; *Mississippian,* April 19, 1996, p. 1.; *Oxford Eagle,* April 19, 1983, p. 1.

216 "This flag": Chancellor's statement to press, April 20, 1983, Sansing private papers; *Mississippian,* April 21, 1983, p. 1; *Clarion Ledger,* April 21, 1983, p. 1, May 6, 1983, p. 8A.

219 "amused and disgusted": *Mississippian,* April 20, 1983, p. 2, April 21, 1983, p. 2.

220 "In spite of our good procedures": chancellor's response to Black Student Union, special Monday report, May 1983, p. 2.

220 passed away: *Mississippian,* June 1, 1983, p. 1.

Chapter 9: The Power of Perception, the Reality of Place

PAGE

222 "This is the University": Gerald Turner interview, June 12, 1996; *Mississippian,* September 26, 1983, p. 1, October 5, 1983, p. 1, April 26, 1984, p. 1.

224 disparaging remarks: *Mississippian,* September 26, 27, 1983, p. 1, November 2, 1983, p. 1.

226 "He had to go": Damon Moore interviews, May 25, June 9, 1996; Jean and Clen Moore interview, June 9, 1996.

227 "remember where you are": Moore interview, June 9, 1996.

228 "an inner message": *Mississippian,* November 13, 1986, p. 3.

228 "abused and mistreated": Turner interview, June 12, 1996; Bailey interview, August 13, 1996; Liggins Willis interview, July 1, 1996; Otis Sanford interview, May 2, 1996.

230 "Awards of Distinction": Michael Edmonds interview, February 28, 1996; Sansing interview, June 13, 1996.

231 "right thing to do": Turner interview, June 12, 1996; Sansing interview, June 13, 1996.

231 "coming full circle": Bailey interview, August 13, 1996.

232 "well, it's insane": Frank Hurdle interview, June 9, 1996; *Mississippian,* April 30, 1984, p. 2.

232 "If you are a white male": *Mississippian,* July 11, 26, 1985, p. 2.

233 "forget morality . . . quasi-racist": *Mississippian,* February 11, 1986, p. 2, February 13, 1986, p. 2.

233 "Wave a flag": *Mississippian,* October 23, 1987, p. 2.

234 his own journey: Thomas "Sparky" Reardon interview, June 11, 1996; Thomas Wallace interview, June 10, 1996.

235 "the house has burned": Reardon interview, June 11, 1996; Wallace interview, June 10, 1996; Turner interview, June 12, 1996; *New York Times,* August 5, 1988, sec. IV, p. 17; *Clarion Ledger,* August 5, 1988, p. 1.

237 goal was $20,000: Stuart Brunson interview, June 6, 1996; William Boyd interview, May 29, 1996; Reardon interview, June 11, 1996.

238 carrying furniture: *New York Times,* October 16, 1988, p. 20; *Clarion Ledger,* August 7, 1988, p. 14H.

239 an open letter: John Ates interview, June 6, 1996; Reardon interview, June 11, 1996; Turner interview, June 12, 1996; *Mississippian,* March 20–April 6, 1989, p. 1, April 19, 1989, p. 2.

240 "KKK . . . I hate niggers": *Clarion Ledger,* September 20, 21, 1989, p. 1; *Mississippian,* September 20, 21, 1989, p. 1; Reardon interview, June 10, 1996; Turner interview, June 12, 1996; Brad Gunner interview, June 6, 1996.

241 "had no idea": *Clarion Ledger,* September 21, 1989, p. 12A.

242 his private school: *Washington Post,* October 5, 1986, p. A11.

242 "it's just not cool": *Mississippian,* October 4, 1989, p. 2.

243 "worst kinds of racists": Michael Harrington interview, June 11, 1996; Michael Harrington, University Studies Program Assessment.

243 expulsion order: *Mississippian,* October 9, 1989, p. 1; Turner interview, June 12, 1996.

244 "The large number": Report of the Chancellor's Task Force on Minority Participation in Campus Life, July 14, 1989; *Mississippian,* April 1989, p. 2.

245 "You'll never make it": Kimsey O'Neal interview, June 6, 1996; Jackson Flenorl interview, May 30, 1996.

247 "earn the respect": Lee Eric Smith interview, June 6, 1996; *Mississippian,* April 26, 1990, p. 1.

247 "You'd be segregated": *Mississippian,* February 6, 1990, p. 6.

248 "I'm the new coach": *Mississippian,* March 31, 1992, p. 1; *Commercial Appeal,* March 31, 1992, p. D1.

248 "the diatribe": *Esquire,* December 2, 1992, p. 108; Meredith interview, March 29, 1995.

248 special issue: *Mississippian,* October 1, 1992, pp. 3–18.

249 University 101: Harrington interview, June 11, 1996.

250 wanted to teach: Cole interviews, July 18, October 17, 1995, May 24, May 25, 1996; Wallace interview, June 10, 1996; Turner interview, June 12, 1996.

251 stop playing "Dixie": *Atlanta Constitution:* November 16, 1974, p. 1, November 1, 1975, p. 11A, November 6, 1975, p. 1.

252 angry reaction: *Mississippian,* March 2, 1993, p. 3, April 1, 1993, p. 1; *Clarion Ledger,* March 4, 1993, p. B1.

254 "I am well aware": *Mississippian,* March 10, 1994, p. 1; Louis Westerfield interview, June 10, 1996.

Chapter 10: Tragedy and Triumph, Shame and Honor

PAGE

256 "I come": Robert Khayat inauguration speech, chancellor's office. April 11, 1996.

256 winced for a minute: Cole interview, June 7, 1996.

257 Two federal lawsuits: *New York Times,* July 2, 1996, p. 12; *Washington Post,* July 2, 1996, p. 1.

259 recruit Mississippians: Khayat interview, July 24, 1996.

260 "It is our dream": *Mississippian,* February 15, 1996, p. 2.

261 "out of his way": Westerfield interview, June 10, 1996.

262 "It is no secret": John Bradley to Dean Robert K. Walsh of the American Bar Association, July 18, 1996.

262 vehemently denied: Jack Dunbar to Professor Erica Moeser of the ABA, July 23, 1996, Dunbar interview, October 21, 1996.

262 "mean-spirited struggle": Erica Moeser to John Bradley, August 28, 1996; Bradley interview, October 11, 1996; Cole interview, October 10, 1996.

263 rude racial awakening: Kenneth Weeden interview, July 30, 1996.

Bibliography

Books

American Association of University Professors Bulletin (Autumn 1965).

Bailey, Thomas Pearce. *Race Orthodoxy in the South—and Other Aspects of the Negro Question.* New York: Negro Universities Press, 1969.

Baker, Ray Stannard. *Following the Color Line: American Negro Citizenship in the Progressive Era.* New York: Harper & Row, 1964.

Barrett, Russell H. *Integration at Ole Miss.* Chicago: Quadrangle Books, 1965.

Bass, Jack. *Unlikely Heroes.* New York: Simon & Schuster, 1981.

Branch, *Parting the Waters—America in the King Years, 1954–63.* New York: Simon & Schuster, 1988.

Brown, Maud M. *The University Greys.* Richmond: Garrett and Massie, 1940.

Cabaniss, James Allen. *The University of Mississippi: Its First Hundred Years.* Oxford, Miss.: University of Mississippi, 1949.

Campbell, Will. *Brother to a Dragonfly.* New York: Seabury Press, 1977.

Chute, William J. *Damn Yankee! The First Career of Frederick A. P. Barnard.* New York: Kennikat Press, 1978.

Cose, Ellis. *Rage of a Privileged Class.* New York: HarperCollins, 1993.

Davis, W. Milam. *Pushing Forward: A History of Alcorn A&M College and Portraits of Successful Graduates.* Okolona, Miss.: Okolona Industrial School, 1938.

Federal Writers Project of the Works Project Administration. *Mississippi: A Guide to the Magnolia State.* New York: Viking Press, 1938.

Foster, Gaines. *Ghosts of the Confederacy: Defeat of the Lost Cause and the Emergence of the New South.* New York: Oxford University Press, 1987.

Franklin, John Hope. *From Slavery to Freedom—A History of Negro Americans,* New York: McGraw-Hill, 1993.

Golden, Harry. *Only in America.* Cleveland: World Publishing Co., 1958.

Lincoln, C. Eric. *Coming Through the Fire: Surviving Race and Place in America.* Durham: Duke University Press, 1996.

Lord, Walter. *The Past That Would Not Die.* New York: Harper & Row, 1965.

Mayes, Edward. *A History of Education in Mississippi.* Washington D.C.: U.S. Government Printing Office, 1899.

McMillen, Neil R. *The Citizens' Council: Organized Resistance to the Second Reconstruction.* Urbana: University of Illinois Press, 1971.

———. *Dark Journey: Black Mississippi in the Age of Jim Crow.* Urbana: University of Illinois Press, 1989.

Meredith, James. *Three Years in Mississippi.* Bloomington: Indiana University Press, 1966.

Morris, Willie. *North Toward Home.* Boston: Houghton Mifflin, 1987.

———. *Terrains of the Heart and Other Essays on Home.* Oxford, Miss.: Yoknapatawpha Press, 1981.

Murphy, William P. *The Triumph of Nationalism.* Chicago: Quadrangle Books, 1967.

President's Commission on Campus Unrest. *Report of the President's Commission on Campus Unrest.* Washington D.C.: U.S. Government Printing Office, 1970.

Reed, John Shelton. *Whistling Dixie: Dispatches from the South.* San Diego: Harcourt, 1970.

Reeves, Richard. *President Kennedy: Profile of Power.* New York: Simon & Schuster, 1993.

Sacks, Howard. *Way Up North in Dixie.* Washington, D.C.: Smithsonian Institution Press, 1993.

Sansing, David G. *Making Haste Slowly: The Troubled History of Higher Education in Mississippi.* Jackson: University Press of Mississippi, 1990.

Scheips, Paul J. *The Role of the Army in the Oxford, Mississippi Incident, 1962–3.* Washington, D.C.: Histories Division, Office of the Chief of Military History, Department of the Army, 1965.

Silver, James. *Mississippi: The Closed Society.* New York: Harcourt, Brace and World, 1964.

———. *Running Scared: Silver in Mississippi.* Jackson: University Press of Mississippi, 1984.

University of Mississippi. *Historical Catalogue, 1849–1909.* Nashville: Marshall & Bruce Co., 1919.

———. *Special Report: The University of Mississippi and the Meredith Case.* University, Miss., 1962.

Vaught, Johnny. *Rebel Coach.* Memphis: University of Memphis Press, 1971.

Waddel, John. *Memorials of Academic Life.* Richmond: Presbyterian Committee of Publications, 1891.

Wells, Larry, ed. *A Century of Heroes: One Hundred Years of Ole Miss Football.* Atlanta: Longstreet Press, 1993.

Wilson, Charles Reagan. *Baptized in Blood: The Religion of the Lost Cause, 1865–1920.* Athens: University of Georgia Press, 1980.

Yates, Gail Graham. *Mississippi Mind: A Personal Cultural History of an American State.* Knoxville: University of Tennessee Press, 1990.

Articles

Bradley, John Ed. "The Man Who Would Be King." *Esquire,* December 2, 1992, pp. 101–110.

Brower, Sidna. "Mississippi Mud." *Nation,* October 27, 1962, p. 266.

Carter, Hodding. "'The Man' from Mississippi—Bilbo." *New York Times Magazine,* June 30, 1946, p. 12.

———. "A Wave of Terror Threatens the South." *Look,* March 22, 1955, pp. 32–26.

Cleghorn, Reese. "Tiger at Ole Miss." *Progressive* (June 1962): 21–24.

———. "Revolt of the Professors." *New Republic,* February 2, 1963, pp. 5–6.

———. *The Reporter.* (October 1963): 42.

"Closed Society." *Newsweek,* November 18, 1963, p. 66.

Davis, Robert N. "The Quest for Equal Education in Mississippi: The Implications of *United States v. Fordice.*" *Mississippi Law Journal* (Winter 1993): 405–507.

Frady, Marshall. "If They Wouldn't Play 'Dixie' So Much." *Mademoiselle* (August 1966): 333.

Gaillard, Frye. "Black Recruiting Increases in SEC." *Race Relations Reporter* (March 1970): 7–8.

Hamblin, Robert W. "The 1965 Southern Literary Festival: A Microcosm of the Civil Rights Movement." *Journal of Mississippi History* (May 1991): 83–114.

Hudson, John B. "The Spoils System Enters College—Governor Bilbo and Higher Education in Mississippi." *New Republic,* September 17, 1930, pp. 123–125.

"Integration at Ole Miss." *Ebony,* May 1966, pp. 29–37.

James, Anthony W. "A Demand for Racial Equality: The 1970 Black Student Protest at the University of Mississippi." *Journal of Mississippi History,* 57 (Summer 1995): 97–120.

———. "Paternalism's Demise, Blind Jim Ivy and Ole Miss, 1896–1955." *Mississippi Folklife* (Winter–Spring 1995): 17–23.

Johnson, Jemmy Grant. "The University War Hospital." *Publications of the Mississippi Historical Society* (1912): 94–96.

Leonard, George, T. George Harris, and Christopher S. Wren. "How a Secret Deal Prevented a Massacre at Ole Miss." *Look,* December 31, 1962, pp. 19–36.

Meredith, James. "I Can't Fight Alone." *Look,* April 9, 1963, pp. 70–77.

"The Mississippi Story." *Saturday Evening Post,* November 10, 1962, pp. 14–17.

"The Mississippi Tragedy—What It All Means." *U.S. News and World Report,* October 15, 1962, pp. 39–52.

Morganthau, Tom, et al. "Race on Campus: Failing the Test?" *Newsweek,* May 6, 1991, pp. 26–27.

Morris, Willie. "At Ole Miss: Echoes of a Civil War's Last Battle." *Time,* October 4, 1962, p. 8.

Murphy, William P. Review of *The Sovereign States* by James J. Kilpatrick. *Mississippi Law Journal* (December 1957): 110–112.

———. "State Sovereignty Prior to the Constitution." *Mississippi Law Journal* (March 1958): 115–157.

"A New Dean at Ole Miss." *Time,* July 19, 1969, p. 53.

"New Misery at Ole Miss." *Time,* August 30, 1968, p. 37.

"New Mood at Ole Miss." *Time,* September 23, 1966, p. 76.

O'Quinn, Sally. "Campus Scourge at Ole Miss." *Life,* July 17, 1964, p. 74A.

"The Pistol on the Steps." *Time,* October 4, 1963, p. 38.

Reed, William F. "Archie Manning and the War Between the States." *Sports Illustrated,* October 12, 1970, p. 14.

Rosen, Jane Krieger. "A Visit to Ole Miss." *Reporter,* December 20, 1962, pp. 18–20.

Rychlak, Ronald J. "Civil Rights, Confederate Flags, and Political Correctness: Free Speech and Race Relations on Campus." *Tulane Law Review* 66, no. 5 (May 1992): 1411.

"Six Weeks Later—No Real Peace at 'Ole Miss.'" *U.S. News and World Report,* November 26, 1982, p. 98.

Smith, Faye McDonald. "*Ayers* Desgregation Suit Has Far-reaching Impact on Black Colleges." *Southern Changes* (Winter 1994): 8–16.

"The Sound and the Fury." *Newsweek,* October 15, 1962, pp. 23–29.

Turnbull, Lucy. "Mississippi." *Bryn Mawr Alumni Bulletin* (Winter 1963): 24–25.

Vinson, Ken. "Mississippi: Signs of Life, the Lawyers of Ole Miss." *Nation,* June 23, 1969, pp. 791–793.

Wilson, Charles Reagan. "The Religion of the Lost Cause." *Journal of Southern History* (May 1980): 169–189.

Wish, Harvey. "Negro Education and the Progressive Movement." *Journal of Negro History* (July 1964): 184–187.

Witherspoon, T. D. "The Appeal of the South to Its Educated Men." Memphis: The Association, 1867.

Unpublished Works

Berry, Trey. "A History of Higher Education for Women in Mississippi." Master's thesis, University of Mississippi, 1987.

Bridgforth, Lucy. "Bomb the Ban—A Study of the Legal Controversy Surrounding Off-Campus Speakers at Mississippi Institutions of Higher Learning." Master's thesis, University of Mississippi, 1964.

Clegg, Hugh. "Someone Jumped the Gun." Unpublished manuscript.

Graham, Hardy Poindexter. "Bilbo and the University of Mississippi, 1928–1932." Master's thesis, University of Mississippi, 1965.

Jones, Myra Hume. "Tenets and Attitudes of an Old-Time Teacher." Master's thesis, University of Mississippi, 1949.

Measells, Dewitt Talmage, Jr. "History of the Expansion of the University of Mississippi, 1848–1947." Master's thesis, University of Mississippi, 1947.

Percy, Anne. "Rebel Land after Meredith." Master's thesis, University of Mississippi, 1994.

———. "The History of the Black Student Union at the University of Mississippi." Course paper, 1993.

Read, James C. "The Williams Chancellorship at the University of Mississippi, 1946–68." Ph.D. dissertation, University of Mississippi, 1978.

Thornton, Kevin Pierce. "Symbolism at Ole Miss and the Crisis of Identity." Master's thesis, University of Virginia, 1983.

Private Papers[*]

Russell Barrett
John Crews
Porter Fortune
John Hall
Verner Holmes
Morton King
David Molpus
William Murphy
Steve Ray
Dottie Quaye Chapman Reed
David G. Sansing
James Silver
George Street
Lucy Turnbull
J. D. Williams

[*]The papers of Hall, Molpus, Ray, Reed, and Sansing are from their personal collections. The others are at the University of Mississippi archives.

Interviews

Dale Abadie, July 6, 1995, Oxford, Miss.
Reuben Anderson, May 24, 1995 (telephone)
Peter Aschoff, December 3, 1995 (telephone)
John Ates, June 6, 1996, Washington, D.C.
James Autry, January 5, 1995 (telephone)
Verna Bailey, August 13, 1996 (telephone)
Coolidge Ball, July 24, 1995 (telephone)
Jack Bass, February 10, 1994, Oxford, Miss.
J. O. Baylen, September 9, 1996 (telephone)
Sheila Putnam Bose, Oct. 31, 1995 (telephone)
Bob Boyd, June 27, 1995 (telephone)
William Boyd, May 29, 1996 (telephone)
John Robbin Bradley, August 17, 1995 (telephone), October 11, 1996, Oxford, Miss.
Patsy Brumfield, Aug. 24, 1995 (telephone), Nov. 17, 1995, Jackson, Miss.
Stuart Brunson, June 6, 1995 (telephone)
Allison Brown Buchanan, March 19, 1996 (telephone)
Nancy Horton Burke, June 5, 1996 (telephone)
Larry Bush, October 11, 1996, Oxford, Miss.

Will Campbell, January 12, 1995 (telephone)

Bela Chain, February 2, 1996 (telephone)

Bill Champion, May 19, 1995 (telephone)

David Clark, November 18, 1995, Jackson, Miss.

Donald Cole, June 18, July 18, Oct. 17, 1995 (telephone), May 24, 25, June 7, Oct. 10, 1996, Oxford, Miss.

John Corlew, May 2, 1995 (telephone)

John Crews, August 16, 1995, Jackson, Miss.

Paul Crutcher, February 15, 1996, Oxford, Miss.

Danny Cupit, September 6, 1995 (telephone)

Robert Davis, June 7, 1996, Washington, D.C.

Walter Dellinger, July 3, 1995 (telephone)

Richard Doss, February 22, 1994 (telephone)

Jack Dunbar, October 21, 1996 (telephone)

Charles Eagles, March 27, 1995, Oxford, Miss.

Michael Edmonds, February 28, 1996 (telephone)

Gene Fair, May 3, 1995 (telephone)

George Fair, August 28, 1995 (telephone)

William Ferris, February 9, 1994, Oxford, Miss.

Rose Jackson Flenorl, February 29, 1996 (telephone), March 30, 1996, Oxford, Miss., May 30, 1996 (telephone)

Mary Thompson Givhan, July 19 (telephone), November 17, 1995, Clinton, Miss., June 18, 1996 (telephone)

Sam Givhan, August 16, 22, 1995 (telephone), October 16, 1995, Starkville, Miss.

Lowell Grisham, December 11, 1995 (telephone)

Brad Gunner, June 6, 1996 (telephone)

John Hall, March 12, 1996, Washington, D.C.

Michael Harrington, June 11, 1996, Oxford, Miss.

Constance Slaughter Harvey, September 1, 1995 (telephone)

John Hawkins, February 13, 1996, May 20, (telephone)

Katherine Webb Heidinger, April 28, 1995 (telephone)

Jesse Holland, February 9, 1994, Oxford, Miss., May 27, 1996 (telephone)

Verner Holmes, February 27 (telephone), March 28, 1995, McComb, Miss.

Michael Horowitz, May 19, 1995 (telephone)

Junie Hovious, December 7, 1995 (telephone)

Katrina Howard, June 7, 1996 (telephone)

James Hull, October 26, 31, 1995 (telephone), February 3, 1996, Oxford, Miss.

Frank Hurdle, June 9, 1996, Oxford, Miss.

Jeanette Jennings, November 21, 1995 (telephone)

Robert Khayat, July 24, 1996 Oxford, Miss.

Albin Krebs, February 3, 1995 (telephone)

Harvey Lewis, March 6, 1995 (telephone)

Trentt Lott, May 15, 1995, Washington, D.C.

Deborah Love, July 23, 1996, Oxford, Miss.

Bonita Terry Malone, February 16, 1996, Oxford, Miss.

Kenneth Mayfield, September 6, 1995 (telephone)

Nola Leggett McKee, July 3, 1996 (telephone)

Eugene McLemore, August 23, 1995 (telephone)

James Meredith, February 17, 1995 (telephone), March 29, 1995, Jackson, Miss.

Ardessa Minor, March 20, 1996 (telephone)

James Minor, February 17, 1996, Oxford, Miss.

Sidna Brower Mitchell, February 13, April 22, 1995 (telephone)

David Molpus, August 21, 1995, Chapel Hill, N.C.

George Monroe, May 5, 1995 (telephone)

Damon Moore, May 25, June 9, 1996, Oxford, Miss.

Jean and Clen Moore, June 9, 1996, Coldwater, Miss.

John Hebron Moore, August 29, 1995 (telephone)

Kent Moorhead, November 29, 1995, January 4, 1996 (telephone)

Burnis Morris, January 2, 1996 (telephone)

Joshua Morse, May 22, 1995 (telephone)

William Murphy, January 6, 1995 (telephone)

Will Norton, March 20, 1996 (telephone)

Charles Noyes, March 20, 1996 (telephone)

Kimsey O'Neal, June 6, 1996 (telephone)

Harry Owens, October 17, 1995, Oxford, Miss.

Randy Patterson, August 9, 1994, Jackson, Miss.

James Payne, July 24, 1996, Oxford, Miss.

Steve Ray, February 23, 1996 (telephone)

William Ray, February 14, 1996 (telephone)

Thomas "Sparky" Reardon, June 11, 1996, Oxford, Miss.

Dottie Quaye Chapman Reed, November 28, 1995 (telephone), February 8, 1996, Atlanta, Ga.

Talley Riddell, March 1, 1995 (telephone)

Steve Riley, May 6, 1996 (telephone)

David Robinson, May 6, 1996 (telephone)

Otis Sanford, May 2, 1996, Memphis, Tenn.

David Sansing, December 16, 1995, February 3, April 17, June 10, June 13, 1996, Oxford, Miss.

Lee Eric Smith, June 6, 1996 (telephone)

Lydia Spragin, February 27, 1996 (telephone)

Nausead Stewart, August 29, 1995 (telephone)

George Street, August 23, September 5, 1995 (telephone)

Willie B. Tankersly, February 16, 1996, Oxford, Miss.

Otis Tims, October 27, 1995 (telephone)

Michael Trister, May 18, 1995 (telephone)

Judith Trott, June 11, 1996 (telephone)

Lucy Turnbull, March 27, 1995, Oxford, Miss.

Gerald Turner, June 12, 1996, Dallas, Tex.

Kenneth Vinson, May 19, 1995 (telephone)
Robert Walker, August 29, 1995 (telephone)
Thomas Wallace, June 10, 1996, Oxford, Miss.
Gerald Walton, July 6, 1995, Oxford, Miss.
Charles Ware, August 9, 1996 (telephone)
Kenneth Weeden, July 30, 1996 (telephone)
Lawrence Weeden, July 30, 1995 (telephone)
Louis Westerfield, June 10, 1996, Oxford, Miss.
Ben Williams, November 17, 1995, Jackson, Miss.
Ed Williams, April 25, 1995 (telephone)
Linnie Liggins Willis, July 1, 1996 (telephone)
William Winter, August 9, 1994, Jackson, Miss.
Patricia Taylor Wise, November 17, 1995, Jackson, Miss.
Charles Reagan Wilson, August 27, 1994, Oxford, Miss.
Kenneth Wooten, February 2, 1996, Oxford, Miss.

Acknowledgments

Anyone interested in the civil rights movement in this country is inevitably drawn to Mississippi because of a history both brutal and ennobling. I am no exception, so when my friend and former *Congressional Quarterly* colleague, Alan Ehrenhalt, suggested one December day in 1993 that the University of Mississippi's passage through this time would be worth exploring, I knew right away he had a good idea. I thank him for prompting me to take on a subject that turned out to be more rewarding and enriching than I had ever imagined.

In my many trips to Oxford, the home of Ole Miss, and other parts of the state, I was unfailingly met with kindness, interest, and candor. David Sansing, emeritus professor of history at the university, was a godsend—patient, encouraging, and thought provoking in our countless conversations. He reminded me whenever I wasn't "thinking like a southerner" and provided valuable suggestions about the manuscript. So did Jack Bass, a member of the Ole Miss journalism faculty who was instrumental in helping me get this project started. Help came too from Alan Ehrenhalt, who generously agreed to read what he had wrought and made it better. My thanks to Lib Sansing for her generous hospitality and support.

Sharron Sarthou and Lisa Speer of the University of Mississippi Archives were invaluable in pointing me to useful collections and books for my research. They were resourceful and tenacious in finding answers to my many questions. DebbiLee Landi and Naomi Leavell helped make my research trips worthwhile, as did Kerry Taylor, particularly in helping me with microfilm work.

I could not have told this story without the help of so many who aided my understanding. I am forever grateful to them for their willingness to give me their time and their insights and to share their memories, however painful, with me. In particular my great thanks go to Quaye Chapman Reed, not only for talking about her experiences at Ole Miss but also for helping me contact others who added much to this effort. And many thanks to Donald Cole, Rose Jackson Flenorl, Sam Givhan, Mary Thompson Givhan, John Hall, David Molpus, Damon Moore, and Steve Ray for their candor and interest and for talking with me whenever I asked. There would have been no book without them.

David Rapp, my friend and sounding board, made me think harder and write better with his penetrating comments on the manuscript in progress. He could see the story when I got lost in the details, and he helped me find my way. My thanks to Jane Abbott, my friend forever, for her wisdom and her suggestions on the early chapters.

At the Free Press my thanks and appreciation go to Adam Bellow, whose insights about how to tell this story made my original idea so much better. He kept me headed in the right direction. Thanks, too, to Mitchell Horowitz and David Bernstein for their contributions, and to Christine Weydig for keeping everything on track.

To Flip Brophy, my agent, my thanks for continuing to believe in me and knowing when to provide an encouraging word. Thanks also to Kristin Kimball for her kindness and support.

My brother, Howard Cohodas, has been there every step of the way. His advice helps keep the keel even. A final and special thanks to Sylvia Cohodas, my mother, who instilled in me a set of values that helped me appreciate this story and, I hope, tell it well.

Index

291